Suzanne,
Cook,

Mom's Family Pie

Memories of Food Traditions and Family in Appalachia

Peggy Ann Shifflett
387—9454

Peggy Ann Shifflett
2006

Mom's Family Pie: Memories of Food Traditions and Family in Appalachia,
© by Peggy Ann Shifflett, 2006.

ISBN: 1-4243-1835-1

Photos courtesy of: Mary, Gary, and Dennis Turner; Hilda Shifflett; Shirley
and Ethel Morris; Dorothy Rowe; Scottie and Bucky Pritchard; Wayne
Cannoy; Nelda Pearson; Winston Rhodes; Keeling Jones; and Lori Bennett.

The people, places and events described in this book are factual. However,
out of respect for family members, in some instances fictional names of
people have been used in place of their real names.

References can be found on page 345.

Printed and bound in the United States of America by:
McClung Companies, 500 Commerce Ave., Waynesboro, VA 22980

Orders should be sent to:
P A Shifflett, Inc.
700 Cherrywood Rd.
Salem, VA 24153
Fax: (540) 831-5464
Phone: (540) 387-9154
Email: Redesther2@verizon.net

Acknowledgements

This book is a result of the encouragement of several people. Dr. Jeanne Mekolichick, a colleague at Radford University, said that it was an important idea and constantly reminded me to get to work on it. My cousins, Charles Morris and Betty Morris Fleming were supportive. Gayle Stoner and Angelica Kaite read several early drafts and offered helpful comments. Both provided moral support and direction, and I thank them. Scottie Pritchard and Evelyn Jordan listened to me read from early drafts and offered encouragement.

Hilda Shifflett, my sister-in-law, Paula Wheelbarger, Hilda's daughter, and my brother, Larry Shifflett, Hilda's husband, sat for hours with me and provided many of the stories. My brothers, John and Warnie, and my sister, Brenda, helped with recipes and stories of evenings around the supper table. Aunt Ethel and Uncle Shirley were incredible resources for recipes, pictures, and great stories. Mary Morris Turner and her sons Gary and Dennis provided information and pictures. I am grateful for their help. I thank Wayne Cannoy for opening his parents' home for me to get pictures of the old spring house and root cellar. I appreciate Dr. Dorothy Rowe for her advice on all aspects of this work, and for allowing me to photograph her old cistern.

I am deeply grateful to the readers of *The Red Flannel Rag: Memories of an Appalachian Childhood*. Many of them asked me to write another book, and this work is a response to those requests. I thank the book sellers, the librarians, and the historical societies for their encouragement. I greatly appreciate the Scott and Pritchard families who invited me to their reunions to speak on the importance of documenting family memories and traditions.

To the men and women on both sides of my family, who exposed me to all the activities involved in feeding their families, I owe a great debt. While this book focuses on Aunt Ethel, Uncle Shirley, and Mom and Dad Shifflett, they represent all the hard working families in Hopkins Gap. Without their successful efforts to survive the seasons, both harsh and mild, my generation would not have eaten as well as we did.

I owe a great debt to my friend, Marsha Jones, for reading and offering suggestions for the organization of this book. Her assistance came at a time when I doubted the worth of the entire project. I thank you, Marsha.

Finally, I want to thank Kim Maselli who did the final editing of *The Red Flannel Rag: Memories of an Appalachian Childhood.* She also edited this book, asked the right questions, offered great suggestions where needed, and did some sketching. I thank you, Kim.

Dedicated

to

Norman Shifflett, my Dad, (1919–1994)

Myrtle Morris Shifflett, my Mom, (1920–2001)

and

Larry Shifflett, my brother, (1942–2006) who spent his life

maintaining food traditions

Table of Contents

Page

Prologue 1

Introduction 7
  Story—Typical Appalachian homestead 10

Chapter 1—Family Pie: Dessert for Busy
Cooks on Busy Days. 15
  Story—Moonshine Mixin' and Sippin' 22
  Story—Fainting at the sight of blood 23

Chapter 2—The Cooks 27
  Story—Can snakes tell time? 49
  Story—Battling the blood-thirsty bedbugs 51
  Story—Grandma's little helper 54
  Story—Mom even fed the convicts 58
  Story—Dad takes a trip and Mom takes charge 60

Chapter 3—The Tools for Cooking and Eating. 67
  Story—Wood ashes for traction on ice 76
  Story—Chicken tracks in the butter 81
  Story—Copperhead snake strikes Hilda 87
  Story—"Movin' on up" with a refrigerator 92

Chapter 4—Everyday Foods 95
  Story—A prancin' cow and a one-legged kick 97
  Story—Cow kicks and bruised crotches 98
  Story—But for the lack of seven hundred dollars 100
  Story—Learnin' about birthin babies 107
  Story—A churn tragedy averted 111
  Story—Bread and milk as medicine 120
  Story—Biography of Larry's Banty Hen, Speck. 136

Chapter 5—Late Winter and Early Spring Foods 147
  Story—Dandelion wine and green cherries 157
  Story—The Old Hirsch Farm 161

Chapter 6—Spring Gardening and Wild Foods 171
  Story—Do potatoes have eyes? 173
  Story—Cherry pickin' and not grinnin' 185
  Story—Cherry seedin', birthin' babies,
    and the bonds of friendship 187
  Story—Kissin' up with cherry winks 191

Chapter 7—Summer's Garden and Nature's Bounty. 195
  Story—Green beans by June 21 197
  Story—Blackberry pickin' and ants in the pants 203
  Story—Little hands make great peach packers. 209
  Story—The peach tree and the tragic childhood of my
    wayward sister. 211
  Story—One touch can kill 216
  Story—Rug houses, corn silk cigars, and corn cob battles 223
  Story—The "Dog Days" of summer. 242

Chapter 8—Fall Harvest 245
   Story—Fussin' over fried potatoes 247
   Story—The potato bin and my arachnophobia. 251
   Story—Sling shot, round green plums, and temptation 257
   Story—The mark of a ripe Bartlett 261
   Story—Aunt Goldie's apple trees, buzzards, and pigpens. . . . 262
   Story—Apple pie and Mom's stroke 266

Chapter 9— Bringing Home the Bacon 279
   Story—Larry adopts a new identity 280
   Story—A tornado hits the farm 291
   Story—Squirrel hunter kills first deer illegally with .22 rifle . 302

Chapter 10—Meal Time: Puttin' It All Together 307
   Story—Breakfast with chicken slop 310
   Story—The cook rebels. 312
   Story—Christmas eve with Mom and Dad 314
   Story—Tomato and peanut butter sandwiches 318
   Story—Stomach linings at supper time. 323
   Story— Finally, the origins of my arachnophobia? 334

Epilogue 337

List of Recipes 341

References 345

Author's Notes 347

About the Author 348

Prologue
Mom Shifflett's Recipe Box

Between two moments, bliss is ripe.
Think in the morning, Act in the noon, Eat in the evening, Sleep in
the night. In seed time learn, in harvest teach, in winter enjoy.
—William Blake

When my mother died in 2001, my siblings and I considered the daunting task of settling her estate. We faced the future sale of our home with dread because Mom didn't throw away much during her lifetime. We knew we would be taking apart the life work of a wife and mother whose sole purpose was to care for her family. From the cellar to the attic we found remnants of her efforts to provide the best life possible for all of us.

In the cellar were several hundred empty canning jars—a verification of the fact that the last years of her life had been spent in bad health that prevented her from gardening, picking, and canning food for her family. She often said to me during those last five years, "You all are usin' up my canned food, and nobody's puttin' any back. When I do get better, I'll have to buy every thing I need." She was right about one thing. Nobody replaced the canned food; but she never got well again. By the time of her death, the canning jars were empty except for about eight quarts of apple butter from the last boiling in 1994.

The wood stove still set next to the electric range in Mom's kitchen; but nobody ever put a fire in it to cook a pot of pinto beans. The wood box sat empty on the back porch, and the kindling box had been removed from its spot by the stove.

For several years after the final stroke that left her partially paralyzed, Mom could tell anyone where to find almost anything they wanted or needed. As time went by, the many caregivers moved things around and didn't return them where Mom had kept them. Because of this, she lost track of her possessions. She cried a lot about everything being out of its place. I soon stopped asking her to tell me where she kept her hand lotion or her band-aids so she could at least be relieved from that stress.

In the upstairs bedrooms, we found three forty-gallon barrels of printed feed sacks—a total of three hundred—in which she had had my dad bring her cow and chicken feed home. She used these colorful sacks to make our school clothes and her dresses and aprons. She made kitchen curtains and a pleated cover for her Singer sewing machine. Toward the end of her life, a neighbor asked her if she would sell her the collection of feed sacks. Mom's answer displayed her hope for the future, "I don't want to sell them because I might want to make somethin' sometime, and I won't have them. Just wait until I die, and you can buy them at the sale if I haven't used them." After her death, I went through the feed sacks. Some had been cut, and I could see what she had made from them. Some of the scraps had obviously been cut in an apron pattern while other scraps were from a dress that I remembered her wearing.

In the steps going to the basement, we found her ancient milk strainer, the large pans she used to boil jams and jellies, and an old milk can that she used to place her milk by the road for Charlie Henkel to pick up and haul to the dairy. These were items I had not thought about for many years. Just touching them brought back a flood of memories.

On top of her kitchen cabinet that held the old flour bin and the pull-down louvered door was a cardboard box about three inches deep. I asked my sister-in-law, Hilda, "What is in this box?" She answered, "That's Mom's recipe box. We've been avoiding going through it to throw stuff away. Why don't you take it back to Salem and go through it." At first glance I said to Hilda, "It looks to me like this whole box could just go in the trash." Hilda responded, "No, I think you had better go through it before you throw it out." A thought immediately crossed my mind. I would finally have access to all the recipes I had asked Mom to give me over the years—ham potpie, sauerkraut dumplings, apple pie, baked sweet potatoes, and many others. I carried the box to my car and took it home with me.

Months went by and I was too busy to look at the recipe box. Finally, during my Christmas break from teaching, I sat down and slowly made my way through the box looking at every item. By the time I reached the last item, I decided that this was much more than just a recipe box—it was a history of my mother's life and her relationship to food and family.

Her recipes dated from the 1940s to the 1990s—from the early years of her marriage until she could no longer cook. There were recipes from my Aunt Ethel and Aunt Goldie, and I suspect that they had just as many recipes from Mom. Some recipes were typed nicely on cards. I remembered typing them for her just after I had acquired my first typewriter. Other recipes were clipped from cereal boxes, flour bags, cake mix boxes, True Confessions magazines, and the GRIT newspaper. Whole sections of magazines and newspapers were also stuck in the box. When I unfolded them, I found recipes that Mom had marked with a pencil, but didn't have time to clip. There were also recipes that my sister, Brenda, and sister-in-law Hilda had given to her.

By noting the dates of various items in the box, I could trace Mom's health problems. She had special diets for high blood pressure given to her by her doctors. I calculated the dates and found that she must have been in her early fifties when she learned that she had high blood pressure. Mom fought a losing battle most of her life with being overweight. At age fifty-seven, she was diagnosed with

Type II diabetes. Special instructions for managing diabetes were included in the recipe box. All these items put together gave me concrete evidence of Mom's struggle with chronic diseases over the years. The most startling thing I noticed as I went through the box were the items included that had nothing to do with food or cooking. I found valentines that she had been given by her grandchildren when they were very young and couldn't spell her name correctly.

She had kept a winning card saying that one of her grandchildren was number one in a spelling bee. There were notes from her grandchildren such as "Dear Grandma, I was going to wait until you got back from milking before I went home, but I have to go now. Love, Randy."

I found fishhooks still in their store wrapping. The fishhooks really puzzled me. Why on earth would she keep them in her recipe box? After much thought I came to the conclusion that she kept the fish hooks there so that she would know exactly where they were when one of us asked for them.

The valentines, little notes, and blue ribbons won by the grandchildren, I recognized as very meaningful to her. She kept them in her recipe box so they wouldn't be thrown out by accident. I can see her reading and rereading them, with a smile on her face, as she visited her recipe box to find a favorite dish.

When I finished sorting through the recipe box, I realized something. None of the recipes for the mouth-watering dishes Mom had cooked for us over the years were written down. She had cooked sauerkraut dumplings and other dishes from memory. At that very moment, the idea for this book was born. I had to write down those recipes or they would be lost to my nieces and nephews, their children and all future generations of my family. I felt compelled to document Mom's efforts to feed her family, and in so doing, document the work of the best cooks in Hopkins Gap while one of them is still on this earth—my Aunt Ethel. I visited Aunt Ethel and asked if she would help me with this effort because she and Mom were best friends and shared all that they knew about cooking with each other. I knew that my sister-in-law, Hilda, had learned all of Mom's recipes and could duplicate them. Both Aunt Ethel and Hilda have been great resources, as you will see.

Mom Shifflett's recipe box inspired me to document the seasonal quest for food and the strategies for preserving, canning, and preparing food. The food traditions recorded in this book are rich in Appalachian culture although they come from Hopkins Gap, a small community in the Allegheny Mountains.

Introduction

"It seems to me that our three basic needs, for food and security and love, are so mixed and mingled and entwined that we cannot straightly think of one without the others. So it happens that when I write of hunger, I am really writing about love and the hunger for it, and warmth and the love of it and the hunger for it...and then the warmth and richness and fine reality of hunger satisfied...and it is all one."
—*M.F.K. Fisher*

My interest in food and family began while I was growing up near Hopkins Gap—a small Appalachian community in the Allegheny Mountains northwest of Harrisonburg, Virginia. The two women who nurtured my interest in food and family were my mother, Myrtle Morris Shifflett, and my aunt, Ethel Crawford Morris. Both of these women grew up in Hopkins Gap. They were born to parents who had migrated to Hopkins Gap from Greene County, Virginia, an area in the Blue Ridge Mountains located between Harrisonburg and Charlottesville, Virginia. These families were forced to relocate during the late 1800's when the federal government claimed their land to establish the Shenandoah National Park. Mom's father, John Wesley Morris, settled in Hopkins Gap around 1895. He met and married Mary Ella Lamb who was born near Singers Glen, Virginia. They birthed a total of eighteen children, and Mom was their fourteenth child.

Aunt Ethel's father, Garfield Crawford, was also born in Greene County and migrated to Hopkins Gap. He married Hattie Dove, and they gave birth to twelve children. Aunt Ethel was their eighth child.

All the folks who migrated to Hopkins Gap from Greene County blended with the original settlers, families that included the Shoemakers, Reedys, Lambs, Carrs, Kirkpatricks, Hoovers, Finks, and Fridleys. Several cultures came together in Hopkins Gap— English, Cherokee, German, Scotch, and Irish. Like settlers up and down the Appalachian Mountain ranges, the folks in Hopkins Gap took the best survival practices from each culture and formed a common Appalachian way of life.

No part of the Appalachian way of life represents the diversity of its origins better than food practices. Joseph E. Dabney, in *Smokehouse Ham, Spoon Bread, and Scuppernong Wine*, said it well:

> In my research and forays over the region, I received instructive insight into our Southern Appalachian foods, particularly the nourishing dishes we inherited from the Amerindians—those based on corn and beans and pumpkins and squash.... ...the region's English and Scotch and Irish food heritage is also rich, particularly the puddings and stack cakes and pies, to say nothing of mountain folk's insatiable love for pork in all of its many dimensions. From the German migrants... came wonderful dumplings and krauts, apple butters, deep-dish pies, and those wonderful Moravian cakes and cookies. ...

The blending of cultures in the mountains allowed the early settlers to recognize and take advantage of the bountiful seasonal foods available to gather throughout the calendar year. Seasonal foods provided diversity and anticipation of good dishes not available every day. The bounty of each season brought the family and community together to forage for the ingredients and to help prepare the recipes. Seasonal foods connected family and community members to each other because at least three generations were usually helping with or watching the work being done.

There were many great cooks in Hopkins Gap who are represented by Mom and Aunt Ethel in this writing. The cooks provided essential continuity, connection, and a loving presence. For the cooks, snapping beans and kneading dough were simple activities that slowed the pace of life and marked the passage of time shared by granddaughter and grandmother, and daughter and mother. History, wisdom, practical information, and concerns were passed from one generation to another as food was hunted, gathered, grown, processed, and eaten. The cooks who most influenced my life were my mother, my grandmothers, and my aunts.

In the early years of my life, Grandma Molly, Aunt Goldie, and Aunt Ethel were always present and quietly passing on their knowledge of food by demonstration. After Grandma Molly's death, Mom became the storehouse of knowledge that she passed on to my sister-in-law, Hilda, whose daughters, Paula and Vanessa, were always present for picking, preserving, and preparing food. Without realizing it, they were training for their future positions within the family and the community. The activities involved in providing food for the family added certainty and continuity to every life.

Fathers and sons always contributed to and learned from these activities. They gathered the wood, fed and butchered the hogs, and killed the wild meat that provided most of the meat for our meals.

The women took care of the everyday foods present at each meal; milk, cheese, butter, and bread. They followed the seasons and gathered wild greens in the early spring and wild fruit in the summer and fall. They gardened all summer and canned fruits and vegetables for the winter. In the fall, they helped with hog butchering and canned the meat. The women cleaned, preserved, and prepared the wild meat brought in by the men. They spent several days gathering and peeling bushels of apples for a multi-generation apple butter boiling and served special dishes at certain times of the year when the wild delicacies were available. After a long winter, the variety of wild greens were a welcome change in March, followed by a special treat of fried morels or "toad stools" in April, wild asparagus with a slice of country ham in May, wild strawberries in early June, and wild blackberries in July. Vegetable gardens provided fresh bounty throughout the summer months. Wild mushrooms and huckleberries were gathered in August. In the fall, the women made sure they picked apples and pears to can for the winter. Aunt Goldie Crawford, Mom's sister, grew a variety of fruit trees and grape vines right in her backyard, which was typical for an Appalachian style farm.

Typical Appalachian homestead...

Appalachian homesteads tended to be small in acreage but large in their food offerings. You could always find a hen house, a corncrib, a pole barn for a cow, mules or horses, a pigpen, a meat house, a springhouse, and a cellar. A large vegetable garden was the center of activity from March until October. Each family grew white potatoes, sweet potatoes, tomatoes, green beans, and cabbage every year because these crops could be preserved in one form or another for the winter food larder. Many other vegetables were grown as well.

A variety of fruit trees were planted over the years—pear, apple, plum, and peach. Wild fruit was abundant on the edges of the forest: red and black cherries, persimmons, paw paws, blackberries, raspberries, and huckleberries. The trees in the mountains provided white walnuts, black walnuts, hazelnuts, beechnuts, and hickory nuts. The mountains and partially cleared land or, new ground with large brush piles, provided shelter for squirrels, raccoon, and rabbits. Deer were abundant along with grouse, turkeys, and quail. Creeks were filled with bass and trout. Wild bees swarmed and settled in hollow trees. Men watched for a "honey tree" while they hunted for game and then returned when the weather was cold to collect the honey to eat with biscuits and to sweeten their coffee. The Appalachian people packed a variety of foods onto small acreage. Those efforts and the bounty offered by the surrounding ridges and hollows provided enough food for very large families and neighbors as well as visitors who were never turned away thirsty or hungry.

November's hog butchering was anticipated by the whole family. The men enjoyed bragging about the size of their hogs, how fat they were, and how much meat and lard they produced. The young men and women looked forward to learning their future roles at the elbows of the seasoned head butchers. The women processed all the meat and closely guarded the lard, as it was the essential grease that ran the homestead for the coming year. In addition to its cooking uses, lard was the basic ingredient in many home cures for both children and animals.

In the chapters that follow, I have salvaged some of the old recipes by describing, through the cooks' words, the ingredients used in the process of preparation and serving traditional Appalachian foods. When possible, I have demonstrated through pictures. I have focused on the best cooks in my family who grew up in Hopkins Gap. These women lived simply in the middle of extraordinary circumstances. They demonstrated great courage, fortitude, and commitment. They were unbending in their fight for survival and their hopes for the future of their families. Although I lived my life differently, the example of how these women lived and where they lived offered important lessons to me and gave me many of the values necessary for success in my chosen profession.

Some of the qualities imparted to me by these cooks are still present in my life. I never go through a summer without "puttin' up" some food that I buy at the farmers' market or grow in my small vegetable garden. In the fall, I buy pork tenderloin at the grocery store, pack it in jars, and process it in a pressure canner. When the cold winter comes, I want to smell tenderloin gravy cooking and then eat it over hot biscuits. I enjoy walking into my pantry and seeing the rows of canned green beans, pickled beets, and golden peaches on the shelves. There is a sense of security and promise for the future that I am sure the women and men of Hopkins Gap must have felt when they went into their cellars and saw the fruits and vegetables from their summer's hard work. The difference between my pantry and their cellar is that I do not have to depend on my efforts to "put up" food in order to survive through the winter. The families in Hopkins Gap survived, year after year, from laborious hunting, gathering, and processing their own food.

In the final pages of this book, I portray Hopkins Gap food culture today as described by my relatives who still live there. While there have been basic changes due to an increasing number of Hopkins Gap women entering the work force, a surprising amount of food traditions live on. The old wood-burning stove has gone by the wayside to be replaced by electric ranges and microwave ovens. But most of the mouth-watering nutritious recipes still remain intact. Memories of the tastes and smells of the foods of my childhood remind me that I can go back home again.

A few mothers and grandmothers in Hopkins Gap are still teaching their daughters and granddaughters the old recipes and techniques of cooking "from scratch" in the traditional way. One evening, as I was leaving Hopkins Gap for my home in Salem, I stopped in to see my Uncle Shirley and Aunt Ethel. Aunt Ethel was teaching her four-year-old great granddaughter, Kylie, how to make an apple pie. I tried to hide my excitement as I asked if I could photograph them. I had been wondering what type of picture I could use on the cover of this book, and there it was—completely unplanned and the perfect fit for both cover image and title.

I hope the reader will relate to or just enjoy the stories, recipes, and characters I have brought to life in these pages. It has been many years since I've have spent a lot of time in Hopkins Gap, and it was a delight for me to return to observe and document the preparation of many of these recipes. Even more so, I enjoyed eating my portion of the dishes after they were prepared. Writing this book has brought me in close contact once more with my relatives in Hopkins Gap—a fine reward for my effort to preserve some of the old food and family traditions. I hope that the recipes and memories I have included in this book will take you back to a time of old-fashioned family cooking and Appalachian hospitality.

Chapter 1

Family Pie: Dessert for Busy Cooks on Busy Days

*"At once impressive and unremarkable, pie can
be complicated and challenging or simple
and homey. Whether ordinary or elegant,
though, a pie is not something to eat by
yourself. It should be made to share,
preferably while fresh and warm."*
—*Lisa Chernasky*

There were two kinds of pies in Hopkins Gap—fancy pies and family pies. Fancy pies had a bottom crust and a top crust. The top crust was decorated with some type of leaf or flower pattern. The decoration had a practical purpose. It served as a vent for air to escape while it was baking so that the top crust didn't bubble. It also allowed any excess juice from the filling to escape rather than spill over the edges of the pie. Depending on the filling, the top crust could be very fancy. For example, Mom placed an inviting lattice crust on top of her raisin pies. Fancy pies were nice and round and were sliced into an even number of perfect triangular pieces—usually six—and served to guests on Sundays and special days such as hog-butchering day.

Few things symbolize the connection of food to family, seasons

This fancy pie is decorated with an abstract pattern of holes. The crust is neatly edged with a fork. This decoration serves to hold the top and bottom crust together during baking.

of the year, subsistence living, hard work, and Appalachian tradition more than the Hopkins Gap "family pie." Family pies were just for the immediate family, and they were not fancy. They had one large crust that was placed in a square pan. Once the filling was poured into the crust, the sides of the crust were lapped over the top of the filling and served as a top crust. There were no decorations in the crust. Family pies were large and probably equaled three or four fancy pies.

They were a practical way to have a nice dessert. After a typical hard day's work and supper, a family would end the day by sharing a dish of family pie.

A family pie was filled with the fruits—cherries, raspberries, blackberries, huckleberries, peaches, or apples—of their labor; and

This family pie is made with a red cherry filling. The bottom crust is lapped up over the filling and there are no fancy decorations on top.

as they sat together at the table to eat the pie, family ties became stronger and family disagreements melted away as the warm pie was consumed.

The purpose of the family pie has not changed as the years have passed. It is still exactly what it says—a pie for the whole family. To this day, I associate the falling leaves of my own silver maple tree with the smell of a family pie made with early fall apples.

I always knew that Mom had been working hard all day when I was greeted by the aroma of family pie. She had probably been in the garden weeding or picking vegetables, or in the kitchen canning and baking bread for the week, or washing and ironing laundry for extra money. (She had to take in laundry when I was in high school so that I could pay my typing fee of $2.50 a month.)

Bread baking days were special because Mom knew we would be hungry after the long walk from the school bus. She always saved some bread dough; and as soon as we burst through the door, salivating from the tantalizing smells, she would ask if we wanted her to fry some dough on the top of the wood stove. Nothing in this world tasted as good as Mom's fried dough. After eating a piece smeared with apple butter or strawberry jam and drinking a glass of fresh milk, we could settle in with our chores or homework and wait for the delicious supper followed by family pie for dessert.

Recently, I stopped in at my brother Larry's house, and I had to smile. When I got out of the car, I was greeted by a familiar scent. Hilda, Larry's wife, had a cherry family pie baking in the oven. I immediately knew she must have hurried home to make dessert after her job of driving the school bus. I thought to myself, "The family pie is still serving as a way to have a tasty dessert for supper when the cook has been busy all day." Hilda, the woman of the house, is now working outside the home to add to the family income, so she is away most of the day. The family pie is quick and easy. It isn't decorative or fussy and requires very little time or attention while baking. A good cook can simply tell when it is done by the smell of the crust.

Hilda explained the speed with which she makes a family pie, "I just mix up a big chunk of pie dough. I flop it up on the counter and roll it out into a large square. While I am doing that, I have my pie filling heating up on the stove. After I roll my dough out in a thick slab, I grab a large baking pan or dish and throw it across the pan and pat it into the corners. I turn to the stove and add a thickener to my filling. It can be any kind of fruit—peaches, cherries, raspberries, blackberries, huckleberries, apples—whatever is in season or available in the cellar or freezer. When the pie filling has thickened, I dump it into the baking pan on top of the dough. Then I take the dough that is hanging over the edges of the pan and flop it across the top of the filling. I don't even try to make it pretty. A family pie is not about being pretty. Then it goes in the oven. While the family pie is baking, I fix the rest of the meal—some meat and vegetables or whatever I'm havin'. Pretty soon the house is filled with the wonderful sweet-scented fruit and baking crust."

Hilda added, "That smell goes out the windows and doors. I can bring Larry in the house for supper without calling him with that smell. He'll come in the back door and ask, 'What's that I smell?' Same goes for anyone else close by; they come in with their appetites whetted. One by one, they will sit down around the table and begin to talk with each other, while they wait for the meal that will end with family pie." Hilda said, "When the pie comes out of the oven, I place it on the counter to cool some while we eat the main meal."

The family pie doesn't have to be sliced and served in nice, neat triangular pieces. When the main meal is over and the dirty dishes cleared, the cook sets out clean dessert dishes and spoons. The warm family pie is placed in the center of the table, and each member of the family serves up their own portion. This method of serving is great for the cook, because she doesn't have to spend time cutting a fancy round pie into triangular pieces and serving them. Also, she doesn't have to try to please each person by serving the amount of pie they want. Each person scoops out as much as they want, and enjoys it while the cook starts to wash the dirty dishes. It is a touching sight to see the hands of three generations helping themselves to a portion from the dish at the same time.

A good thing about family pie is that often there was leftover pie. My daddy would eat a man-size portion of family pie for his dessert, and then later, long after Mom had cleaned up the supper dishes

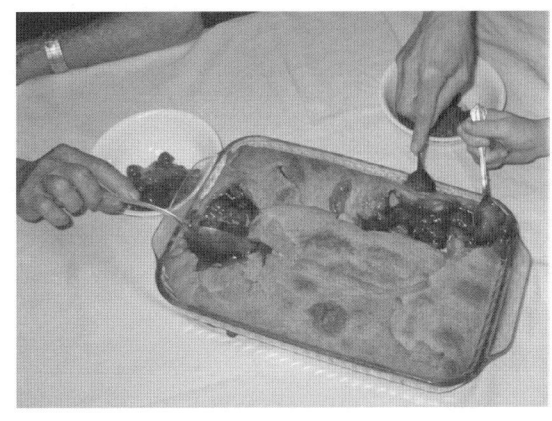

Granddad Larry Shifflett, his daughter, Paula Shifflett Wheelbarger, and granddaughter, Kylie Wheelbarger, are each dipping their portion into a small dish.

and collapsed into a chair, he would slip back into the kitchen. He would locate the leftover family pie that always sat on the back of the cooling wood stove, and, taking a clean saucer from the cabinet, he would help himself to a bed time snack. Mom reacted to his habit as if she was mad about him eating more pie; but in fact, she was so tired from the day's work that she couldn't stand the idea of Dad dirtying more dishes. She would fuss and say, "I can't stand to get up in the morning to dirty dishes in the kitchen." After Dad went to bed, she would go into the kitchen, wash his dirty bowl, and put it back into the cabinet.

My daddy always claimed he didn't like raspberries in a family pie. On one occasion, after having raspberry family pie for dessert at supper, he went into the kitchen for his bedtime snack and ate a second huge portion of the same pie. When he finished, he came back into the living room rubbing his stomach with a very satisfied look on his face. Mom asked, "Did you eat more of that pie?" He said, "Yes, I did." He was often defensive because she didn't like him dirtying more dishes. Mom frowned at him and said, "Norman, that is raspberry pie." He rubbed his belly again and said, with a serious look on his face, "Damn! It's no wonder I didn't like it."

In the past, families in Hopkins Gap had large numbers of children. These adult children, along with extended family, neighbors and friends, often dropped in unannounced, but always welcomed, at meal time. The cook had to be prepared for these guests and the family pie was a quick, easy, and delicious dessert to serve them. Hopkins Gap families are much smaller today in terms of numbers of children. However, it still holds true that folks are likely to come visiting right around meal time.

Like families everywhere, Hopkins Gap families were warm and close; but at times they also had fights and arguments. Sometimes my kin folks didn't speak to each other for weeks at a time. Often just the smell of a family pie drifting around the house and out the windows and doors might be enough to tempt them all to the table again. Differences were resolved while the meal was consumed.

I recall one occasion in my early childhood when a family pie was not enough to settle a family disturbance. We always went to church; and afterwards Dad drove us through Hopkins Gap searching for Sunday dinner. Sometimes we stopped at Uncle Jim and Aunt Hazel's house or Uncle Shirley and Aunt Ethel's house. These were relatives on Mom's side of the family. Other times we stopped at Grandma Molly and Grandpa Austin Shifflett's house or Uncle Jake and Aunt Bessie's house. These were Dad's kinfolks. Uncle Jake was his brother. Mom always fussed when we stopped at Uncle Jake's because she just didn't like him. She would always warn Dad, "If we go in there and they're drinkin', I am not stayin'. We can go somewhere else for dinner." The problem was that Mom couldn't drive, so if Dad wanted to stay, she was stuck.

We never knew where Dad would stop to visit, where we would eat, or whose kids we would be playing with before and after Sunday dinner. Everybody in Hopkins Gap knew that the cooks at these houses would cook huge dinners with heaping plates of fried chicken, piles of mashed potatoes, gravy, green beans, fruit salad, and banana cake, and dozens of fancy pies. All we ever knew was that we were eating Sunday dinner somewhere in Hopkins Gap and that there would be plenty of food and family members with whom to eat it.

I often thought it was strange that since Mom was such a good cook, she never hosted a Sunday dinner at our house. In recent years I have come to the conclusion that it was because we didn't actually live in Hopkins Gap. We lived just across Little North Mountain outside the Gap. Our Sunday trips to church and after church visits, I believe, were a demonstration of Mom and Dad's attachment to their family members who never moved out of the Gap.

When I was still very young, Mom and Dad drove down through Hopkins Gap after church and stopped to have Sunday dinner at Uncle Jake's house. Grandma Molly and Grandpa Austin were there. Uncle Jake and Aunt Bessie had three children. When Mom, Dad, my brother, Larry, my sister, Brenda, baby John and I arrived, there was the possibility of a pleasant three-generation family gathering.

The women were bustling around the kitchen, catching up on the past week's gossip, and sharing meal preparation. The sounds of crackling and popping came from the wood stove as the dry wood burned. An iron skillet was sizzling with country ham slices. Green beans bubbled on the back of the stove, and the boiled potatoes were ready to be mashed. The warmth from the stove and the smell of the country ham made a great atmosphere for a multiple generation family get together.

I was too young to understand that there was another activity going on that threatened this peaceful setting. All the adults, except Mom, were sipping a clear liquid from a quart-sized canning jar. Mom might have been sipping at the jar too except that she quit drinking when she was breast feeding me several years earlier. I am sure Mom knew what was happening, but she had probably decided to keep quiet about it.

I later learned that they were drinking moonshine. Homemade whiskey often warmed up our family gatherings, and other than

Mom fussing about the drinking, most occasions went very smoothly. Mom especially hated to be around Grandma Molly when she was sipping at a pint of moonshine. "I can tell every time she's drinking," Mom said, as she shook her head in disgust. She constantly picks up her apron and wipes her mouth like she's hidin' somethin' while she's tryin' to cook Sunday dinner. She must think I can see the whiskey on her mouth. Sometimes I've seen her rub her chin raw tryin' to hide her drinkin'."

Moonshine Mixin' and Sippin'...

Part of Mom's duty as a young wife and mother was to mix Uncle Rob's moonshine so that it held a perfect "bead" indicating that it was 100 proof. She told me, "Rob's whiskey was so good; you could drink it by the tea cup full. While I was mixin' it with good cold spring water, I would dip my cup in and take a big swallow."

One time, shortly after I was born, she had swallowed a few times too many and was more than a bit tipsy. She was trying to breast feed me, and I strangled on breast milk. She was too drunk to raise my left arm to clear my throat. She confessed to me later, "Goldie had to take you from my arms, and get you to breathe again. I got so scared when I couldn't get you 'unstrangled,' I swore I would never drink again." As far as I know, she stuck to her word and became a model for the temperance movement in that she hated drinking and loathed being around people when they were drinking.

Sometimes a family member or two would drink just a little too much and bring up past grudges or current problems to fight about. On this day, Uncle Jake's wife, Aunt Bessie, and Grandma Molly were putting the food on the table, when Uncle Jake, who had had a bit too much to drink, got into an argument with Aunt Bessie about her "runnin' 'round" with another man. They yelled bad names and slapped each other around. My cousins and I came into the kitchen to see what was going on. I immediately realized that I needed to get out of the way. I stood in the corner near the pie safe and watched. The smaller kids started crying.

As we watched in horror Uncle Jake grabbed the quart canning jar, still half filled with moonshine. He drew his arm back and shouted, "I'm gonna knock yer damned head off." Aunt Bessie ran for the back door. Uncle Jake's arm came forward, and we watched helplessly as the can flew through the air, missed, and hit the door jamb next to Aunt Bessie's head. It splintered into hundreds of tiny pieces. Aunt Bessie's face was cut and little streams of blood were running down her face. She was screaming that her eye was cut. Mom went over to Aunt Bessie and saw a tiny piece of glass sticking in the white of her right eye.

Grandma Molly started yelling at Uncle Jake, "Now, look what you did. She might go blind." Uncle Jake suddenly stormed from the house slamming the door behind him. Mom helped Aunt Bessie get the glass out of her eye by gently touching it with a clean white cloth. That image was the last thing I remembered until a few minutes later when I found myself on Mom's lap.

Mom told me about this incident many times as I was growing up. "When I got the glass out of Aunt Bessie's eye, I heard Grandma Molly saying, 'What happened to that kid? Did she get hit?' I looked around and saw you layin' on the kitchen floor white as a sheet and not movin'. I didn't know what happened to you. I grabbed you up and checked to see if you had been cut, and yelled for your daddy. I told him, 'We're goin' home right now.'" Mom held me tight to her chest, and I started to cry. "We are not going home right now," Dad said, "I'm hungry, and we are going to eat before we go home."

Fainting at the sight of blood...

Mom told me some years later, "I figured out that you fainted when you saw the blood runnin' down Aunt Bessie's face because you fainted one other time when you was about nine years old. I took you to town with me that day, and we went over to Hobe's restaurant to eat a hot dog for our dinner. Buck and Conard was back in the pool room playing pool, when all of a sudden I heard some yellin'. I looked back there, and they were knockin' each other around.

One of them, I think it was Conard, used steel knuckles and hit Buck in the head above the eyes. His forehead split open into three gashes. Blood flew all over the mirror behind the pool table. I heard a plunk beside me, and there you was layin', on the floor beside the bar stool. I gathered you up and we went next door to Layman's restaurant to eat a hot dog."

After Aunt Bessie got straightened out and stopped crying, she helped Grandma Molly finish putting the food on the table, and we all ate dinner. Uncle Jake never came back in the house to eat. As I recall, there was talk about him while we ate. "He's probably in the barn sleepin' it off, and "we'd better leave him alone until he wakes up on his own."

During dinner, I sat on the bench beside my Cousin Sis. While we were eating, Dad started comparing my hair to my Cousin Sis's hair. He told Mom, "I like Sis's haircut. Why don't you cut Peg's hair like that instead of lettin' it hang down all stringy?" My hair was golden blonde and hung down to my shoulders in waves. Sis had a haircut that looked like Uncle Jake had set a cook pot upside down on her head and cut all around the edges. Mom just glared at Dad, and I knew there would be hell to pay in the car on the way home. We ended the meal with a regular fancy apple pie that Aunt Bessie had baked on the previous day.

Just as we were getting in the car to leave for home, we saw Uncle Jake coming out of the barn with a feed sack wrapped around his left hand. Mom looked at him and said, "Look at that dumb head. I wonder what he did to his hand. Dad sneaked a glance toward Uncle Jake but kept quiet as he drove us up the road toward home.

On the way down the other side of Little North Mountain,

Mom finally broke the silence. She brought up the remark that Dad had made about Cousin Sis's haircut. She told him, "You mind your own business about how I fix Peg's hair. I'll be damned if I am going to let her walk around with a "piss pot" haircut. You just say that kinda stuff when you're with your family. You think I won't argue with you about stuff like that, but I am warnin' you. You had better stop it, or the next time I am gonna let you have it right then." Dad drove on home without a word as he often did when he knew Mom had had all of his family that she could take for one day.

The following Sunday when we went to Hopkins Gap for dinner, Grandma Molly told us that Uncle Jake felt so bad about what he did to Aunt Bessie, that he had gone out to the woodpile and chopped off his thumb with an axe so that he couldn't pick up a glass jar and throw it at her again. Aunt Ethel visited her sister, Aunt Bessie, the day after the big fight. She told me, "I saw Jake's thumb layin' beside the choppin' block. It was all shriveled up. I don't know what happened to it. I reckon the chickens picked it up and carried it off."

For the rest of his life I remembered that fight every time I saw Uncle Jake. On hog butchering day I watched Uncle Jake clean hogs' heads without his thumb. He was right-handed, and he had cut off his left thumb. As I grew older, I tried to make sense out of this. I wondered how he thought cutting off his left thumb would stop him from throwing a quart of whiskey with his right hand. After a lot of pondering I made sense of the situation for myself by assuming that he thought his missing left thumb would remind him not to throw something at Aunt Bessie with his right hand.

In that extreme family disturbance, I don't believe the smell of a family pie baking would have sobered up Uncle Jake or averted this disturbance. Uncle Jake was an unfortunate soul who was more susceptible to the powers of alcohol than to an excellent meal and family fellowship. I am happy to say that very few family gatherings were preceded by a nasty family fight, and none were as memorable as this one.

Chapter 2

The Cooks

"We may live without friends;
We may live without books;
But civilized man cannot
live without cooks.

—*Meredith Owen*

Hopkins Gap children spent their lives in the company of many strong women and great cooks. Grandmothers, mothers, and aunts were the gatekeepers of food and family traditions in Hopkins Gap. By hanging around at the elbows of these women, many generations of females have learned how to hunt, gather, cook and preserve food for their families. Just one generation before mine, young girls were often orphaned at very young ages for several reasons. Their mothers married very young—eleven to fourteen years of age. They became pregnant immediately and spent the majority of their remaining years having babies. They had large numbers of children with only the care of a midwife. Many of them were exhausted by their mid to late thirties and died soon after, leaving behind adult children as well as under aged children. The younger children were taken in by older sisters; and, in some cases, they assumed the duties of the household which included cooking, cleaning, and caring for their young nieces and nephews.

After the incident at Uncle Jake's house, Mom wouldn't let Dad stop there. Since we rarely ate Sunday dinner at home, he would choose among three other possibilities: Aunt Hazel and Uncle Jim's house, Grandma Molly and Grandpa Austin's house or further down the road to Uncle Shirley and Aunt Ethel's house.

Each place had a special appeal to me. If we stopped at Uncle Jim's house, I could go back to the Shoemaker River and pretend to be a hermit living in a shack. Sometimes Uncle Jim had an old broken-down car setting just outside the kitchen window. He would work on the motor all afternoon with me hanging over the fender to watch. Occasionally, he would shock me by taking my hand and touching it to the car battery. He always got a good laugh out of that trick. As I look back, I think he probably wanted me to get my nose out of his way so he could work.

If we stopped at Grandpa Austin's house, I could play in the field we called the "bottom" with my cousins. We invented all kinds of games and carried them out as we explored the woods and the creeks. If there were enough of us, we would split into teams for a ball game.

Uncle Shirley's house was my favorite place to stop for dinner. He had nine children all around the same ages as we were. A lot of other families stopped at his house too. Sometimes there were enough children to have several softball games going at once. In the summer, we would lounge in a water hole in the river just below his house, and keep a keen eye out for snakes along the river bank.

Uncle Shirley collected old junked cars. He kept them in a small field behind his house until he had time to chop them up to haul to the steel mills in Pennsylvania. I loved to get in them and pretend to drive. We all searched under the seats for coins and often found some. We immediately would run up the road to Ress Kirkpatrick's little store and spend our findings. My favorite thing to buy was a bottle of orange crush. We didn't get much pop to drink because Mom and Dad didn't have the money.

Because very few households had telephones, I don't recall any communication during the previous week that would have warned a household that we were coming for Sunday dinner. It was just a fact that wherever we stopped would have a huge dinner, prepared with enough food for an extra family—Mom, Dad, and five children.

We weren't the only family that just picked a place to eat Sunday dinner; the cooks just knew to prepare a huge meal for whoever decided to drop in to eat. The cook, at whichever house we landed, had a plan to keep enough clean plates and forks for folks who arrived after the first table of eaters. Someone was assigned the duty of picking up the dirty dishes and washing them for the next round of guests. Often we would be handed a plate and a fork that was still warm from the dishpan of soapy, scalding hot water.

Sometimes Dad let Mom know where we were going especially if it was to Grandpa Austin's and Grandma Molly's house, because she didn't like to go there too often. She fussed and complained, "When we go there for Sunday dinner, it just puts extra work on me." Mom would bake a few pies on Saturday to make a contribution to the Sunday meal. She added, "They don't go anywhere all week or talk to anybody so there's nothin' to talk about. I get tired of sittin' and watchin' them rock back and forth and spit snuff. Nobody has anything to say to each other."

Aunt Lena, my dad's sister, lived with Grandma Molly and Grandpa Austin. Neither Grandma Molly nor Aunt Lena knew how to bake pies, although time and time again Mom had taken the ingredients with her to teach them how to make a pie. Mom told me, "They are dumber than bake wood split crossways. It's like they can't learn anything different from what they already know." So Mom kept trying to teach them, fussing, and baking pies to take with us when we visited them.

Mom enjoyed going to Aunt Ethel's house because Ethel could drive a car and did get out of the house during the week. They often went to the grocery store together. There was never a dull moment when those two were together in the kitchen. They whispered to each other and laughed like school children. They had a close bond. Aunt Ethel often tells me, "Myrt was more like a sister to me than any sister I had."

*   *   *   *   *

Most of the women in Hopkins Gap were good cooks, and in fact, I never met a bad cook in Hopkins Gap, except for Grandma Molly and Aunt Lena. They weren't really bad cooks; they just cooked the same thing all the time. I did hear some gossip along the way about one or two women who "couldn't boil water" or "fry an egg." Mom always said, "Some women are just too lazy to cook, and some women, like Lena and Grandma Molly, are just too dumb to cook." She said, "I don't understand what's wrong with them. Anybody can cook. There's not that much to it." I never met those women who were too lazy to cook, probably because my daddy was smart enough not to drop in at their houses for Sunday dinner.

Two of my family members stand out in my mind as having influenced me the most when it comes to cooking and eating. These two women hunted and gathered, planted gardens, preserved food, and cooked the most delicious meals you could find anywhere. Both were born in Hopkins Gap and carried on the food tradition that had been handed down from their mothers and grandmothers. They, in turn, passed those same food traditions on to their daughters, granddaughters, and daughters-in-law who continue to provide delicious meals for their families. The two women were Myrtle Morris Shifflett, my mother, and Aunt Ethel Crawford Morris. They are known to this day as the "two best damned cooks in Hopkins Gap." Occasionally they are referred to as the "two best damned cooks in the Shenandoah Valley" indicating that their reputations have spread beyond the little gap in the Allegheny Mountains.

Many people have sat around Mom's and Aunt Ethel's tables and consumed their meat and vegetables and their pies--both fancy round pies and family pies. I often asked them how they could cook such fine dishes. They stared at me and, most of the time, didn't answer. I now believe it might have been the same as me asking a flower how it blooms or a bird how it flies. Cooking to Mom and Aunt Ethel was just a part of who they were.

Neither Mom nor Aunt Ethel bothered with a lot of measuring or fussed too much about details. I asked them to give me their recipes. They nonchalantly named the ingredients. I asked, "How much flour and how much salt? They both had the same answer, "Oh, I don't know, enough for a good mess, a couple of handfuls maybe, a pinch of salt. It depends on the size of the pan you're using." In frustration, I tried to pry out of them the ingredients for four people. My answer was a confused stare from them and finally a statement such as, "Well, I can't tell you that. You'll just have to try it out a couple of times until you get it like you want it." I finally convinced Aunt Ethel to show me what a "pinch of this or that" looks like. She let me photograph her hand with a "pinch" and a "handful." I asked her to show me a "dash of this or that." Aunt Ethel said, "Just think of a 'dash' as the same as a 'pinch' except that you throw a 'dash' into the ingredients. A "dash" might be a little less than a "pinch.'" Although I'm still not sure of my 'pinches' and 'dashes', I was very honored that she took the time to show me.

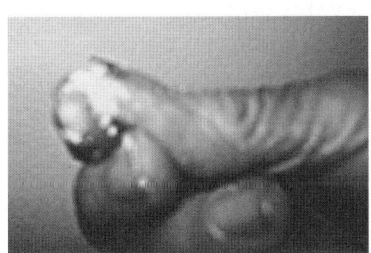

Aunt Ethel showing me a pinch of salt

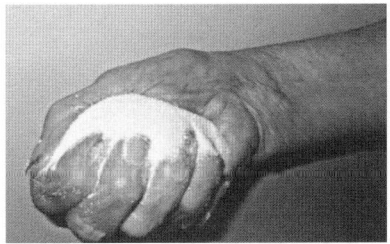

Aunt Ethel showing me a handful of sugar

Mom and Aunt Ethel were great cooks because they began cooking when they were little girls and would become all puffed up with pride when folks rubbed their stomachs after a meal and bragged about their cooking. As people consumed their dishes, both

Mom and Aunt Ethel kept their ears open for compliments. When they heard a person say they liked a particular food, that person could be assured the same food would be prepared for them over and over again. Once, I was hunting deer with Aunt Ethel. She packed a lunch of sausage sandwiches with mustard and sliced dill pickles. I raved about how much I liked it. To this day, every time I go to visit Aunt Ethel, she fixes me a sausage sandwich with mustard and dill pickles. She has been doing this for over forty years.

Mom and Aunt Ethel's approach to cooking was simple because most of their foods were simple and fresh from the fields, woods, and gardens. Gourmet cooks, who are highly respected today for cooking with fresh vegetables and herbs, have nothing on these two cooks. They always cooked the same basic survival foods that had brought them through the Great Depression and the hard times of drought when gardens failed and the harvests were lean.

Mom hated President Hoover. She blamed him for having to eat "water gravy" during the Depression. She told me, "Many times Rob and Goldie didn't have anything to cook with but flour and potatoes. I put a little lard in a skillet and browned some flour. When I should have been pouring milk into the browned flour to make a pan of gravy, I had to pour in water. We ate it over fried potatoes. We would have all starved if President Roosevelt hadn't got in office."

*   *   *   *   *

Large families were common in Hopkins Gap during the time when Mom and Aunt Ethel were born. Their mothers married at age fourteen and eleven, respectively, and began having children right away. This was very typical of the women of Hopkins Gap. It was common for a married couple to have between eight and twelve children. Some of their first born daughters had married and were having children of their own before their mothers stopped having babies.

Both Mom's and Aunt Ethel's mothers died when they

were very young, one died several months after giving birth to her eighteenth child. The other one spent the last years of her life in bed and finally died there. Her living children told me she was just worn out. This was common in Hopkins Gap at the time. There were few doctors, and most folks depended on Granny Women and midwives for their medical needs. By the time my generation was born, there was one doctor, Dr. Charles Watson, who would travel all the way from Broadway—probably twenty-five miles from Hopkins Gap—and assist the midwives in complicated births. Later births in my generation occurred in a hospital in Harrisonburg under the supervision of Dr. Watson.

The young mothers who died often left a number of minor children behind to be cared for by older siblings or by other families in the Hopkins Gap community. Mom and Aunt Ethel found themselves in these circumstances. Their mothers died at age thirty-nine and thirty-seven, respectively. They both moved in with an older married sister at age ten; and both took over much of the child-rearing and cooking duties in their new homes. Mom moved in with her sister, my Aunt Goldie, and Ethel moved in with her sister, Hazel. When I asked Mom and Aunt Ethel where they learned to cook, their answer was essentially the same, "I ought to know how to cook. I've been doin' it all my life." This answer made a lot of sense to me after I learned the details of their early lives.

*   *   *   *   *

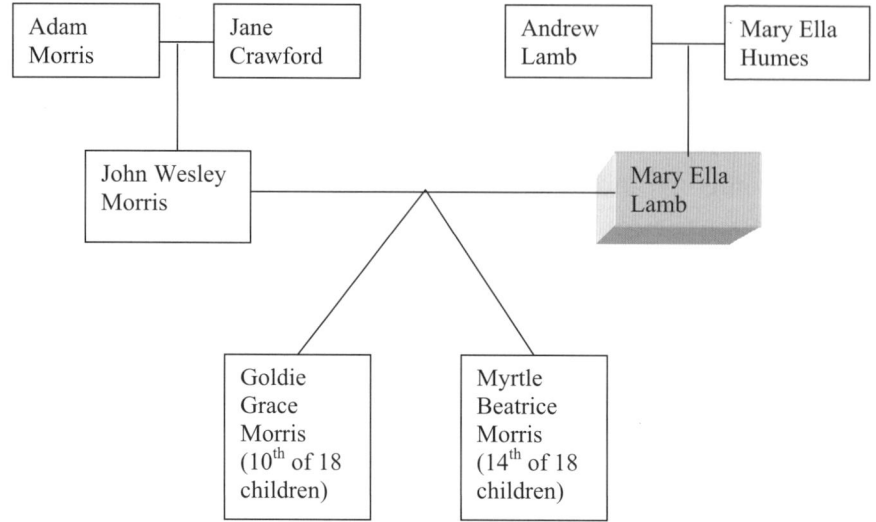

| Adam Morris | Jane Crawford | | Andrew Lamb | Mary Ella Humes |

| John Wesley Morris | | | Mary Ella Lamb |

| Goldie Grace Morris (10ᵗʰ of 18 children) | Myrtle Beatrice Morris (14ᵗʰ of 18 children) |

Mary Ella Lamb Morris (1887–1926)

Mary Ella Lamb Morris was the mother of Carl, Zilla, Charles, Stella, Warren, Gilbert, James, Dorothy, Goldie, Shirley, Gladys, Myrtle, Russel, Vivian, and Richard. She was born to Andrew Lamb and Mary Ella Humes on June 4, 1887 (Bennett) She married John Wesley Morris on August 25, 1901 at the age of fourteen. John was born in Greene County, Virginia, on March 20, 1880, and migrated with a group of relatives, over the Blue Ridge Mountains and across the Shenandoah Valley, to settle in Hopkins Gap in the late 1800's.

Mary Ella Lamb Morris at age 17, holding her third child, Charlie

Mary Morris gave birth to her first child on April 15, 1902. She celebrated the birth of her first born before she had a chance to celebrate her first anniversary and before her fifteenth birthday. During their twenty-five year marriage, Mary and John continued to have children until they reached a total of eighteen. They raised twelve of their children to adulthood. Others were stillborn or died at very young ages. John and the attending midwife buried the stillborn children in the back yard wherever they lived at the time.

Uncle Shirley Morris, often told me, "When we lived up on the hill across the river from my house, they buried two of the dead babies at the back of the yard. You can still hear those babies crying if you walk through there at night." At the time of her death, Mary left six children under the age of twelve. John died four years later having cut his hand in a butchering accident. He left three children under the age of thirteen.

Mom was only five years old when her mother died, but she often described her as a pretty woman who worked very hard. Mom would tell me, "She was skinny with a waist as thin as a wasp. She made her own clothes out of bright colored cloth and always wore an apron that she pinned to her breast. I remember her holding me against her chest, and I could feel the pins against my face. My favorite memory of her was at the clothes line hangin' up line after line of clothes that she had boiled in a black kettle and rubbed on a washin' board. She could put a good meal on the table when she had something to cook. Sometimes all she had was pinto beans, potatoes, and flour. She would stretch the beans over several suppers by making some biscuit dough and cutting it into thin strips about the size of a pencil. She chopped them up and put them in the beans. She called it beans and rivils. She was always pregnant."

I asked Uncle Shirley if his mama ever made any special dishes. He told me, "There was no such thing as special dishes. She cooked what she had and we ate what she cooked. We were glad to have whatever it was."

Grandma Mary always raised a garden. Uncle Shirley told me about a time when he tried to get smart with his mother. "She raised potatoes every year, and there were enough of us kids to put one on each row to pull weeds. One time I finished my row before anybody else and went on in the house. Mama asked, 'Have you finished weedin' your row? If you finished already, you didn't do a very good job of it.' I tried to sass her back and said, 'If you want it done any better.......WHACK!!!! Her hand landed across my nose. I ended up back in the corner with a bloody nose and busted lip where I finished my sentence under my breath, '....you can do it yourself.'"

Not only did Mary have eighteen children of her own, but she was known as an exceptionally good midwife. In studying my dad's birth certificate, I was surprised to see that his future mother-in-law, Mary Ella Morris served as the midwife at his birth. With a few calculations, I learned that Grandma Mary was pregnant with my mother when she assisted my dad's entry into this world.

Mary never recovered from the birth of her last child. She was thirty-nine years old when Richard was born in May, 1926. Mom often told me the story as it was told to her, "My daddy was scared Mom would get pregnant too soon again, so he asked Lansy Knight and his wife, Victoria, if they would keep Mom until she got over havin' Richard. She moved in with them just across the mountain, but she died in their house four months later of heart dropsy." (Congestive heart failure in today's medical terms). The date was September 24, 1926. Aunt Goldie was eleven years old and Mom was five years old when Mary died.

* * * * *

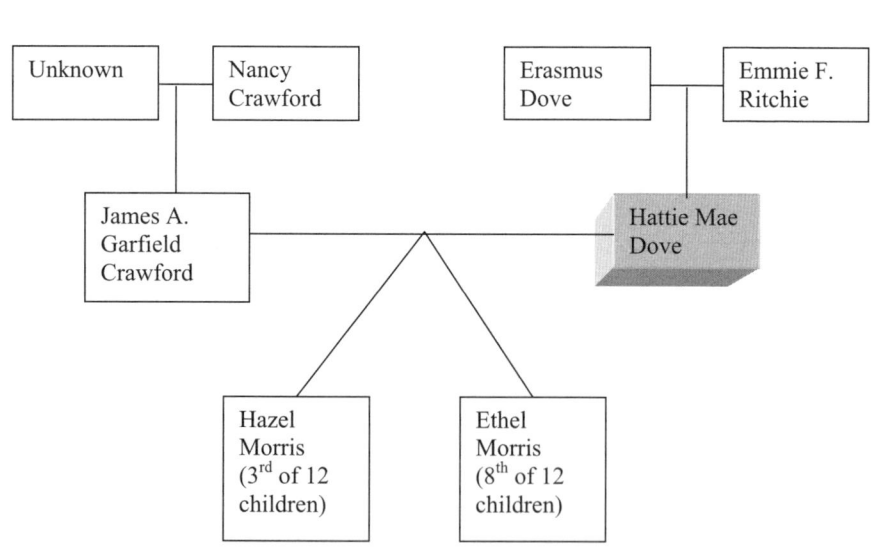

Hattie May Dove Crawford (1898–1937)

Hattie May Dove was mother to Melvin, Hazel, Russell, Beulah, Howard, Amy, Ethel, Robert, Genevive, Sherman, and Otis (Skip). She was born to Erasmus F. Dove and Emmie F. Ritchie on May 7, 1898 and died on July 20, 1937 at age thirty-nine. She married James A. Garfield Crawford on December 20, 1909 at age eleven (Bennett). Garfield, as he was known, was born in Greene County, Virginia. He moved with family and relatives to settle in Hopkins Gap in the late 1800s.

Hattie Crawford at age 13, holding her first child, Melvin

The first of Garfield and Hattie's children was born on December 30, 1911. Hattie was twelve years old. She and Garfield went on to have a total of twelve children.

Hattie was a very sickly woman for the last ten years of her life but apparently had four children during those years. She was often bedridden and too weak to cook for her family. I have often heard that Hattie suffered with consumption (tuberculosis). One of her sons was her main caregiver. He was only ten years old. He told me, "My momma was a big woman, but she had lost so much weight that I could lift her out of bed and set her on a chair until I changed her sheets. So, you know she was really sick. She was nothin' but bones. When I put on clean sheets, I lifted her back in the bed." He told me, with sadness in his voice, "One day she felt good enough to get up. She went straight to the kitchen and mixed up a big cake of warm bread. It tasted so good. We all thought she was gonna get better." When Hattie died, she left five children under the age of twelve. The children were taken in by the community at large and moved from house to house to find shelter, food, and clothing. Mr. Crawford was not able to provide a home for his underage children. He died when his house burned down in Hopkins Gap on December 22, 1958.

Aunt Ethel told me recently that her mother, Hattie, was known as such a good cook that the Shenandoah Valley farmers asked her to help their wives cook the noon meal on days when a large number of men were needed to harvest a big crop of wheat or barley. Aunt Ethel said, "One time John I. Myers [a well-known farmer and friend of Hopkins Gap folks] saw me in town. It was long after Mom had died. He said, 'Ethel, if you are half the woman your mother was, you are a fine person. Before you were born she helped my wife, Ada, do the cooking for the men who came to help me with thrashing. She was a wonderful cook, I tell you.'" Aunt Ethel went on to say, "I never knew much about Mom. She got sick when I was four years old, and I went to live with Hazel and Jim."

*   *   *   *   *

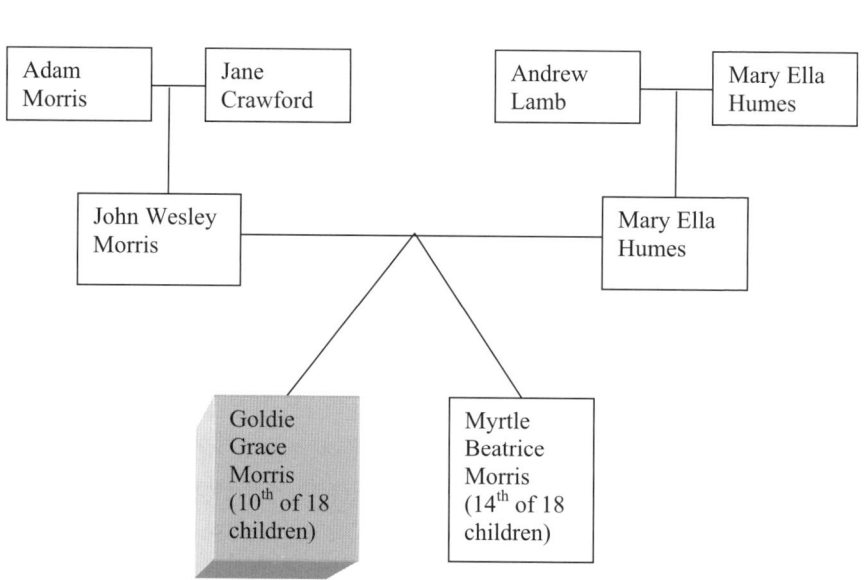

Goldie Morris Crawford (1915–1987)

Goldie, the tenth daughter of Mary Ella Lamb Morris, was orphaned at age eleven by the death of her mother. Goldie remained at home with her father, John, until he married Ivy Lam. When she had just turned thirteen, she married Robert Noah Crawford. She always described him as "the love of my life." She said with a sweet smile, "I had my eye on him from the first time I saw him." Uncle

Rob, as he was called, was twenty-one years old when they got married.

Within a year after Aunt Goldie married Uncle Rob, her father, John Morris, died. His remaining three underage children were scattered among the older brothers and sisters, uncles, and aunts. After a period of time, Mom moved in with Goldie and Rob. She helped to raise their children and did most of the cooking for the family. She remained with them until she married my dad, Norman Shifflett, in 1940.

Goldie Morris Crawford, standing in the kitchen on a Sunday afternoon after church

Aunt Goldie was widowed in 1946 at age thirty-one. She and her husband, Uncle Rob, had bought a small farm just outside Hopkins Gap. He made his living with a saw mill that he bought and set up in one of the pasture fields that he called the "blue grass" field. When Uncle Rob died of complications from gall bladder surgery, Goldie lost his income. She had four young children still in school. In spite of the fact that she could not read or write, Goldie learned to drive and went to work in a silk mill in Harrisonburg. With her factory income, she did an admirable job of raising her children and was able to hold on to her farm. She kept it in good repair until her death in 1987.

*   *   *   *   *

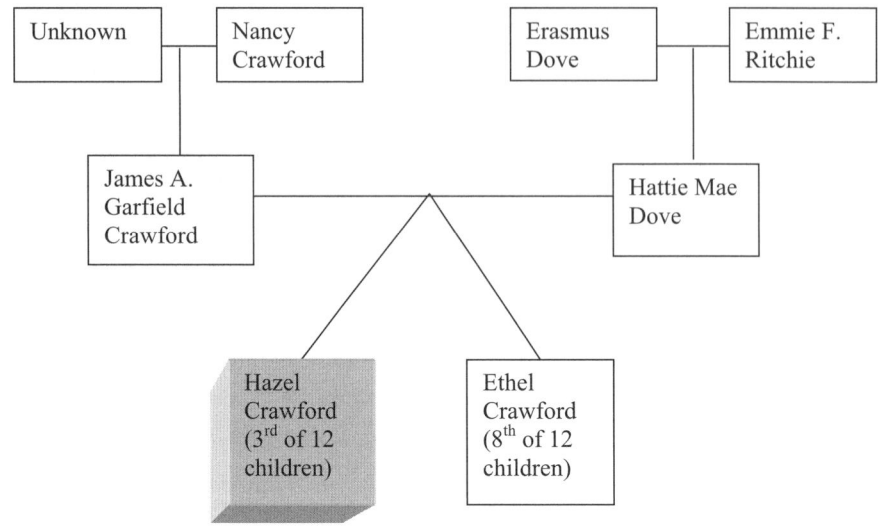

Hazel Crawford Morris (1916-2000)

When Hattie May Dove Crawford died, her third daughter, Hazel, was already married to Uncle Jim Morris--Aunt Goldie and Mom's older brother. Aunt Hazel and Uncle Jim took in Aunt Hazel's younger sister, Aunt Ethel, when she was four years old because Hattie, her mother, could no longer care for her. By age ten, Aunt Ethel was doing most of the cooking for Hazel's family.

Aunt Hazel and Uncle Jim raised Aunt Ethel until she married Uncle Shirley Morris, Uncle Jim's younger brother, at age fifteen. Aunt Hazel and Aunt Ethel had living arrangements similar to Aunt Goldie and Mom. Aunt Ethel, like Mom,

Hazel Crawford Morris is resting in her easy chair.

helped with Aunt Hazel's and Uncle Jim's children and did a lot of the cooking for the family.

The lives of Aunt Hazel Morris and Aunt Goldie Crawford took a different turn from that of their mothers. They both lived fairly long lives and, most importantly, expanded the possibilities for women in Hopkins Gap. Aunt Hazel was one of the first women to learn to drive a car. She regularly drove from Hopkins Gap to Harrisonburg, where she worked in poultry processing plants for many years. Her older daughter, Christine, learned to cook at a young age. She did much of the cooking while Aunt Hazel worked for wages. Aunt Hazel used her income to help support her family and to modernize her home. She had one of the first indoor bathrooms in Hopkins Gap.

*　　*　　*　　*　　*

The "Two Best Damned Cooks in Hopkins Gap"

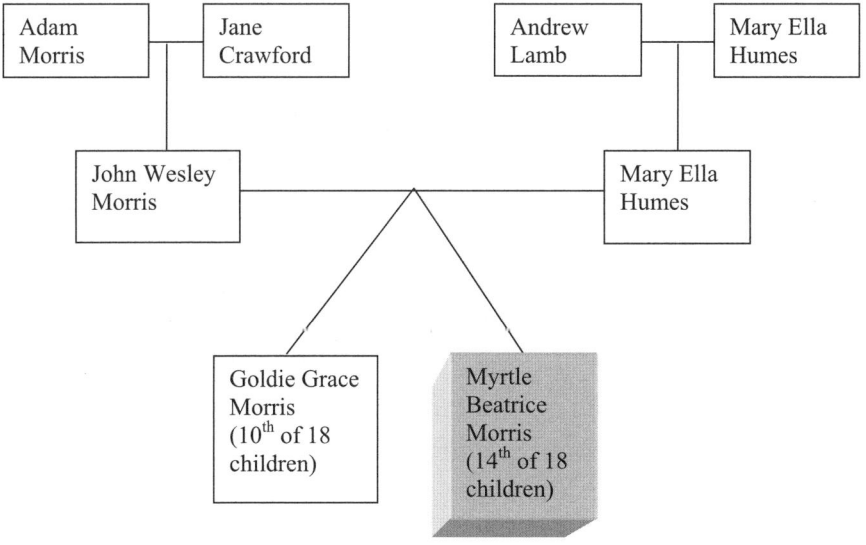

Myrtle Morris Shifflett (1920-2001)

Myrtle (Mom) met Norman Shifflett, my dad, and married him in 1940. She was 19 years old and he was twenty-one. They set up housekeeping and started their family nine months and ten days later, with my birth in 1941. Even before Mom was married she had gained a reputation for being a very good cook.

Myrtle is in her kitchen, mixing dressing for cole slaw in 1994.

She always glowed with pride when people bragged about her food. She responded, "I sure had enough practice. I started cookin' when I was ten years old and ain't stopped yet." Then she would launch into stories about the young men who tried to court her because of her cooking skills.

Mom often told the story of Rob Craig who loved her biscuits and sausage gravy and wanted to court her. "He might've liked me, but I thought he was ugly. One time he come up behind me when I was slicin' ham. He reached under my arm and felt my titty. I took the butcher knife and hacked him across the knuckles. The blood just flew. He never touched me after that."

Mom frequently described the painful four years after her mother died. "My daddy tried to hold the household together for us younger kids." Two of his young daughters, Aunt Dorothy and Aunt Goldie, did the cooking for John's family. Mom often related sad stories about how they either undercooked or overcooked everything they put on the stove. She never recovered from the frustration she felt about Dorothy and Goldie's efforts to cook. She often said, "I loved my daddy so much. I wanted to cook for him, but I was only five or six and too little to reach the stove. I worried about him when I saw him set down at the kitchen table for supper. He would eat a little, then get up from the supper table, and go out on the front porch. I wondered if he was missing Mom as he looked down the ridge toward Uncle Joe's house. He never talked about Momma around us kids. I think he knew it would upset us too much."

For two years John Wesley Morris lived alone with his children just across the road and up the ridge from his brother, Joseph Morris and his sister-in-law, Millie. According to Mom, "No matter what time of year it was, smoke from Aunt Millie's wood stove curled out of the chimney toward the sky. When the wind was just right, the smell of her home made bread, brown beans, and fried cabbage drifted up the ridge to our house."

"Sometimes Aunt Millie would come out to her yard gate and call my daddy to come down to eat with them," she continued. "I can still see her standing there just outside the garden gate. In the summer, her yard was filled with flowers—hollyhocks and zinnias and snow ball bushes—waving gently in the wind. Her yard was a great place for bees and butterflies to land. The seeds from her flowers provided a lot of food for all kinds of songbirds in the fall and winter."

"Aunt Millie would wipe her hands on her apron, look up the hill to see if my daddy was on the porch. She would call to him, 'John, come on down and eat we have aplenty.'"

After a moment of remembering and gathering her thoughts, Mom continued, "Sometimes he went on down to eat when she called him, but not all the time. I don't remember her ever invitin' us kids. We understood that she didn't have enough food to feed

Millie Morris standing at her yard gate with hanging plants on fence and upside down milk crocks on the fence behind her.

all of us, and my daddy worked hard and needed to keep up his strength." Finally, Mom added at the end of her story, "When Aunt Millie would bake, she made some extra light rolls or a loaf of bread. She sent it home with my daddy, so we could all have milk gravy and bread for the next morning's breakfast."

Although many years had passed, and there had been many "tellings" of this same story, Mom's eyes always filled with tears. Sometimes she would break down and sob. When this happened, I would cry too, as I thought about what it must have felt like to lose a mother at age five.

John lived a hard life for four years after his wife, Mary, died. He barely kept his family together for the first two of those years. One day he went down the road about a mile and asked John Lam if he could marry his daughter, Ivy. John said yes because Ivy was "gettin' some age on her" and no other Hopkins Gap man was showing any interest. She was already twenty-two years old!! Grandpa John and

Ivy got married, and Ivy took over the household chores and the cooking. Mom always claimed that her daddy did not sleep with Ivy. "He didn't want her for that. He just needed somebody to keep house."

John died two years after he married Ivy. His household broke up and the remaining underage children were scattered in several households around Hopkins Gap. Ivy, his widow, went back down the road to her parent's log cabin home. She cared for her parents until they died and then lived the remainder of her life there. Mom described the day her daddy

John Wesley Morris and Ivy Lam Morris on their wedding day

died; "He was across Little North Mountain butchering for somebody and sliced his thumb open. By the time he got home, he had lost a lot of blood and was complaining about the pain. He kept on takin' aspirin for the pain and the bleedin' never stopped. He took thirty aspirin that day to kill the pain." She continued, "We know now that the aspirin thinned his blood so he couldn't stop the bleeding. He lost so much blood that he had a heart attack and died after he went to bed. He was only forty-nine years old."

Myrtle Morris Shifflett was nine years old and in the third grade at White Hall School at the time of her daddy's death.

After John died, Mom moved in with her sister, Aunt Zilla, who was married to John Raleigh Carr. They already had eight children of their own, but they made room for Mom, who was nine years old, and her sister, Aunt Dorothy, who was sixteen. All her life, Mom told stories of how Aunt Zilla was terribly mean to her. Aunt Goldie often told me, "Me and Rob knowed Zill was mean to Myrtle, so we took her in after a year."

*   *   *   *   *

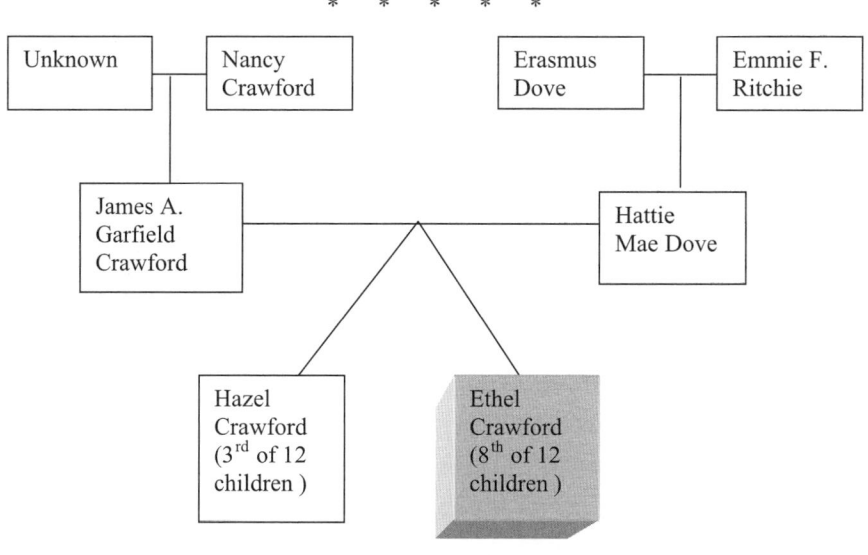

- 45 -

Ethel Crawford Morris (1926–)

Aunt Ethel was ten years old when her mother Hattie died. She was taken in by her older sister, Aunt Hazel Crawford Morris and Uncle Jim Morris. Aunt Ethel said, "Hazel expected me to take over most of the cooking when I moved in with her and Jim. I was just learning how to cook, and Hazel and Jim went to Harrisonburg to buy groceries. I decided I was hungry for pie, so I made up some dough and tried to bake a blackberry pie. When Hazel got home, the pie had bubbled out all over the oven because I didn't know how to seal the dough over the

Here is Aunt Ethel, in 2005, with her ancient rolling pin; rolling out yet another dough for egg custard pies.

top of the pie. Hazel cracked my head with her knuckles and fussed at me for wasting flour and fruit. Jim jumped all over Hazel for crackin' my head. He told her, "You leave her alone. At least she tried to bake a pie." Aunt Ethel soon learned how to bake a pie, and she has never forgotten to this day.

Mom and Aunt Ethel, the "two best damned cooks in Hopkins Gap" had very similar early life circumstances. Both were orphaned at an early age by the death of their mothers and forced to move in with an older sister where, as they told the story, they were treated much like Cinderella was treated by the "ugly" sisters. Both were ten years old when they took over many of the household chores and began their Cinderella roles. They each report being "cracked on the head" with their sisters' knuckles when the food they cooked was burned, undercooked, or didn't taste just right. Mom told us many times, "I learned to cook in the school of hard knocks. Rob told me if I didn't fry potatoes to suit him, he was going to beat my ass. He taught me a lot about cooking. He didn't cook himself, but he knew how he liked his food done."

Aunt Ethel shared a story about "getting tired" of doing all the work. "It was hot summer time, and Hazel told me to go to the garden to dig potatoes for supper. The garden had weeds taller than my head, and I didn't want to go because I was afraid of snakes. I pretended I couldn't find the hoe, and I said, 'Where in the hell is the damned hoe?' Hazel heard me say that and told Jim. He whipped my ass real hard, and said, 'I will show you where the damned hoe is. Now go dig some taters for supper.' I cried my eyes out and went into the tall weeds to dig some taters."

Aunt Ethel stayed with Aunt Hazel and Uncle Jim until she fell in love with Uncle Jim's brother, Uncle Shirley. Mom had just gotten married to my daddy, and they had set up housekeeping on Muddy Creek in John I. Myers' rental house. Aunt Ethel moved in with Mom and Dad when she was fourteen years old. She married Uncle Shirley when she was fifteen and continued to live with them for a while after she was married.

She told me, "I learned a lot about cookin' from your mom while I lived with her. She taught me how to cook brown beans, and Shirl said I cooked the best brown beans because the broth got thick. Myrtle taught me how to tell when beans was ready for the seasoning. The skin had to be coming off the beans and stickin' to the pot above the broth. Myrtle said, 'Don't put your lard, salt, and pepper in until you see the skins sticking above the beans. After you season them to taste, cook them hard again for about half an hour. If you do this your broth will get nice and thick.'"

Many Sundays I have sat in Aunt Ethel's kitchen and listened to Mom and her carry on some interesting conversations while they cooked dinner. They would slide their pots and pans around on the top of the wood stove searching for the right temperature for each stage of cooking, while they talked and shared food stories and recipes.

In between food stories, they kept each other up on the latest gossip, including recent pregnancies and births, along with vivid descriptions of the birth pains, the length of the labor, and what the woman said while the baby was being born. Midwives were not sworn to secrecy in those days. They brought each other up to date on which women in Hopkins Gap were committing adultery and with whom.

Mom and Aunt Ethel described certain women and referred to them as "whoring around." They were very serious during these exchanges and condemned the women to hell. So I asked, "What about the men, Mom?" She answered with a demonstration. She picked up a pencil and told me to hold my hand up so she could stick the lead into my palm. Of course, in anticipation of the pain, I moved my hand. She explained, "See, if a woman don't lay down and hold still, a man can't stick it in her."

I wasn't ever satisfied with that answer, but I let it go for the time being and returned to my chores. My job at these Sunday dinners was to cut up fresh and canned fruit for fruit salad that would be spooned over banana cake for dessert. I listened to all their discussions as I quietly filled the fruit bowl.

No matter where we ended up for Sunday dinner, each dish that was put on the table had a memory or a story to accompany it. The fried chicken brought back memories of the previous week when the unsuspecting chickens were walking around the yard, picking at the grass and scratching for bugs. I especially remember how awful the wash house smelled when we cleaned the chickens on Saturday. It was the same with squirrel, or venison, wild turkey, or rabbit. While we sat around the table and ate, the hunters shared detailed descriptions of the kill and the field processing, and the struggle of "dragging" the dead deer out of the Hog Pens; a nearby mountain range. They described the sly manner in which the turkey had been "called" within shooting distance, or how cold, wet, or foggy the morning had been when the squirrels were hunted.

Aunt Ethel would remove the lid to stir the green beans and see if it was time to move them to the back of the stove. As she determined if the beans were tender enough to eat, she told a story about picking them. She said, "It was so hot yesterday when I picked these beans, I thought I would die. But the beans were ready to pick, and it had to be done. I waited until the sun went down and set on the back porch after supper to string 'em."

Sometimes the stories were more exciting. Grandma Molly often shared the experience of killing a copperhead snake who was basking in the hot sun between the bean rows. She would say, "I figured I'd run into a snake, so I took my hoe with me and kept my eyes ahead in the row. Sure 'nough there laid a copperhead. I whacked his head off with my hoe and went on pickin' beans."

Aunt Ethel shared stories of being greeted, on many occasions, by one or two rattlesnakes at her cellar door. Grandma Molly and Aunt Lena often found copperhead snakes wrapped around their fruit and vegetable jars when they went into the cellar. Their cellar was a welcome resting place for snakes because it was simply a space dug out into the side of a low-lying ridge. It was framed up on the back and sides with logs and boards crudely nailed together. Even though the entry door was always shut, snakes could crawl in through a myriad of cracks. The women never went to the cellar for canned food or potatoes without arming themselves with a hoe to chop the head off an unsuspecting snake.

Can snakes tell time....?

It was not unusual to find snakes in some of the houses in Hopkins Gap. Mary Turner related a story of her mom and dad, Joe and Millie Morris, finding a copperhead snake living behind and around

their clock on the living room wall. Mary still has the clock. It is a beautiful, handmade antique clock.

My step grandmother, Ivy Lam Morris, lived in a log cabin. She told everyone who visited her about hearing the snakes crawl in through the logs and go into her dresser drawers to rest among her clothing. She said, "They don't bother me, and I don't bother them.

Food was not just eaten to satisfy hunger and meet the energy and nutritional needs of Hopkins Gap families. Food connected family members at the Sunday dinner feasts. When it was time to eat, the men were called to the table first, signifying their dominant place in the families. If there were spaces left after the men were seated, the children were called to the table. The women tended the others; keeping the dishes filled and meeting the needs and requests of the men and children. Once everyone else was fed, the women cleared the dirty dishes, and sat down to eat. Many times, the chicken plate was empty. I have watched Mom and Aunt Ethel take partially uneaten pieces of chicken off the children's plates after they had finished eating. They cleaned slivers of meat off the bones so that they would have some meat with their meals. The cooks, who had gathered the raw products and prepared the meal over a hot wood stove, were often left to forage for their own meal. This seemed very unfair to me when it happened. Watching this as a young girl was a strong factor in my decision not to live the life that my mom and Aunt Ethel had chosen for themselves.

*   *   *   *   *

Mom never worked outside our home. As a homemaker, her daily travels were limited in area, but diverse in responsibility and results. She spent the early hours of each morning down the hill at the barn where she fed and milked her Jersey cows. She had five cows at one time, each in varying stages of pregnancy and milk production. Before and after meal time, she was working in front of her stove and sink. In the summer, she weeded the garden or picked vegetables until the sun got too hot. In the afternoons, she canned her produce while her supper simmered on the back of the stove. Those same hours in the winter were spent sewing, patching my dad and brothers' britches, or making comforters for our beds or to sell. A lot of Mom's time was spent processing the milk from her cows. She made butter, cottage cheese, clabber (described in Chapter 4), and butter milk. She washed and ironed all our clothes and hung them on the line while bragging, "My clothes are whiter than anybody's I've ever seen."

Battling the blood-thirsty bedbugs....

For many families in Hopkins Gap, the warm days of May meant it was time to battle the bedbugs. My introduction to bedbugs occurred shortly after I was born; therefore, I don't remember how it felt. When I was old enough to be hanging around with Mom when she was changing the bed sheets, she showed me a bloodstain on the corner of the mattress on which she and dad slept. The stain was as large as a fifty-cent piece. Mom said, "That's your blood. When you were a baby, we had bed bugs. You slept with us because you were still nursing. One night you kept whining and wiggling. I lit the lamp and looked around to see what was the matter. Two bed bugs were biting your shoulder. They were full of blood when I mashed them. That is your blood on the mattress."

I don't remember when the bedbugs bit me, of course. I was too young, but Mom kept that bloody mattress for years until she could afford another one. She showed me the bloody spot every time I helped her change the sheets. I remember thinking that if I died, she would have something by which to remember me. I told her one time, "If I die, you will have this spot to remember me." She said, "Here grab that pillow case and let me show you how to put it on the pillow." I was hoping she would say something about me being special and important to her and that she would cry every time she saw the bloodstain.

When I was old enough, I asked her, "How did you get rid of the bed bugs?" She said, "That was the hardest thing me and Goldie ever had to do. When I lived with her we slept on straw ticks. That's what we called the cloth that we sewed together to hold the straw. So we had to rip the ticks open, dump the straw, and burn it."

"We built a fire under the iron washing kettle that we kept down by the river to wash clothes. When the bed bugs got too bad, we filled the kettle with water and poured in some lye and started a hot fire. We boiled the ticking so the hot water and lye killed all the bed bugs and their eggs. Then we filled the ticking with new straw and sewed up the ends again."

"We carried the bed springs outside. They had coiled springs that closed up when you put your weight on them so the bed would be comfortable. The bed bugs hid inside the coils. So we had some of the kids to stand on each coil so they would close up. Then we took a big chicken feather and dipped it in kerosene. We rubbed the feather down into each coil as it closed up with the kid's weight. The kerosene killed the bed bugs."

My cousin, Joyce, told me she was the kid who helped get rid of the bedbugs by standing on the bed spring coils. She said, "I just jumped from coil to coil. When my weight closed the coil, Mama would dip the feather into a can of kerosene and wipe it all around the coil. Mama and Aunt Myrt worked all day tryin' to get rid of the bed bugs. It wouldn't be any time until we had them again. My daddy always had men comin' in to help him on the saw mill, and they must have carried the bed bugs in their clothes. At least that's what Mama said. Now I just wonder if they ever really killed all the bedbugs and their eggs."

Mom continued, "Before we brought the clean springs and straw ticks back into the house, we had to clean the cracks in the walls and in the floor. We had walls made out of plaster and horse hair and they cracked real easy. Bed bugs hid in the cracks during the daytime and came out to bite at night and suck our blood. That was also a good place for them to lay their eggs. We took another chicken feather dipped in kerosene and rubbed it back and forth in the cracks in the wall."

"Our floors were made out of rough wood and there were cracks in them. The bed bugs hid in those cracks too. Goldie boiled some water and put lye in it. She scrubbed the floors with the hot lye water and let it soak into the cracks."

"Finally, we took four tin cans, like Vienna sausage cans, and put each leg of the bed frame in the can. Before we put the clean springs and straw ticks back on the bed, we poured a little bit of kerosene into each tin can so if we missed a bed bug and it tried to get in the bed with us, it couldn't because it would have to crawl through the can with kerosene in it."

Joyce told me, "We stopped sleepin' on straw ticks when Daddy could afford to buy mattresses. Then the bed bugs hid in the tufts, seams, and folds of the new mattresses. We couldn't put kerosene or lye on the mattress, so we had to use our fingers to separate all the hiding places in the mattress. When we found bed bugs, we mashed them between our fingers. It was a bloody mess because they were full of our blood they had sucked out the night before. Our mattresses didn't stay new for very long." She went on, "I was just a kid, so I smelled my fingers after mashing the bugs. They smelled really, really bitter. People don't know how lucky they are today that bedbugs seem to be a thing of the past."

Mom cast a powerful image from those settings—an image that is burned into my mind. When I see her in my memory even today, she is wearing her colorful summer dresses that she bought on sale at Roses or Kmart. Her favorite color was purple, so many of her dresses had some purple in the patterns. She always wore a homemade feed sack apron over her dress. No matter where she was around the house, from Monday until Saturday, she wore a feed sack apron. She took her apron off to go to Harrisonburg to the grocery store and to go to church on Sunday (the few years that she attended church). Her apron was her "homemaker's uniform." When I go to the drawer where I keep one of Mom's aprons, I can conjure up wonderful images of her in the kitchen washing dishes or cooking yet another meal.

Mom is standing in her favorite spot—between her wood stove and the kitchen sink. She sewed her own aprons from feed sacks, and the stain across the belly is evidence of her hard work and long hours of rubbing against the stove and sink as she cooked for the family. (1974)

After my brother, Larry got married, his wife, Hilda, accompanied Mom in her kitchen. Larry married Hilda when she was fourteen years old and brought her home so Mom could teach her how to prepare the foods that he enjoyed. They lived with Mom and Dad for several years and eventually built a house just down the road from home. Soon there were babies—a boy, and eventually, two girls. Hilda visited often, and as soon the children could crawl or walk they were also in the kitchen with Grandma.

Grandma's little helper...

Larry and Hilda's oldest daughter, Paula, loved to be around Mom and Hilda when they were cooking. From the time she could talk, she claimed she was their "helper." Mom realized Paula's interest in cooking quite by accident one day. Paula was still in diapers and just learning to walk and climb. Paula was wearing a little blue dress over her diaper when she dragged Mom's split bottom rocking chair to the front of the electric stove. She climbed up on the chair and then onto the stovetop. She sat down on the largest burner where she could reach the knobs used to turn on the heat. From her perch, she turned the knob for the burner under her butt. Mom and Hilda were busy with food preparation and didn't notice Paula as she sat on top of the stove. Hilda told me, "All of a sudden, I smelled rags a burnin'. I turned around and smoke was coming off of Paula's dress. I grabbed her off the stove. She had the rings of the burner scorched into her blue dress. We were just lucky she didn't have a burn on her legs."

This potential tragedy was a sure sign of Paula's interest in learning to cook from her Grandma. As soon as she was old enough, she spent many Saturdays in Mom's kitchen. She said, "Grandma taught me a lot of stuff. We would just pick a recipe book off her shelf and choose a recipe we had a taste for that day. We made yeast doughnuts, cold oven cake, and any cookie recipe you can imagine. I'll always remember what she taught me one time when I burned myself while I was gettin' cookies out of the oven. She grabbed a jar of apple butter and rubbed a glob on my burn. It really helped. I've always done that for my kids too."

Paula shared some her favorite recipes that Mom taught her how to prepare.

Grandma's Oatmeal Cookies Recipe…

Ingredients

1 cup raisins	1 cup lard
1 cup packed brown sugar	2 eggs
2 cups all purpose flour	2 cups rolled oats
1 teaspoon ground cinnamon	½ teaspoon ground allspice
½ teaspoon ground cloves	½ teaspoon baking soda
½ teaspoon salt	

Place raisins in a small bowl; cover with boiling water. Let stand for 10 minutes; drain, reserving 6 tablespoons liquid. Set raisins and liquid aside. Cream lard with the brown sugar in a mixing bowl. Add eggs; beat well. Combine dry ingredients; add to creamed mixture with raisin liquid. Fold in the raisins. Drop by teaspoonful onto a dry cookie sheet. Bake at 400 degrees for about 12 minutes. Makes about three dozen.

Yeast Doughnuts Recipe....

Ingredients

2 packs of yeast	½ cup warm water
1 cup milk	½ cup sugar
2 teaspoons salt	2 eggs beaten
1 teaspoon lemon juice	¼ cup melted lard
5 cups of flour	½ teaspoon nutmeg
Lard for deep fryer	powdered sugar

Dissolve yeast in warm water and set aside. Mix all dry ingredients, except powdered sugar, in a large bowl. Add yeast mixture, milk, lemon juice, eggs, and melted lard. Mix until a dough forms. Set dough aside and let it rise. Pinch off pieces of the dough and, using a rolling pin, roll them to about ½ inch thick. Cut out the doughnuts and set aside to rise for one hour. Drop the risen doughnuts into a deep fryer of grease at 375 degrees. Let them fry until brown on one side and turn them over to fry on the other side. Dip the doughnuts out of the grease, drain them on a cloth, and then sprinkle with powdered sugar.

Cold Oven Cake Recipe....

Ingredients

1 stick of butter	1 cup lard
3 cups of sugar	5 eggs
3¾ cup flour	¼ teaspoon salt

½ teaspoon baking powder   1 teaspoon vanilla flavoring
1 teaspoon lemon flavoring   1 cup plus 1 tablespoon milk

Cream the butter, lard, and sugar. Add eggs (all at once). Beat well. Sift dry ingredients, and add creamed mixture. Fold in vanilla and lemon flavoring. Pour into greased and floured tube pan. Put in cold oven. Turn oven on to 325 degrees. Bake 1½ to 2 hour.

Today Paula still shows her appreciation of Mom's efforts to teach her how to cook. In her kitchen, she has what she calls "Grandma's corner." In that place she has Mom's pie safe, her split-bottom rocking chair, her original rolling pin that someone gave her as a wedding gift in 1940, her flour sifter, and many other items that Mom used in her cooking.

Mom and Aunt Ethel never took a vacation from feeding their families as well as anyone else who dropped in at meal time. The word "vacation" meant nothing to them except that more folks would be dropping in to eat their sumptuous meals. Even when Mom went to somebody's house for Sunday dinner, she helped with the cooking and stayed until every dish was cleaned and in the cabinet. It was the same for Aunt Ethel. The few times in her life that she went to someone else's house for a meal, she either took a dish or two or helped with preparation and the clean up.

The number of meals Mom and Aunt Ethel cooked is staggering. I calculated the number of meals Mom cooked in her lifetime. She began to cook for and feed Aunt Goldie's family at age ten. Because she was not totally responsible for all the cooking, I have eliminated those years from my calculation. She got married when she was nineteen years old. She and Dad started their own household immediately. At the end of her life, she was not able to cook for her family for five years. That leaves fifty-seven years during which she cooked three meals a day. The total number of days is twenty thousand, eight hundred and five. Multiple that by three and Mom hunted and gathered, planted gardens, preserved food, and cooked sixty-two thousand, four hundred and fifteen meals for her family, those who dropped in to eat, and all other folks who might be hungry, tired, or thirsty.

Mom even fed the convicts...

Mom even fed the convicts who worked on the gravel road that passed in front of our house. She could see them from the front window; and if it was hot during the summer time, she would say, "I'll bet those convicts are burnin' up. They must be thirsty." Or if it was cold in the winter time, she said, "I'll bet those convicts are freezin'. They could use a cup of hot coffee." After a speech about how they obviously were criminals or they wouldn't be in jail and how they were still human beings and had normal human being feelings, she would march herself out to the road and approach the surly prison guard. He was dressed in a uniform with his arms folded across his chest; holding a menacing twelve-gauge shotgun to use in case one of the convicts tried to escape.

There was a big flat limestone rock at the corner of the garden near the road. That big flat rock, still there today, was a useful part of our property. When we were children, we played with our toys on the rock. We sat on the rock and ate little sandwiches that Mom prepared for us. I stood on the rock to watch our neighbors, Fanny Jane and Lloyd Myers, go by the house. Standing there made me feel tall, important, and more in control. The rock was always in the way when visitors parked their car in front of the house; and, upon occasion, some of our visitors had a little too much to drink and would drive their car into the rock and later leave with a dented fender or mangled bumper. I often saw Mom standing on the rock and wondered if it made her feel taller like it did me—she was just five feet tall.

When Mom approached the prison guard to ask if she could feed the convicts, she would stand on the big rock for height and safety. She asked, "Hey Mister is it okay if I give these men something to drink and eat?" He answered, "That's awfully kind of you ma'am, but we provide food and drink for them." Mom's response was, "Well, it is cold [or hot] out here, and it's a while before dinner time. I have fresh coffee and some homemade cookies I could give them, and you can have some too." Sometimes she offered them a slice of fancy pie left over from Sunday dinner.

No matter if the weather was hot or cold, the guard broke down and said, "Yes, you can bring something to drink and some cookies, but keep back a ways from the prisoners. Just place it on the rock there and each man can help himself." Well, that was all Mom needed to hear. In a flurry, she went back into the kitchen and gathered up the coffee and cookies, or sometimes homemade pie, iced tea, or whatever she had available. She carefully placed the food on the big rock; and when she walked away so the prisoners could help themselves, the rock had become a bountiful table filled with delicious food and drink. As they stopped their work and walked to the rock to eat and drink, they each said, "Thank you, Ma'am." Mom received her reward because their facial expressions told her how good it all tasted as she stood a safe distance away, outside the kitchen door, and watched them eat.

Sometimes, in my childish ignorance, I was ashamed when Mom did things like feed the convicts. I thought she went overboard with her sharing of food, but I came to believe she considered it her responsibility to see that anyone who came within range of her house had to leave with a full belly and quenched thirst or she had failed to do what she was put on earth to do—cook and feed the masses.

Mom and Aunt Ethel both loved to discover new recipes they thought their families would enjoy. One of them would prepare the new dish and tell the other one how it turned out and whether or not the family had liked it. Aunt Ethel had a lot more freedom to try new recipes on her family because Uncle Shirley and her children were open to different foods. Mom was limited, most of the time, by Dad's simple taste in foods which he had acquired from Grandma Molly and Aunt Lena. He liked the basic foods, prepared in the same old traditional ways.

Dad takes a trip and Mom takes charge...

One time I remember Dad going away to Wisconsin for a week to learn how to vaccinate turkeys and chickens. He had received a promotion from mixing feed to field technician at the Rockingham Milling Company where he worked. Mom had been asking him to let her tear out an old stairway that came down from the upstairs into the dining room. It took up a lot of space so that she could set the table only one way in the room. She always liked to move her furniture around in each room for an occasional change.

The old stairway was never used and had a strong dead-bolt lock on the outside of the door that opened into the dining room. Mom asked Dad, "Norman, can I have Skip tear out that old stairway so I can have more room?" He always answered, "No, you can't tear it out. What if the house catches on fire and we have to get out that way?" Her response was the same each time, "Yeah, and if we ran down that stairway, we would all burn up because the door is always locked on the outside." The discussion would end there because Dad wanted to keep the stairway. The next night I would have a nightmare about all of us being trapped in the dark stairs.

When Mom found out that Dad was going away for a week, she made plans with Skip and some other helpers to tear the stairway down and patch the ceiling. She told me, "I'll bet your daddy won't even notice the difference when he comes home." Removing the stairway was not all that Mom planned for the week. She went through her recipe box and pulled out all the recipes she had clipped from here and there. She was excited and told me, "I am gonna try every recipe I ever wanted to while Norman's gone. I'll cook dinner and supper for Skip and the workers and try all these recipes."

During that week, Mom made fancy casseroles and pastries. We ate like royalty, and Skip's bragging about her food at every meal just made her cook more. She made a delicious broccoli casserole that we all raved about. Dad came home and, as expected, did not realize that the stairway was gone and the dining room table was turned in the opposite direction. He finally noticed after we kept glancing up at the new tiled ceiling. He didn't say too much. He just rolled his eyes and warned Mom about all of us dying in a fire because we no longer had another way to get down stairs if the front stairs were burning.

A week or so later, Mom baked the broccoli casserole again and set it on the table in front of Dad. He looked at it and said, "What in the hell is that? It looks like dog puke." I said, "It's a broccoli casserole, and we all like it." He pointed his fork at me and yelled, "You're bringin' new ideas like this in here from college. Well, I am not eatin' that crap, and you stop tryin' to change things around here." Mom took the casserole off the table and warmed it up the next day for our dinner. Needless to say, she went back to the old recipes she had stored in her head. When Dad wasn't around, we all sat around the table and reminisced about the wonderful food we had enjoyed the week he was in Wisconsin.

Because Mom never worked at a formal job outside our home, she practically remained in front of her stove for her entire life. I still see her in my mind's eye, and I can almost taste and smell the food she prepared, especially my favorite--the coconut cream pie she made for special occasions, such as butchering day.

If Aunt Ethel lives another two years, she will have cooked about the same number of meals as Mom. She started at age ten and is still cooking three meals a day for Uncle Shirley and often for her children, grandchildren, and great grandchildren who live nearby and visit often. You can find her in her kitchen most of the time. When she is not cooking, she is cleaning and wiping her counter tops. There is always a homemade pie in the pantry or in the freezer so that she can entertain guests with a hot cup of coffee and a slice of apple, blackberry, or coconut cream pie. Folks, including myself, just drop in and take a seat at the kitchen counter.

Aunt Ethel remains devoted to and absorbed in the work of caring for family and friends, and she is recognized by those around her as very skillful at what she does. I recall visiting her one summer afternoon in August, 2005, and watching her bustling about, still taking care of everyone. She made sandwiches for the men who were paving her driveway; she made a sandwich for me, remembering from years ago when we used to hunt deer together that I like sausage sandwiches with dill pickle; and she tended to her elderly husband, Uncle Shirley while at the same time calling her daughter, Betty, to pick up Uncle Shirley's medicine when she left her work. In between it all, she made ham potpie so I could photograph the stages of preparation and measure the ingredients while she talked about family problems and her attempts to negotiate any uncomfortable interactions in her family.

All of their lives, Mom and Aunt Ethel paid attention to many people at once. They observed their activities and planned how to respond to them. They kept track of sounds—men talking, children playing—and used what they heard to determine their family's needs and to respond to them.

In the middle of this hot August afternoon, I asked Aunt Ethel how much time she spends thinking about and planning the next meal. She responded with a surprised look on her face that I interpreted in two ways. First, she was wondering how I knew to ask that question, and secondly, she had never thought about the question herself. After a moment, she answered, "All the time. I am always thinking about what I will make for supper or breakfast the next day. As the weekend comes, I think about what kind of pies I will make on Saturday for Sunday, who might come for Sunday dinner, what their favorite pies are, what I might have on hand for making pies, and do I have go to the store for anything. Food and meal planning for family and friends is always on my mind."

Aunt Ethel and Mom used to go to the grocery store to buy

staples such as flour, salt, pinto beans, and sugar. Most everything else they needed had been preserved in some form or fashion, so all they had to do was walk to the cellar or, later on, to the freezer. Now that Aunt Ethel is older and caring for Uncle Shirley around the clock, she doesn't have time to raise a big garden. She now buys a larger variety of foods when she goes to the grocery store.

Aunt Ethel and Bun Morris pose for me in Ethel's kitchen in 2005. Her dish cloth is readily available in the lower left hand corner of the picture for wiping the countertop. Bun was working nearby and just stopped in around noon for "dinner." Ethel served him two sausage sandwiches with a big slice of tomato and several glasses of iced tea.

As I sat there listening to Aunt Ethel and taking notes, her son called and asked if she could make dinner the next day for the workers who were paving his driveway and her driveway. She said, "Yes, I guess I can come up with enough to feed them." At least he gave her a day's notice. Many times, folks just arrive at meal time, and somehow Aunt Ethel finds enough food to feed them.

Mom related to food and family in the same way as Aunt Ethel. She was constantly thinking about what to have for the next meal and for several meals to come. I often heard her say, "If I cook extra brown beans tonight for supper, I will have some for tomorrow when Wayne Hartman comes to plow the garden." Making sure that family and friends enjoyed their favorite foods was her job. When she learned that my cousin Randy loved her sausage gravy, she made it every morning so he could drop in on his way to work to have breakfast. Occasionally he didn't come by, and it was obvious that her feelings were hurt as she said, "I wonder where Randy is this morning."

At age seventy-six, Mom suffered a stroke and was forced to spend most of her time in a chair. That didn't stop her, though, from teaching each of her children and granddaughters how to cook their favorite dishes. She knew that her time was short and she wanted her traditional foods to be enjoyed after her death.

Mom taught Warnie, her youngest, who was divorced at the time, how to make homemade bread. She called it "light" bread. She sat in her wheelchair at the end of the dining room table and guided him through every step of the process. I remember noting how strange his big male hands looked with pieces of dough stuck to his fingers as he mixed the flour and lard. I had never seen a man's hands all sticky with bread dough before.

She taught my brother John how to cook pinto beans and make jelly. She had my sister, Brenda, load her and her wheel chair into the car and take her to his house, where she talked him through each step of cooking dried pinto beans. He is very grateful to this day, as pinto beans are his favorite food. Mom wanted John to have flowers around his home after she was gone, so she had Brenda buy azaleas and rhodendron and plant them in his yard while she supervised from her wheelchair.

Since I am single, Mom felt the need to teach me how to cook something. I told her I could cook as much as I needed, but she insisted on teaching me how to make cherry dumplins'—a recipe she clipped off a cake mix box many years ago. I knew she had an ulterior motive for teaching me the cherry dumplin' recipe when I think about it now. She absolutely loved cherry dumplins'.

She sent me to the kitchen and told me to look inside the cabinet door for the recipe. The recipes she liked and used most often were taped inside her cabinet doors. Over the years, the cherry dumplin' recipe had grown yellow with age. It had burned spots where it had been laid too close to the stove burner, and it had grease spots from Mom's fingers that had touched it after being dipped into the dough in the early stages of preparation.

Although Mom is now cooking in heaven, as I drive past our old home, I imagine I can still smell the smoke from the wood stove, the aroma of the hot rolls, pinto beans, fresh coffee, and ham potpie that would tickle my appetite as I got off the school bus and walked past the big rock and made my way to the kitchen through the back door.

Aunt Ethel is still cooking the recipes she and Mom used to make. She always offers something to eat and a cup of percolated coffee to everyone who walks into her kitchen. Then she leans on the other side of the counter and catches up on the news from "up or down the road" in Hopkins Gap or, in my case, "across the mountain."

Chapter 3

The Tools for Cooking and Eating

In the childhood memories of every good cook,
there's a large kitchen, a warm stove, a simmering
pot and a Mom.

—*Barbara Kostikyan*

The Kitchen Stove

Central to all cooking is heat, and in Hopkins Gap the kitchen stove provided not only the means for cooking, but it also met many other needs of the family. My memories of food and family began with the wood cook stove. We all knew that Mom ruled the household with her knowledge of how to cook, and we quickly learned not to mess with her stove without her permission.

Most homes had a wood cook stove with what looked like smooth iron tops with different sized round holes recessed in the top. Each hole had an iron lid with a small notch. To raise the lids to add wood or to set your iron pot directly over the fire, you had to use a stove hook. The hook had a silver handle with metal rings around the part where you held it and a tip that fit perfectly in the lids of the wood-burning cook stove. Without the hook, the cook was rendered helpless when it came time to start a fire to warm the house and cook breakfast.

The silver metal rings on one end of the hook allowed air to circulate through the top of the handle so it stayed cool enough to hold in your hand. The hook lay on top of the warming closets above the stovetop. When I was visiting in Hopkins Gap and growing up at my parents' home just outside Hopkins Gap, I saw many a child get in serious trouble for playing with the stove hook and misplacing it. I watched what happened to other children, and I certainly knew better than to play with the stove hook and not put it back on top of the warming closets.

The wood cook stove was designed to have different levels of heat on the top. The cooks who learned how to use the stovetop turned out to be the best cooks. The two lids to the left of the stovetop were directly over the firebox where the wood was burned. The early stages of cooking—getting the boiling started slowly so the contents didn't burn—were done directly over the firebox. Then, once the draft up the stove pipe was just right, the pots were slid onto the two burners to the right, that were the hottest and offered the most even heat. The middle stage of cooking was done on these hot burners.

Next to the firebox, and under the stovetop, was the oven. This part of the stovetop was used to slow the cook pots down to a simmer, while foods that took less time to cook were placed over the hottest part of the stove. Most of the wood stoves had a water reservoir to the far right. The heat from the stove kept a readily available source of hot water for use in cooking and washing the dishes after a meal. Once the food was finished cooking, it was slid over to the top of the water tank, where it was kept warm until the other dishes were ready to serve.

I heard the comment many times, "Myrt and Ethel cook the best pinto beans. The broth is so nice and thick. Other people's beans have watery broth." Mom and Aunt Ethel learned at an early age to bring their pinto beans to a boil over the firebox. When the draft was just right, they would slide the pot to the hottest burners on the right. The beans boiled at a steady pace for several hours until the hulls were deposited in a ring around the inside of the pot above the broth. The cooks then added the seasoning—country ham, lard, or pieces of cooked bacon, salt and pepper. The beans were left on the hottest burners to boil hard for another thirty minutes. Finally, the bean pot was slid over the water reservoir until supper. The broth thickened up very nicely while the beans slowly simmered over the low heat.

One of my favorite memories was watching and listening to the expertise of Mom and Aunt Ethel as they slid their cook pots back and forth across the stove, searching for the perfect level of heat while they prepared Sunday dinner and talked and laughed with each other. Through years of experience, both women knew exactly where to slide their cooking pots, depending on which food they contained. They knew that different parts of the stovetop had different temperatures, and they used that knowledge to time the food so that everything was ready for the table at the same time.

One of the first foods I cooked for myself was fried eggs for breakfast. I put the iron skillet on the hottest part of the stove, placed a tablespoon of lard in it, and waited for it to get hot before breaking my eggs. My fried eggs never tasted as good as Mom's. One morning, she was coming in from milking the cows as I was breaking my eggs into the skillet. She looked at the skillet and looked at me. "No wonder your eggs don't taste as good as mine," she said. "I thought you were just too lazy to cook for yourself. Let me show you how to fry eggs."

She pulled the skillet off the hottest part of the woodstove and moved it to the middle section where the heat was moderate as she explained, "You have to cook eggs over lower heat. Eggs cooked at a high temperature are tough and leathery. Fry your eggs in a little grease on the right hand side of the wood stove."

If Mom and Aunt Ethel wanted to remove something from direct heat but needed to keep it warm, they had two choices. They could move it over on top of the water reservoir at the side of the stove, where simmering water would keep the food warm; or they could move the pan to the warming closet—a shelf above the back of the stovetop. The warming closets were used to hold bread dough while it was rising. The rising dough was placed on top of the warming closets or over the water reservoir. Dishes that needed to be kept warm were placed inside the warming closets. When the cooks' backs were turned, I thoroughly enjoyed sneaking open the warming closet and reaching in for a bite of whatever was waiting inside.

Grandma Molly Shifflett's wood cook stove in 1958. She has her pots placed where they are receiving the appropriate heat. The coffee pot sets on top of the warming closet. The coffee stayed warm and readily available for drinking.

The woodstove was hard on pot handles—wooden or plastic ones—because the stove is hot all around the pan as well as under it. Wooden handles were often scorched and plastic handles didn't last long before they melted. Mom, of course, had a solution for ruined pot handles. Since she was also a fine seamstress, she had lots of wooden thread spools around the house. She sawed the larger ones into two pieces, removed the burned handle, and screwed the wooden spool on top of the pot lid. She never wasted a thing that I can remember.

The oven of a wood stove was to the right and next to the firebox. It was heated by hot air circulating from the firebox over, down the far side, and under the oven. Ovens vary from one woodstove to another and with the type of wood that is burned. The weather and the altitude also affect the wood stove oven. Mom knew her oven like the back of her hand and knew the heating process varied with the kind of wood she was burning. When she borrowed a recipe from the Grit newspaper or the back of a cereal box, she always said, "I'll have to adjust the baking time to my oven."

When Mom's oven stopped heating or was heating unevenly, she knew exactly what the problem was. She got her ash bucket and her stove scraper. She removed the top of the wood stove and scraped the soot off the top and sides of the oven. She opened a little door under the oven and scraped the soot and ashes from that area. She always emptied her soot in the garden, because she thought it improved the soil for next year's planting.

The oven temperature on a wood stove was hard to work with, but Mom knew how to tell when the oven was hot enough for various baked foods. After so many years of experience, she could stick her hand into the oven and sense the temperature. If she thought it was too hot, she cracked the door open to let it cool before she put her food in to bake.

Eventually, the sliding of pots and pans around the stove top was replaced by control knobs on a new electric stove—one for each burner ranging in levels of heat from high to simmer. Mom and Aunt Ethel, as well as all the cooks in Hopkins Gap, eventually bought electric stoves on which to cook. I know that Mom never liked her electric stove. She complained at least once a day, "It is either too hot or heats too slow." After she got her electric stove, she struggled with the knobs and never seemed to adapt to a "knob" that replaced the parts of a wood cook stove top. Aunt Ethel recently told me, "Shucks, I wish I still had my wood stove. I don't like that old electric stove. You can't keep nothin' warm on it." Her youngest son was visiting, and he spoke up. "With a wood stove, the men could come in late from work or huntin' and find the pots still warm on the wood stove. Now you gotta wait for Mom to heat the food up again on the electric stove. It makes it harder on her now."

One funny, but scary, time in Mom's kitchen occurred when she tried to bake a banana cake in her new electric oven. After three failed attempts to make the layers so that they wouldn't fall when she took them out of the oven, she threw the cake pans in the floor, cake dough still in them, and stomped them flat. We were all in the kitchen with her, hanging around her elbows as she baked. I was older and knew to stay out of her way as she got madder and madder. The younger children were hit by flying half-baked cake dough, and the smallest child started screaming and crying out of fear for her life.

Mom calmed down quickly and cleaned up the mess, while muttering to herself out loud, "I can't control the temperature on that electric stove. I didn't have near the trouble with my old wood stove. I am gonna get me another wood stove, you mark my words." She was never satisfied until she found a small wood stove and set it up right beside her electric stove. It stayed there until she died. It was mainly used for heat as the years passed by, but on cold winter days while she was heating the kitchen, she cooked a pot of delicious pinto beans or her famous vegetable soup or venison stew. She and my brother John claimed the pinto beans tasted better if they were cooked on a wood stove. I couldn't tell the difference, but then both John and Mom loved pinto beans and had their taste buds fine tuned to any variations in flavor.

In the summer time, the cooks would remind the men of the house that they needed to start gathering the winter supply of wood. Mom always reminded Dad that the wood had to be a certain length and not one half-inch longer or she couldn't use it. Once in a while he forgot to saw it to the right length, and there was hell to pay until he got the wood to the right length.

Every Hopkins Gap home had a wood yard. The man's responsibility ended when he got the winter wood cut into blocks and piled on the woodpile. Then it was up to the older children to split the blocks into smaller pieces that would burn quicker and hotter. Being the oldest child, I had the job of chopping the wood until my brothers were old enough to take over. One of our important chores when we got home from school each evening was to carry in enough wood for the next day's cooking and heating. None of us liked to chop and carry in wood, so we fussed and put it off until nearly dark all the time. It was really hard to do the job after nightfall. Mom told us a black widow spider could bite us if we waited until after dark. That threat got my butt moving toward the wood yard way before dark, because I was deathly afraid of spiders.

Mom needed really dry wood for kindling. Green wood, or wood that is still damp with tree sap, will burn okay in a big fire, but it mostly produces a lot of smoke as it smolders in a wood stove. To make kindling out of green wood, Mom had us split blocks of wood into small pieces. She placed them in the oven of the woodstove to dry them out so they would be good to start her morning fires.

Kindling was cut with a hatchet because the smaller pieces of wood would not stand up by themselves. Mom had to hold them up with her left hand and chop with her right hand using a short-handled hatchet. She explained as I watched, "You can lose a finger or two if you try to use a long-handled axe to chop kindling." She continued, "When I first started choppin' kindlin', I realized I would have to learn to aim really good or let go of the wood just seconds before the hatchet blade struck, so that my fingers were out of the way."

Mom had three different wood boxes. She had a long wooden box that she built herself and placed under the windows on the back porch. It was about eight feet long, and twenty inches wide and two feet deep. It held about enough wood for a week. One of my chores was to carry wood in from the wood yard so Mom could fill her wood box. At first she showed me how to place the wood in the box. She took the wood from my arms and arranged it in neat stacks, grouped by graduated sizes, with the really small kindling on the left the larger sized wood on the right. She explained, "I need different sizes of wood sometimes, and I don't want to have to dig down through the pile to find it. It will save me time if you stack it like I want it in the first place. If you don't want to do it right the first time, then you'll have to 'lick your calf over'." She always threatened us with "licking our calf over." One time I asked her what it meant, and she explained, "Well, when a cow has her calf, she turns around right away and licks it until it is dry. She does it right the first time or the calf won't get up and start sucking so it can live. I have tried to teach you kids how to do a job right the first time so you don't have to do it over again." With the mental images of me licking a calf and remembering what it was like for her to stand over me and supervise while I did the chore over again, I usually did things right the first time.

A smaller wood box sat beside the stove in the kitchen. That box had to be filled once a day by carrying wood in from the big wood box on the porch. It was about two feet wide, three feet long, and two feet deep. It was made without a bottom so Mom could lift it up and sweep out the chips and dirt from the wood without having to carry the box outside to dump it. She threw all her paper-type trash in that box for starting fires and kept her kindling at one end.

Mom kept another small wood box, about the size of a shoe box, near the wood stove. It was always full of small slivers of rich, oily pine knots. The men gathered the pine knots from the woods while they were hunting. When we got old enough, my brother Larry and I were responsible for keeping the pine box filled. We used the short-handled hatchet. Remembering Mom's warning about losing a finger or two, we laid the pine knots down on the chopping block and chopped them into small slivers.

When Mom made her morning fires, she layered the wood in the stove by placing paper on the bottom, followed by pine knot slivers, then kindling, and finally, large pieces of split wood on top. One match held to the paper soon ignited the oil rich pine knot slivers. The flames licked up through the kindling. Soon the larger pieces of wood were afire and sending heat throughout the kitchen.

I often wondered if Mom ever slept. I never saw her go to bed, and when I got up in the morning, she was making fires to warm the house and cook breakfast. I will never understand how she managed, day after day, to get up in the icy house, leaving Dad and us in warm beds. When I got out of bed on cold mornings, I started out by sitting on the top of the wood stove. As the stove began to heat up, I slid away from the firebox over to the top of the water reservoir. When that spot got too hot, I leaned against the stove for warmth. When the stove was hot enough that I couldn't lean on it any more, I felt thawed out enough to get ready for school.

As the slivers in the pine box warmed, a rich aroma wafted through the kitchen and the dining room. The smell of pine was clean and inviting. It generated a feeling of comfort and safety for me as a child. I also knew that shortly after that pine scent began to fill the house, I would smell pork sausages, milk gravy, and fresh coffee. My stomach was ready and, it was never long before the table was filled with steaming food.

Mom used her wood stove in many ways. She "clabbered" her milk for cottage cheese on the back of the stove. When she knew Uncle Rob was coming to visit, she had a dish of clabbered cream for him to eat on the back of the stove where the heat was low. The spring chicks, or "peepies" as they were called, lived the first part of their lives in a box on the floor behind the stove. Later, they graduated to the back porch, then into the yard. Piglets that had been abandoned by their mothers were brought into the house and placed in a large box near the wood stove. Occasionally, John I. Myers would give Mom a lamb that had been abandoned by its mother. Mom would let us feed the lamb and keep it in a box by the wood stove.

Every wood stove I saw in the homes in Hopkins Gap had a tea kettle of hot water steaming on the back of the stove. Many times I saw Mom and other women take the lid off the tea kettle and stick a bottle of milk in the hot water to warm before giving it to a baby. As the bottle warmed, droplets of steam settled on the nipple. Mom told me, "A baby can stand a lot of cold if it's kept wrapped in a blanket and gets warm milk in its belly. You don't feed a baby cold milk, and you have to keep it out of drafts or you won't get a minute's sleep at night because of colic. A colicky baby cries all the time but worse at night."

Mom saved the ashes from the wood cook stove, and every two years or so she fired up an iron kettle in the yard and made homemade lye soap. She loved to use lye soap to wash clothes. The soap was made with wood ashes, rancid hog lard, and lye. She cooked the ingredients in the kettle and then let them cool and get hard. She used an old butchering knife to cut the hard soap into usable chunks.

Wood ashes for traction....

It used to snow a lot when I was growing up. Dad always insisted on getting his car out on the roads to go to work no matter what the weather was putting down. While he was a smart man about many topics, he simply did not know how to drive in the snow. He would get in the car, put it in gear, stomp the gas, and rev the motor. Of course, the tires never had a chance to get traction on the ice because they were turning so fast. Mom always knew exactly what was going to happen. On snowy and icy days, she would wait inside the house until she heard him revving the motor and spinning the tires. She said, time and time again, "He'll never learn to drive on ice. I have told him a thousand times over to just give the car a little gas so the tires can take a hold. Listen to him out there. He'll rip the transmission out of the car."

While Mom was telling us children this, she would head for the back porch where she kept a coal bucket full of ashes from the stove. She would pick up the bucket and march out to the car. After yelling loud so Dad could hear her over the roaring motor, she would tell him to wait a minute. He let the motor idle while Mom sprinkled ashes in front of his tires. Like magic, the ashes from the woodstove allowed the tires to get enough traction to get the car going down the road and Dad off to his work.

Mom built a tall wooden box that fit just behind the stove and next to the chimney. She kept the wash pan on top. She kept warm water from the stove reservoir in the pan so we could all wash our hands before meals. A chunk of homemade soap sat in a dish beside the pan. In the winter, every place in the house was cold except the kitchen and the area around the coal stove in the living room. Because the kitchen was the warmest spot, my sister, Brenda and I took our morning sponge baths in the wash pan beside the wood stove. We brought our school clothes down from the icy bedroom upstairs and hung them in the living room near the stove so they would be warm when we dressed for school. We took a bath in the kitchen and dashed through the cold dining room and jumped into our warm clothes by the stove in the living room.

Sometimes I forgot to bring my clothes downstairs, so I hurried with my bath and stole my sister's warm clothes. I realize now that I used my power as the oldest one of the children to cover up my laziness. I have since apologized to my sister for her having to go upstairs and get cold clothes to put on for school.

On Saturday nights, the area in front of the wood stove became a bath room. Mom dragged in the large oblong zinc tub, known as the "big tub" and filled it with hot water from the reservoir on the stove. She opened the oven door to add heat to the area in front of the stove; otherwise any body parts not under the warm water would soon be shivering.

All five of us children took turns getting into the "big tub" for our weekly bath. Mom put the boys in first because she said they weren't as dirty as the girls. I always resented that I had to crawl into their dirty bath water. To keep the water hot until five children got a scrubbing,

After we put in a bathroom in 1969, Mom let the grandchildren "swim" in the big tub in the summer time. Curt and Kent are posing for the camera.

Mom would add hot water to the tub between baths. After all of us children were scrubbed and chased off to bed, Mom emptied the tub, filled it back up, and got in for her bath. I guess Dad got in the tub too, but it was long after I was asleep.

The wood cook stove served many, many functions in my family. While I know it was old fashioned, I do believe the wood cook stove was more suited to family living and cooking than any modern stove I've seen.

Pots and Pans

Mom and Aunt Ethel never owned a full set of cookware. They each put together a set that was suitable to their every need. They bought a few pieces here and there at estate sales, took other women's hand-me-down pots, and ordered some things from the Sears catalog. When they needed a pot such as a double boiler, they devised a way to meet the need with the pots they had on hand. Mom just got a big pot, filled it with water, and put a smaller pot inside to fix her egg custards and other foods requiring a double boiler.

When I got my first job, I bought Mom several sets of pots and pans that I thought she would like to have. They usually stayed in their boxes. She seemed really happy to get them, but she always said, "I will save these until my others wear out." Her pans were ancient and dented. Occasionally one handle would be missing, but she knew them like she knew the back of her hand. She knew how they would heat, whether or not they cooked evenly, and which dented lid fitted which pot or pan. When she died, my sister, sisters-in-law, and I carried to our homes, several new sets of pots and pans that had never been used.

Both Mom and Aunt Ethel had a set of cast iron skillets that they preferred for frying meat, potatoes, and making gravies for breakfast. Mom always said,

"I know how to cook with my iron skillets. I know exactly how long I can leave my milk gravy cooking while I get another pan going to fry eggs. Once I got used to them, I never burned another thing." Mom could tell when it was time to turn over her fried potatoes because of the crackling sound coming from the skillet when the bottom layer of potatoes were turning brown.

Recognizing the important role of his future wife, Dad gave Mom two Griswold No. 10 cast iron skillets for her wedding present. She used those skillets everyday of her life until she couldn't cook anymore. She often told me, "On our wedding day your daddy handed me these brand new skillets and said, 'One is for fixin' sausage and ham, and the other one is for fryin' taters—my favorite food."

After Mom knew she would never cook again, she offered me one of the skillets. She had tears in her eyes as I gladly took the skillet and left for my home. It is my most prized possession, and I often make myself sausage gravy or fry some potatoes in it. Needless to say, using the skillet does not make my cooking taste like Mom's.

Mary Turner showed me her skillet that she got from her mother, Millie Morris, who got it from her mother, Ginny Riggleman. Great pride showed in Mary's face when I told her the skillet looks brand new. She said, "I take good care of it because it was my Mom's favorite."

In the early days in Hopkins Gap each cook had at least one cast iron

Well taken care of, this old skillet is as good, or perhaps better than it was when it was brand new.

pot with four little legs on the bottom. The pot fit perfectly into one of the wood stove holes so it sat directly on the fire. My cousin, Joyce, remembered her first cooking experiences with the four-legged iron pot. She said, "After Aunt Myrt got married and left our house, Mom [my Aunt Goldie] got appendicitis, and while she was laid up in bed, she turned the cooking over to me. I was twelve years old. From her sick bed, she showed me how to peel potatoes and told me how to cut cabbage. I got the potatoes frying and the cabbage boiling, and then Daddy [my Uncle Rob] came in from the sawmill to season the food. So, I started cookin' for my daddy and the sawmill helpers. Daddy bragged on my food to the sawmill men, and I gladly took over most of the cooking after that." Joyce stepped into the shoes of my mother and is now also known as one of the best cooks from Hopkins Gap.

Plates, Dishes, and Glasses

Just like her pots and pans, Mom's eating plates, serving dishes, and drinking glasses were a mixture of odds and ends she had collected over the years. All of my life, I remember using those same plates. Some had a faded flower pattern, but most were plain white. All of them were cracked and had chipped edges. The cracks had turned dark over the years. Considering that those same plates were used three times a day and washed in hot dishwater three times a day for over sixty years, it is no wonder they had discolored cracks in them.

Mom had a set of saucers that she had collected out of soap powder boxes and oatmeal boxes. They were also cracked and chipped from use. Her serving dishes were the same—odds and ends that had seen better days. Each serving dish had a special purpose. There was the fried potato dish, brown bean dish, cole slaw dish, the gravy dish, and so forth. I asked her several times why she had to use the same dish for specific foods. Her response was quick, "When I make a pan of gravy in this skillet, I know exactly which dish will hold all of it without spilling." The reply didn't explain my question in detail, but I accepted it.

The only eating utensils we laid out were forks—just as ancient as the plates—and we put them on top of the plates rather than beside them. Our teaspoons were kept in a tall cut-glass container in the middle of the table. They were removed after each meal and placed in the open kitchen cabinet. We never used napkins while we ate. We rarely put out knives on the table. Since we didn't have knives at the table, we all dipped into the butter dish with the side of our fork.

Chicken tracks in the butter....

One time all of us children were chased away from the table for making "chicken" tracks in the butter by using the tines instead of the sides of the forks. My sister, Brenda was the instigator of this mischief; and the rest of us followed suit. We had already started to giggle when Mom came in from the kitchen with the last dish of food for the table. She saw what we had done to the butter. She yelled, "My god, it looks like the chickens have been scratching in the butter." That was it—we were all laughing so hard we couldn't stop. Dad didn't like any kind of silliness at the table and, of course, Mom knew that we were probably going to get our heads slapped. We could not stop laughing, so she ran us out of the house. We ended up in the pasture field, rolling in the grass still laughing.

It was a long time before we got ourselves together enough to go back to eat. The table had been cleared, and the food was back in the pots setting on the back of the stove. For years, we laughed about that and often discussed why it was so funny. All of us remember the "chicken" tracks in the butter incident from years ago.

We never had a complete set of drinking glasses. Mom saved jelly jars for glasses. She also saved coupons for sets of glasses with Disney characters on them. We broke drinking glasses so fast that she gave up on having matching glasses and just used her jelly jars.

Mom did have a nice set of dishes that she had saved coupons to get. They were very pretty; with a dark blue ring around a flower design in the middle of each plate. There was also a thin gold line around the blue ring. The cups and saucers had a similar design. This set of dishes stayed in the dining room china cabinet and never in my life did Mom take those plates out and use them. She had other fancy dishes that Uncle Rob gave her when she first got married. One gorgeous dish was maroon-colored with tiny legs on it. If you wanted to suffer, you let Mom catch you in the China cabinet looking at that dish with the intent of touching it. It was never used in Mom's lifetime. I asked many times, "Mom, why don't we use those dishes in the china cabinet sometime?" "We don't need to get those dishes out," she answered, "Food ain't gonna taste any different on them. We've got plates to eat off of. Besides, I promised that set of dishes to Warnie after I die. I don't want any of them broke."

The Pie Safe

The pie safe was a common piece of furniture found in the kitchens of Hopkins Gap families and served as storage before the days of refrigerators. Pie safes were made by hand, mainly from poplar or pine but sometimes from walnut, cherry, maple, or chestnut wood. The doors, and occasionally the sides of the cabinet, had pierced-tin panels that allowed air to circulate inside the cupboard while protecting the contents from houseflies.

The pie safe that I remember best was in Grandma Molly Shifflett's kitchen. It contained mostly dishes of apple butter, jams, and jellies that were put on the table for each meal. Grandma Molly and Aunt Lena also stored the pies that Mom made for them in the safe. The wood of the pie safe seemed to absorb all the cooking odors over the years, so when I opened the door to sneak a spoonful of jelly or jam, I could smell ham and sausage, brown beans, fried potatoes and fried cabbage—which is about all that Grandma Molly and Aunt Lena ever cooked. Today when I enter an antique store, I revisit Grandma Molly's kitchen by opening the door of an antique pie safe.

Grandma Molly was stingy with food. If she had something special in her pie safe, such as some leftover pie that Mom had baked for her, she opened the pie safe very carefully and placed her body in front of the door to hide the contents. Once, one of my nephews saw

This pie safe belonged to my great Aunt Millie Morris. It is made of pine and poplar. It is now owned by her daughter, Mary Morris Turner, and is being used for storage of her jams and jellies and canning jars.

her open the door and, before she could stop him, he crept under her arm to see what she had in there. He saw a half of an apple pie and asked her if he could have some. I will never forget what she said to him, "You didn't see no pie in thar boy." She slammed the door shut with him looking up at her as if he were wondering if he was seeing things. It was sad and funny at the same time.

One of my cousins, Gary Turner, described the contents of Aunt Millie Morris's pie safe. "She always had a dish of apple butter in there. When we got to her house, the first thing I did was open the pie safe. I took a spoon and raked back the dried crust on top, and got me a spoon of the fresh apple butter. It was delicious, and it is my favorite memory of going to Grandma Millie's house. She also kept leftovers from meals in the pie safe—a plate of fried meat and a dish of brown beans."

Kitchen Table, Oilcloth, and Split-Bottom Chairs

Kitchen tables in Hopkins Gap homes were nearly always rectangular and rather large because of the size of the families. The table sat in the middle of the room or against the wall; with enough room for a bench behind the table. I remember this arrangement at Grandma Molly and Grandpa Austin's old house. I also remember Uncle Rob and Aunt Goldie's kitchen table with a bench behind it where the children sat to eat. It was not until later in my life that I realized why most Hopkins Gap houses had benches behind the kitchen table. Of course, a bench allowed more room for the children to sit at the table. It was possible to squeeze six small children's behinds onto a bench when six chairs would not have fit into the same space.

The kitchen table was always covered with oilcloth. Oilcloth is a vinyl that is bonded and supported with a woven cotton mesh. It was considered the best table covering for feeding a lot of children because the surface could be wiped clean using a warm, soapy cloth then wiped dry with a soft cloth. When Mom bought a new oilcloth for our table, the whole room smelled funny for days until the creases worked out and the food smells replaced the oilcloth smell.

Split Bottom Chairs

The grownups sat on split-bottom chairs made of white-oak splits. My family used these chairs during most of my younger years. The splits were thin strips of wood that were peeled off the main trunk of a small white oak tree and then woven around the oak rungs to make the seat of the chair. The frame of the chair was carved from oak wood and very sturdy. The split bottoms had some flexibility so they made for comfortable sitting. Each split-bottom chair had a sound of its own depending on the weight of the person who sat down on it. The splits made a unique sound as they stretched to accommodate a sitter.

Split bottom chairs were great for tilting back and leaning against the wall, but the stress placed on the chair eventually weakened the frames. It was very common to see split-bottom chairs with rubber from a tire inner tube carefully wrapped around the back legs of the chair where they met the floor. This prevented the chair legs from cutting through the linoleum on the kitchen or dining room floor.

In our house, the person who always leaned his chair back against the wall was my cousin Randy. When he came for breakfast, he leaned his chair back against the wall in front of the stove, after he

Oliver Day demonstrates how to make the first split in a white oak log to start the process of making white oak splits for split-bottom chairs. (1975)

Mr. Day splits the oak wood in another step toward the thin oak splits he needs for making a chair bottom. (1975)

had eaten his fill of Mom's sausage gravy and homemade bread. He got that habit from his daddy, Uncle Rob. My cousin Joyce told me that Uncle Rob leaned his split bottom chair back and held himself in place by bracing his knees under the edge of the table. He sat that way while he ate his meals.

Mom usually fussed about Randy leaning her chairs against the wall after he left for work, and she examined her kitchen linoleum for dents made by the chair legs. She said to us, "I don't want to

The thin splits are wound around the oak frame of the chair and then woven through the first splits in a basket weave pattern. (1975)

catch you all leaning my chairs back. You see these dents in the floor. That's what causes it." It never crossed her mind to ask Randy to stop leaning his chair against the wall because she enjoyed him complimenting her sausage gravy way too much to offend him.

The Spring

During my childhood, Hopkins Gap kitchens did not have water piped into them. Most families who lived in the Gap got their water from springs that seeped out of the sides of the Allegheny Mountain ridges. A spring is a place where water literally comes out of the ground and seeps through rocks and moss to form a pool. It was a real blessing to find a spring on the hillsides or in hollows or valleys and to be able to use the water for cooking and drinking. Spring water was always very cold, clean and clear—all the way to the bottom of the pool. I could see crawdads moving in and out of the mud stirring up tiny mud clouds. Water spiders skipped across the top of the water making little tracks of ripples behind them.

The water seeps through the rocks and moss and forms a pool for dipping. During dry seasons, the water just drips and sometimes dries up; but during wet seasons, it can overflow into a stream. (Courtesy of Bucky and Scottie Pritchard, Grayson County, VA, 2006)

Many Hopkins Gap homesteads had springs. Some folks like my Grandma Molly, improved her spring by digging it out so that the water seeped through the rocks and formed a nice pool of sparkling clear water that could be dipped out. Other folks made sure they built their homes and outbuildings down hill from the spring. They sunk a pipe in the spring to catch the water and let gravity pull it downhill closer to the house. Most of the springs in Hopkins Gap are now gone or filled up. Very few folks even remember where they were located.

When we visited Grandma Molly, after I got old enough, I was sent up the hill to the spring to fill the water bucket. The springs were always cool because dense brush and tall trees surrounded them. Grandma Molly kept a dipper by the spring. She always told me, "You watch for snakes. Now be sure to rake any leaves off the top of the water before you dip, and don't you dare bring any water spiders in here either."

It was not uncommon to come face to face with a snake when you raised your head up from dipping water. Hilda recently told me, "I went to the spring for Grandma Dove one time. I squatted down and dipped my bucket full of water, and when I raised my head to stand up, I was eye-to-eye with a large copperhead snake. He was no more than a foot from my face. I just kept my eyes on him as I placed the dipper back on the rock, stepped back, picked up my bucket, and walked down the ridge toward the house."

Copperhead snake strikes Hilda...

Hilda wasn't so lucky the second time she faced a copperhead snake. He bit her in the ankle. She didn't know she had been bitten until her foot swelled up to twice its size. In earlier times in Hopkins Gap, Grandma Molly would have split open a live chicken and placed it on the bite to draw out the venom. Or she might have sliced an onion and laid the slices on the bite until the venom was gone. However, Hilda was taken to the hospital and received a shot for her snakebite. To this day she is allergic to certain common medications because of the shot of snake-bite serum.

I loved to hang out a while by Grandma Molly's spring and

watch the water trickle from the mountainside into the pool. Green moss grew along the cracks in the rocks where the water seeped out of the mountain. Droplets of water hung in the moss. The sun occasionally peeped through the dense trees and turned the water droplets into sparkling diamonds as they became larger and larger and finally dropped into the pool below. After I had spent some time enjoying the sights in and around the spring, I carefully placed the dipper into the water and filled the bucket.

The Dry Sink and Water Bucket

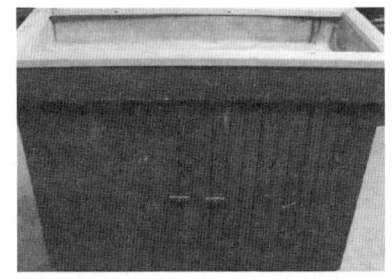

When I got back to the house, Grandma Molly would take the bucket from my hands and put it into a dry sink. The dry sink was commonplace and functioned like a fully-plumbed sink in a modern home. Most of the time it was used with a pottery basin and pitcher because it offered a recessed well on top to prevent the water from splashing out while washing or shaving.

This dry sink is very similar to the one Grandma Molly had in her kitchen. The top is built so that the water bucket sat down about three inches in the top. (1976)

Grandma Molly put the drinking dipper in the water bucket. As we got thirsty, each person used the dipper to get a drink. I had problems with that because Grandma Molly dipped snuff all the time, and Grandpa Austin chewed tobacco. I never saw a toothbrush around, so I was sure they didn't keep their mouths very clean. I rarely took a drink of water at their house. I tried to wait until we got home. We had the same arrangement with the drinking water bucket, but I didn't mind drinking after anyone living in my house.

I asked Mom, "Do Grandpa Austin and Grandma Molly brush their teeth?" Her answer was another lesson in the history of Hopkins Gap. She said, "Yes, they use twigs from a birch tree to brush their teeth. Grandpa Austin walks up on the mountain and gets a bunch, and Grandma keeps them on the shelf in one of her empty snuffboxes. That's how everybody cleaned their teeth when I was growin' up. There was no such thing as a toothbrush. My daddy always carried some birch twigs in his pocket. I watched him after he ate. He went out on the porch and did it. He took about a half inch of bark off the end of the twig then chewed the wood until it shredded up like a brush. He rubbed the brushy wood all over his teeth and threw it out in the yard when he was done. His breath always smelled fresh and right after he brushed his teeth, it smelled sweet and spicy."

Of course, I started watching Grandma and Grandpa when we visited them for Sunday dinner. After Grandpa finished his meal, he walked to the shelf and got a twig. He did the same thing that Mom said her daddy had done. Grandma did the same thing after she ate. Grandma died with her natural teeth, and I don't remember if Grandpa Austin had false teeth. Although I learned that they did clean their teeth, I still waited until I got home to have a drink of water. I still imagined a bit of snuff or tobacco spit got into the bucket every time they replaced the dipper after drinking.

The Spring House

Hopkins Gap homes did not have modern conveniences to keep their food from spoiling. Probably by accident, someone discovered that perishable foods did not spoil so quickly when they were kept cold. Many of the homesteads backed up against either Second Mountain or Little North Mountain near a spring that seeped through the rocks and crevices. Springs furnish an abundant supply of cold running water. Because of the cool water temperature, the surrounding air is often cooler as well. An enclosure surrounding the spring took advantage of this by capturing natural refrigeration for fresh meat, milk, eggs, and butter. Until refrigeration reached the mountains, the family had to be creative when it came to preventing foods from spoiling.

Hopkins Gap families constructed several types of small

buildings over their spring so they would have a dry and animal proof place in which to keep their foods cool. Aunt Millie Morris's daughter, Mary Turner, described how her mother and father used a cold spring on the bank of the Shoemaker River that flowed behind their house. Their springhouse was very simple. It was covered with boards that were nailed together and placed in such a way that the spring water pooled inside the boards. The enclosure was covered with a wooden lid.

Mary told me, "Mom kept her butter and milk in the spring. She used gallon crocks and set them down in the cold water. She

This spring house is a one room building built on top of a flowing spring. The foundation has an opening for the water to flow on through the building. (Courtesy of Wayne Cannoy, Grayson County, VA, 2006).

The inside of the springhouse has a square concrete box in the floor that stays about half full of cold water. This is the storage area for crocks of liquid foods such as milk. The shelves above the water were used for butter, cheese, and other foods that had to be kept cold. (Courtesy of Wayne Cannoy, Grayson Co, VA, 2006).

loved to drink the water from her spring. The last Christmas that Mom was living she wasn't feeling well. She told me she craved a drink of water from the spring that had long since been gone. She said she thought she would get better if she could have some of that good, cold water."

Other Hopkins Gap families had more elaborate springhouses. They were small and enclosed one-room buildings that were built above the spring, but allowed the water to run through at the bottom. The springhouse I remember best was at Grandma Molly's rental house. She and Grandpa Austin rented a house from Brian and Edith Conley before they built their own place. The springhouse was only about four feet high at the roof level. Even Grandma Molly had to bend over to enter, and she was only four feet and nine inches tall. It was a simple little building with a red oak shingle roof and a wooden door latched by a hook and eye. Her springhouse had a hole on one side so the spring water could escape without rotting the wood. There was a wooden trough that sat in the spring. It was about four feet square, and the boards had cracks in them so a shallow pool of water stood inside the box, but didn't fill it to overflowing. Crocks or jars of milk, butter, eggs, cottage cheese and anything else that Grandma Molly needed to keep cold was placed in the shallow water within the trough or on flat rocks above the water. It was one of my childhood pleasures to go to the springhouse with Grandma. She taught me a lot of valuable lessons as we walked down the path to the springhouse and carried food back to the house for Sunday dinner. There are no spring houses in Hopkins Gap today. They are a vanishing relic of those days before mechanical refrigeration.

The Ice Box

The icebox replaced the springhouse. The icebox was kept in the kitchen in most houses and was cooled with a big block of ice placed in the bottom. Ice was delivered once a week from Cassco Ice in Harrisonburg. Food was kept cold by placing it on the shelves above the ice.

Aunt Millie kept her icebox on the front porch. This picture shows a simpler design with only two doors. The bottom space held the block of ice shelving for food storage. The upper door opened to additional shelving for foods that needed to be kept cool. A split-bottom chair sits in front of the icebox.

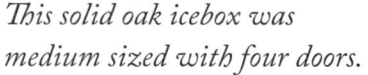

This solid oak icebox was medium sized with four doors.

The icebox had a drain that removed the water as the ice melted over time. The water dripped into a pan under the icebox. A hinged board covered the pan so it was not visible. When the pan was full, the board was lifted to remove the pan for emptying. Woven metal shelves allowed the cool air from the ice to circulate around the food. After mechanical refrigeration became available, spring houses and ice boxes soon became obsolete.

"Movin' on up" with a refrigerator....

My cousin, Joyce, told me that Uncle Rob built his own ice box so he didn't have to buy a refrigerator for Aunt Goldie. Joyce said, "For some reason he didn't want to buy a refrigerator when they first came out, but Mom wanted one real bad." So daddy dug a big hole in the back yard just below the pear tree. He framed it up and poured cement for the sides. He fixed a pipe in the bottom so the water could run out as the ice melted. He built a heavy lid to cover the ice box. Every week he went to Cassco Ice in Harrisonburg and bought a huge block of ice. He used saw dust from his saw mill to cover the ice so it would not melt too quick."

Aunt Goldie used the home made ice box for many years to keep her food cold. Joyce said, "In the summer time we all liked lemonade. Mom would make a big container with sliced lemons and sugar. Daddy would get his ice pick and go to the ice box for ice. I watched him chop off a big hunk and take it to the cistern and pump water over it to clean off the saw dust. He dropped that hunk of ice into the container of lemonade, and that was the best lemonade I ever tasted."

Uncle Rob died in September, 1946. He was just thirty-six years old. Joyce told me, "The first thing Mom bought after Daddy died was a new refrigerator. It was one of those little General Electric refrigerators. We thought we was somethin' else. We felt rich, and found every excuse we could to open the door and look in at the food on the shelves. Mom made payments on it until she got it paid off."

The Cistern

My home was located a mile or so away from the mountains, so we did not have a spring to provide our water. We had a cistern at the back edge of our yard from which Mom filled our water bucket by pumping the water out of the cistern. A cistern was a big hole dug into the ground and lined with bricks or cement. It was filled with rainwater that ran off the roof into gutters. The gutters were set to empty into down pipes mounted on the edge of the roof, and into the cistern.

This cistern is very typical of the one my mother was using when the lightning struck. (Courtesy of Dorothy Rowe, Weyers Cave, VA, 2006).

There was a metal hand pump setting on top of the cistern. The pump had a pipe coming out the bottom that extended down into the water. The pipe had a chain inside of it with rubber suckers every two feet. When the pump handle was turned, the chain dipped into the water, the suckers captured the water, carried it up the pipe, and pushed it out through the waterspout into the bucket.

One of my most horrifying memories was when Mom went to get a bucket of water during a thunderstorm. She was pumping away when a bolt of lightning hit the pump. Luckily she had just released the pump handle and was turning to come back into the house when the lightning hit. I was watching from the back door and saw her body surrounded by blue light. She screamed from fear and ran to the house and up the steps into the kitchen. She was in a lot of pain for several days. For the remainder of her life, she was deathly afraid of a thunderstorm. When she saw a dark cloud coming over Little North Mountain, she gathered all of us into the living room. She closed the curtains and made us sit quietly on the floor until the storm was over. We all grew up very scared of lightning.

Cisterns are still used in many homes and farming operations in the Shenandoah Valley. The major difference is that now the water from the cistern is pumped into the house by an electric pump.

Running Water in the House

Eventually people were able to get water piped into the kitchen. This was made possible in two ways. Some folks were able to place a pipe in the spring and use gravity flow to bring the water into the house. They controlled the water with a single tap where the pipe entered the house. The other way was to pipe the water from a cistern or a spring into the house and mount a pump on the sink. Having water in the kitchen made the cook's life much easier, as water was always available, and there was no danger involved in securing it.

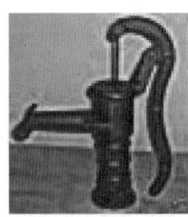

This pump is similar to ones mounted in the kitchen to bring water into the house.

Chapter 4

Everyday Foods

Good bread is the most fundamentally satisfying of all foods; and good bread with fresh butter, the greatest of feasts.
—*James Beard*

Everybody knows that a good cook maintains, on a daily basis, a supply of the basic foods that are served with every meal or that are the necessary ingredients in the preparation of the family's favorite dishes. This list includes milk, butter, cheese, bread and eggs. All the mothers, grandmothers, and aunts in Hopkins Gap had their own cow or cows, a hen house with built-in nests where the hens laid their eggs, a butter churn, a cheese cloth to hang their clabbered milk on the clothes line to drain for cottage cheese, and a flour barrel or kitchen cabinet with a flour bin.

Milk Cows and Milking

All up and down the Appalachian Mountain range, the love of milk and milk products was a given. Hopkins Gap households each had at least one milk cow and, when affordable, two cows were kept so that when one went "dry" (stopped producing milk) before giving birth to a calf, the family's milk supply could come from the extra cow. Milking the cow twice a day was usually the cook's job. Very few men in my family and extended family ever milked the cow. In fact, Mom would not let a man get near her cows. She said to my Dad many times, "You talk too loud, and the cow stops "giving her milk down."

Mom liked to be alone in the barn when she milked. She said many times, "It's peaceful in the barn with my cows. It is a time for me to pray and work out my problems. My cows don't talk back to me." Occasionally Dad would be upset about his job, and he would go into the stall where she was milking and start yelling and cursing. She would stand up from the cow and threaten him with her milk bucket or milk stool. "Get the hell out of here," she yelled. "You're scarin' this cow, and she won't give her milk down." Needless to say, Dad shut up pretty fast and left the barn when he pictured the milk stool slamming on top of his head. He had seen Mom use the milk stool to whack the cow across the back if she didn't stand still to be milked.

Mom had a cow named Ole Dot that she swore was possessed by the devil. She had an unusually large knot on the top of her head that Mom wondered about. Ole Dot always had a hard time giving birth to her calves. She wouldn't stay in one place to give birth so that Mom could watch her and help if she needed help. Ole Dot would keep walking with the calf coming out, inch by inch. Finally, the calf would come all the way out and fall to the ground behind its mom. Mom said, "Look at that old cow. I've never seen anything like her. That calf is going to break its neck when it falls out on the ground."

The calves always fell to the ground. Then Ole Dot would turn around and start licking them. Mom asked the veterinarian about Ole Dot standing up to give birth. He laughed and told her, "That is probably why Dot never loses a calf. The fall knocks the phlegm out of the calf's throat and it starts breathing faster than if it had been born with her lying down."

A prancin' cow and a one-legged kick...

Sometimes Ole Dot just wasn't in the mood to be milked, and she would prance around with her back feet. Mom always started warning her, gently at first, "Stop prancin' Dot," she would say quietly, as she put her hand on the cow's leg. If the quiet words didn't make the cow stop, she yelled louder. After the third or fourth time of asking both gently and loudly, Mom calmly stood up, moved her milk bucket out of the way, picked up her milk stool and slammed the old cow across the back. This action was worth the effort because it usually got good results. Mom would then put her milk stool back in place, put the bucket between her knees, and calmly finish milking the cow. I saw her do this many times. Afterwards, Ole Dot would stand still, and sometimes her back legs would be shaking, but she never moved her feet while Mom finished milking.

There was one occasion when Ole Dot fought back. Mom went through the whole routine to get her to stop prancing and nothing worked. She stood up picked up her milk stool, and whacked the cow across the back. In response, Ole Dot lifted her leg and stepped on Mom's foot and refused to move. Dad was just outside the stable. Mom yelled, "Norman, come in here and push this cow off my foot!!" Without moving toward the barn, he yelled back, "Kick the bitch!!!"

Mom told me later, "How in God's name did he think I could raise one leg and kick while a cow was standing on my other leg?" I had no answer for her.

When I reached the age of eleven or twelve, Mom taught me how to milk. She took me to the barn with her and sat me on the milk stool beside Ole Jerse. She put my little hand around the full teat then placed her hand over mine. She began the squeeze with her index finger and then added the strength of the middle finger. By the time she reached the end of the teat, she had all four fingers and her thumb in the squeezing action, and my little hand was crunched under the pressure. Mom then watched me as I learned the steps in the squeezing process. She often said, "Your little hands were made for milkin'. They fit just right on a cow's teat." Of course, I swelled up with pride from her bragging about my milking skills and wanted to help milk all the time for a while.

I loved being around cows, and I enjoyed milking. The thing I liked least about it was the smell that was left on my hands. I usually helped milk the cows in the evenings. I would wash my hands with soap when I got back to the house, but the next morning on the school bus, I could still smell the cows on my fingers. I looked around in Mom's things and found some perfume called "Evening in Paris." I put a drop or two on my hands, but the perfume didn't take the smell away. It just blended with the cow smell. The odorous result was a smell even worse than the cow smell. I just had to learn to keep my hands tucked in my pockets or under my arms, because I knew that the cow smell would prevent me from having friends and that I would certainly never have a boyfriend. I still wonder occasionally if that is why I never dated in high school and never married.

Cow kicks and bruised crotches...

One summer when I was in college and taking a swimming class, Mom had surgery on her foot to remove a bone spur. She was laid up for eight weeks. I had to get up very early to get the milking done and make my swimming class by 7:30 a.m. At that time she had a Jersey cow, named Ginger, who had just had a calf. Mom had sold the calf as a baby, so Ginger was producing about four and a half gallons of milk morning and evening. I had to take a regular milk bucket that would fit between my knees and a big bucket to pour the milk into when the small bucket was filled. One morning I was sitting beside Ginger squeezing the milk into the bucket, when I fell asleep. I quickly learned that Ginger didn't like to have two hands hanging on her teats unless they were relieving the pressure from her milk bag. She raised her back foot and swiped it close to my head as a warning. She woke me for sure, but before I could shake the sleep out of my eyes, she raised her foot again and kicked me in the groin; knocking me back into the corner of the barn with the milk bucket upside down on my chest. I was soaked with warm milk, but I crawled out of the corner and finished the job.

By the time I got to swim class, I was almost bent over with pain. I had a very large blue and reddish bruise extending from under the front of my bathing suit out onto my upper thighs near my groin. I saw the swimming coach look at me, but she didn't want to say anything because the bruise was suspiciously located in a very personal place. Over the next three weeks, the bruise changed colors as bruises do—from blue to green to yellow. Finally, one day, the swim coach could not resist. She said, "How in the world did you get that bruise?" I looked at her and said, "I thought you would never ask. A cow kicked me." She lowered her head and looked away. Not another word was said about the bruise by either of us. I am not sure she believed my explanation.

Mom got her first cow while Dad was in Germany fighting in World War II. She was a small Jersey heifer that Pop May, our landlord who lived next door, donated to my mother out of sympathy for her plight as a single mother of three children trying to survive the absence of the bread winner in the family. Pop May provided food and shelter for "Ole Jerse." He fed her hay and sheltered her, but allowed Mom to keep all the milk and consider the cow hers.

Mom bred Ole Jerse to Pop May's bull; and when the time came, she was in the barn on her knees

This is Ole Jerse, Mom's first cow. She kept horns all of her life. Mom said, "She can keep her horns because she knows how to use them.

helping with the birthing of the calf. She fed Ole Jerse a little grain twice a day when she sat down to milk her daily. In return, the cow provided milk for Mom's babies—Larry, Brenda, and me—while Dad was overseas and for many years after he returned.

Ole Jerse moved with us to Aunt Goldie's house after Uncle Rob died, and two years later, she moved with us to our permanent home. She lived to the ripe old age of twenty-three years, having survived many difficult birthings and even a broken hip from one of the last times she was bred. Bulls were always difficult for her to stand up under, but this particular bull was especially heavy, and his weight snapped her hip. Usually a cow had to be killed if she had a broken leg or hip, but Mom nursed Ole Jerse by keeping her in the barn away from the other cows. Her hip healed, but she always walked with a limp.

Ole Jerse was a bountiful milk provider who gave more milk than Mom needed in her cooking and to feed her babies. Pop May came to the rescue again and arranged with the local milkman, Charlie Henkel, to bring Mom a five-gallon milk can in which to put her milk. The milkman hauled her milk to the dairy and sold it for her until he died of a heart attack in 1957. His son, Wendell (Sonny) Henkel took over the milk hauling business, and continued to haul Mom's milk for many years. Each month she received a check large enough to pay her rent to Pop May and buy a few staples that she needed to supplement her bountiful garden produce and her canned food from the previous year.

But for the lack of seven hundred dollars...

Because of her milk sales, Mom was able to save a large portion of Dad's army allotment. Before he came home from the war, she had saved two thousand dollars—a small fortune in 1945! Meanwhile, a small farm that adjoined Pop May's land came up for sale. It had all the amenities that Mom had always dreamed about and was the ideal place to raise her children. She told me later in my life, "It had a nice house in good repair. The barn was perfect for the cows I wanted to have. There was a feed room attached to it and a couple of outbuildings. A little hen house sat between the house and the barn. The garden was three quarters of an acre and flat. It was right outside the kitchen door. It had a grazing pasture behind the house and up the hill that was full of limestone outcroppings. Below the house were two ten-acre fields that I could've used to raise hay for my cows. Best of all, the place was located a quarter of a mile from Goldie and Rob. I could raise my kids close to them." I saw your daddy in that big garden every spring planting potatoes and saw myself growing vegetables to can for the winter. I saw about four Jersey cows givin' enough milk for my kids, for making butter, for cooking, and for making cottage cheese."

Mom was such a go-getter. She checked on the price of the little farm and found it was two thousand and seven hundred dollars. Since she already had two thousand dollars, she asked Uncle Rob if he would loan her seven hundred. She said, "He told me, 'I can't loan you that much money.' He really didn't give me a good reason why he wouldn't loan me the money. I figured he thought your daddy might get killed in the war, and that I would bite off more than I could chew as a young widow. I didn't have the education or any way to get myself to a bank to borrow the money. In fact, I was so disappointed that Rob wouldn't loan me the money that I really didn't think about asking anybody else if I could borrow seven hundred. I'll bet John I. Myers would have loaned it to me or even Pop May. I just let my dream slip away."

I was upset as she told me that Uncle Rob wouldn't loan her seven hundred dollars. I felt the sorrow she must have felt because I knew she wanted to surprise Dad when he came home by having moved into her own home. I remarked, Uncle Rob should have known you could pay him back since you had already saved two thousand." She reminded me, "Don't be mad at Rob. He did a lot for me when my daddy died. If he hadn't let Goldie take me in, it's hard to tell how I would've ended up."

When the little farm was sold, it was split into two parcels. John I. Myers bought the two hay fields, and another man bought the house and grazing field to use as rental property. After several years of renters moving in and out, the house was torn to pieces. The barn, the hen house and the other outbuildings were rotting away.

Dad did return from the war in 1945. A year later, Uncle Rob died in September. He had crops that needed to be harvested shortly after his death. Aunt Goldie asked us to move into her house, so that Dad could help her teenage sons, Randy and George, get the corn cut, shucked, and into the corn crib. She moved into her washhouse that was set up as a living space. I remember watching Dad and Goldie's sons cut the corn and arrange it into shocks. After the corn ears ripened in the cool October air, we all helped take the shucks off the ears, toss the golden corn onto a wagon, and haul it to the corncrib.

I used those days to explore the corncrib and the barn. I found a horse collar hanging on the wall of the corncrib. It had cobwebs in the middle where it went over the horse's neck. Nearby hung harnesses for a workhorse. As I looked over the cracking leather, I remembered Uncle Rob's big workhorse, Ole John, and how when I was barely two years old, someone had sat me up on his haunches. One time, I slid off. I remember it felt like I was moving in slow motion as I headed for the ground. I could hear somebody in the background was yelling, "Get that baby. Ole John will stomp her to death!!!" I landed on my back and felt my little head hit the hard ground. Ole John never moved his hind feet.

We continued to live in Aunt Goldie's house for several years. Mom bought more cows because she had enough land to graze them. That is where I learned to milk. Aunt Goldie's chicken house had cracks in the walls through which Mom and I watched Hommy have a calf, and I learned about birthing babies. Mom took over Uncle Rob's chicken houses and raised chickens to sell. She took care of her chickens just like she took care of her babies. When the poultry buyer came to buy her chickens, he always gave her the top price available at the time. Mom had almost achieved her dream of having a little farm, but she was just renting from Aunt Goldie.

In the early months of 1953, Mom's dream farm was back on

the market. It was now in ill repair and the two hay fields were not included in the sale. Dad was working at the Rockingham Milling Company, and Mom was selling chickens, milk, homemade butter and cottage cheese. They easily came up with a small down payment, and the bank loaned them the rest of the sale price of two thousand and eight hundred dollars. We moved into our new home in August of 1953.

The house was so damaged that we could see light coming in through the walls and could see the cellar through the cracks in the kitchen floor. Mom said, "winter is comin', and if we don't fix these cracks, we will all freeze stiff."

She began to tear old rags and stuff the cracks in the wall. She bought some cheap linoleum and covered the kitchen floor to keep the cold from coming up from the cellar.

Dad had me help him move Mom's winter hay from Aunt Goldie's barn to our own barn. We moved several loads, and just as we were putting the last load into the loft, the whole loft caved in with us. We were both buried under two hundred bales of hay. The hay probably saved both of us because it prevented the beams above our heads from falling on us.

The first winter was terrible. We did nearly freeze stiff, as Mom had predicted. Warnie was a baby at that time and suffered from allergies. On several occasions, Dad had to rush him twenty miles over a gravel road to Broadway to see Dr. Charles Watson.

Mom often said to me, "If I had just had another seven hundred dollars, I could have had this place when it didn't need so much work, and it would have had two hay fields. I feel like for the lack of seven hundred dollars, what I wanted for my family had to be set back a long way. It will take us a lot of years and money to get this place in shape, and we paid more for it than it would've cost me with twenty more acres of land."

Mom used her cows much the same way folks used a hog—
"everything but the squeal." The most unusual way she used them
was to predict the severity of an upcoming thunderstorm. When a
black cloud would roll over Little North Mountain, Mom would
look out the kitchen window to see what the cows were doing. If
they were quietly grazing or chewing their cuds, she said, "There
won't be much to that storm. Don't close the windows until we see
if we get a hard rain." But if her cows were walking fast toward the
barn, she called all of us children into the house. She would say,
"There's a bad storm comin'. Go upstairs and close the windows and
stay away from any metal." Often the "bad" storm cloud did not
look very black, but the cows were always right. When they headed
for the barn, we often got a very dangerous storm with high winds,
thunder and lightning, and hail.

Another way she used Ole Jerse was to baby sit. When Dad
went to the war, he left her with three small children. I was three years
old, Larry was a year and a half, and Brenda was six weeks old. Mom
had to go to the barn to milk Ole Jerse. The barn was a fair distance
from the house and way out of earshot of three young children. Our
house was far out in the country, where our only neighbors were the
elderly Pop May and his wife, Minnie. Our nearest relative, Aunt
Goldie, lived a mile away, and Mom couldn't drive the car to take us
there. There was no one around to watch us while Mom went to the
barn twice a day to milk.

Being an ingenious problem solver, Mom came up with a
scheme for babysitting us in the warmer months of the year. When I
think of how she accomplished babysitting and milking at the same
time, I just have to shake my head and smile. Twice a day she walked
to the barn with Larry in one arm, Brenda in the other arm. I walked
by her side. She had the handle of the milk bucket in one hand and
her milk stool in the other hand. In her milk bucket she had about
two inches of warm water, a clean cloth, and two small baby bottles
with nipples.

When we arrived at the barnyard, Ole Jerse would be waiting

with a swollen milk bag and full teats. The cow stopped chewing on the hay Pop May had put out for his cows, and stood very still waiting to be milked. Mom put Larry down to stand beside me and held Brenda close to her chest while she placed her milk stool beside Ole Jerse. "Back your leg," she told Ole Jerse who, without fail, stepped her right hind leg back so Mom could get to her full teats. Mom took

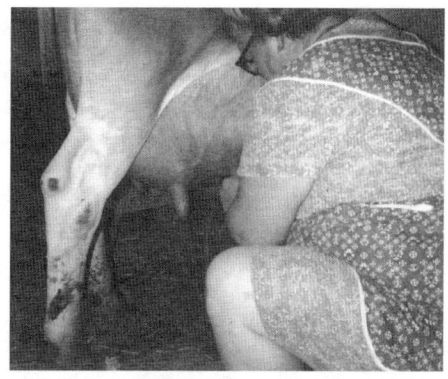

Mom is milking Ginger, offspring of Ole Jerse. She is dressed in her homemade feed sack dress and apron. (1968)

the cloth from the warm water in her milk bucket. Using her free hand, she wrung out most of the water and used the wet cloth to wash Ole Jerse's bag and teats. She laid the dirty cloth on the ground beside her and dumped the rest of the clean water out of the bucket. (When I was learning to milk some years later, Mom told me to use a warm cloth to wash the cow's bag and teats so she would "give her milk down" quicker and the milk would be cleaner.) Mom placed the milk bucket under the full teats, and placed Brenda on her lap across her knees and told Larry and me to stand still.

I recall that standing still was difficult, because there were so many things going on in the barnyard. Chickens wandered around pecking in the cow piles. Some of the hens had babies, and Larry and I wanted to play with them. Larry was just learning to talk so he was naming all the animals. Mom started milking, and once some of the pressure was released from Ole Jerse's bag, she would pick up the baby bottles and fill them with milk straight from the teat. She then put the nipples on the bottles and would hand one to me and one to Larry. The milk was so delicious—warm and foamy—that nothing going on in the barnyard could distract us.

We each had one or two refills before Mom emptied Ole Jerse's heavy bag. It took some time for us to empty two or three bottles of milk. I remember us leaning our heads back and holding the bottle high to get the last drops out of bottle. By the time the milking was finished, we had bellies full of warm milk. Mom helped us make our way back to the house. Her load was heavier now with the bucket full of milk.

Later in my life, Mom described those times to me with great pride in the way she had solved her baby-sitting problem. She said, "We were all lucky that Ole Jerse was such a good cow. She could have kicked all of our brains out, but she acted like she knew that I needed her to be gentle. I even taught you and Larry a game to play when you got bored. I told you that if you held on to Ole Jerse's tail and pumped it gently up and down while I was milking, she would give more milk. That old cow put up with a lot and never once lifted her foot to kick."

Ole Jerse had many calves during her lifetime. Mom kept one of the female calves and raised her to be a milk cow. She named her Hommy. She grew up to be a huge cow, much larger than her petite mother, and she had a totally different personality. Mom had Hommy's horns removed as soon as possible. Hommy looked mean, and sometimes she was mean. She would occasionally kick the milk bucket over and refuse to be milked.

Hommy had a problem with various people who got near her, and she would take her head and butt them out of the barn. It never failed, when my sister, Brenda, got near Hommy there was trouble. She would push Brenda against the barnyard fence and hold her there with an occasional butt with her head. The cow didn't seem to really want to hurt Brenda, but she wouldn't let her get away either. Brenda was trapped and had no alternative but to scream as loud as she could until somebody rescued her. Mom would come out of the barn and yell. The cow would back up and walk away as if to say, "I don't like that kid. Keep her out of my space."

Learnin' about birthin' babies....

When I was twelve years old, Mom told me it was time for me to learn about where babies come from. Hommy, the cow, was about to give birth and had chosen a somewhat private spot—a narrow space between the barnyard fence and the back of the chicken house—to have her calf. Mom took me into the chicken house so we could watch the birth through the cracks in the boards.

We watched the birth while Mom compared each step with the birth of a human baby. When the calf's feet appeared, she said, "The nose is coming next. If that was your baby, it would be the crown of the head. Human babies are born face down when there's no problem." She went on, "Sometimes a human baby is born butt first. That's called a breech birth. The doctor has to go up inside and turn the baby so it can be born head first." Mom continued to explain each part of the birthing of Hommy's calf. She said, "Sometimes I had to help Ole Jerse. One leg of the calf would come all the way out, so I would push it back in and grab the other leg to get them together. If the one leg comes way out, it can break the calf's neck, so you gotta try to help to save the calf."

After that lesson in birthing, I was able to help Mom with her cows when I was home. Because Jersey cows are small, they often have calves that are too big to be born naturally. Mom would grab a burlap sack and get down on her knees behind the cow. The burlap sack allowed her to get a grip on the slimy calf. When the cow had a birthing pain, the legs and nose would push out. She wrapped the sack around the legs and pulled. Then she would wait for the next birthing pain. Gradually, she got the calf out far enough for me to grab on and pull. "Get down on your knees with me", she said, "and help me pull." When the calf finally fell free, Mom would clean its nose and mouth with her hand and make sure it was breathing. Then she would look at me across the slimy calf and grin because we had just saved a calf and maybe a cow.

Mom had a few cows for the remainder of her life. Not too long after Dad returned from the war, she bought another Jersey cow so that she would have milk all the time. When she had to let Ole Jerse go dry in preparation for the birth of her calves, she had another cow to give milk. Mom always said, "No other cow's milk tastes as good as Ole Jerse's milk." She judged her cows by how much cream rose to the top of the milk as it cooled in the icebox, and later, the refrigerator. "Ole Jerse gives the richest milk," she would say as she eyed the level of cream. "I get more butter off of a gallon of her milk than any other cow," she often bragged.

Mom absolutely hated milk from a Holstein cow. She called it "blue john" because the milk had very little fat in it and gave off a bluish hue when she strained it into a glass jar. She ranked cows by breed according to how much cream they gave. "Jersey cows are the best," she said. "If I had to choose, the next best would be a Guernsey, but I wouldn't give a nickel for a Holstein. They give a lot of milk, but it ain't no good for makin' cheese or butter. Probably the best cow might be a cross between a Jersey and a Holstein. Then you would get a lot of milk, but it would be richer."

When we moved to our permanent home, Mom was able to buy a Holstein heifer crossed with a Jersey. She named her Betsy. She loved Ole Bets because she gave a lot of very rich milk just as Mom had predicted she would. One day Ole Bets got into the hog feed and ate too much. She bloated and died right in front of Mom. That was not an easy few days for anybody. Mom always got mad when she was grieving the loss of a cow.

Everyday Milk-based Foods

When Mom got her fresh milk into the house the first thing she did was strain it. She had a commercial milk strainer. It was a large metal bowl with holes in the bottom. A ring fit in the bottom to hold down a paper filter disk. The disk trapped any hair or dirt that might have fallen from the cow's bag into the milk. After it was strained, Mom she set aside a portion of the milk for us to drink and for her to use in cooking. She processed the rest into various products. In the early years, she cooled the milk in an icebox. (See Chapter 3) When the milk cooled, the cream would rise to the top and settle in a golden ring around the glass jar. Ole Jerse gave such rich milk that the ring of cream was often one third of the contents of the jar.

Mom skimmed most of the cream off the milk and put it in a separate container. When she had enough cream, she churned it into butter. She had a "modern" churn—a step up from the wooden churn with a dasher that you had to lift up and down until the cream turned into butter. Mom's modern churn was a glass jar with a metal top and crank, attached to two wooden paddles that stirred the cream as the crank was turned. When she was about ready to churn butter, she took the cream out of the ice box and let it warm to room temperature. Then she set the churn on the floor and had me sit on the floor with the churn between

This "modern churn" or paddle churn, belonged to Aunt Millie Morris, but Mom and other cooks in Hopkins Gap replaced their old wooden churns with this same type of churn.

my outstretched legs. I would begin cranking the handle. At first, the crank turned without tiring my young arms, but when the butterfat began to separate and turn into chunks of butter, I would start to cry because I was tired. Mom would reassure me, "Keep on turnin'. You almost have butter." I would gather my strength and turn one or two more cranks, and then she would pick up the churn and make a few turns. Almost immediately the butter would appear. I remember thinking she knew everything and could do anything. It seemed magical how quickly she would get butter. I wondered if I would ever be able to do what she did.

I have always enjoyed the old Appalachian songs of singer and songwriter, Jean Ritchie. In one of her songs, she describes the scene above and takes me back to those early days in Mom's kitchen.

There now, don't you cry
Hush your crying by and by
Then we'll make the butter fly
Mommy's baby don't you cry.
Churn, churn, makes some butter
For my little girlie's supper...
—*Jean Ritchie*

Mom had another rhyme that she taught us to say while we were churning butter for her:

Come, butter come
Come, butter come.
Peter standing at the gate
Waiting for a butter cake.
Come butter come.

Sour Cream Butter Recipe....

Allow the raw milk to cool so that the cream comes to the top.

Collect the cream from each day's milking until you have enough to fill the churn one-half full.

Let the cream sour by placing it on the back of the wood stove—a low heat area—for about four hours.

Let the sour cream cool to between 50–68 degrees. The cooler the cream, the longer it will take to get butter.

Put the cream in the butter churn and begin to churn in a steady but methodical motion. If you have a paddle churn, turn about one revolution per second.

This process could take 30 minutes or a lot longer.

When the cream begins to feel, thicker and harder to churn, it is about to separate the butter from the butter milk.

When it separates, the chunks of butter will be floating in the butter milk.

Separate the butter from the buttermilk. (Mom used her hands to do this while some Hopkins Gap folks had a butter paddle.)

Place the butter in a bowl and remove all the buttermilk from the butter.

Using your hand or a butter paddle, work the butter back and forth on the sides of the bowl, then wash the butter to remove all traces of buttermilk. Use cold water and work it with your hands or a butter paddle.

Sprinkle in 1 tsp. of salt per pound of butter and mix it in.

Put butter in molds—be sure to get rid of air bubbles. Take the butter cake out of the mold by pushing the false mold bottom. Wrap in wax paper and keep cold.

The milk that was left in the churn after dipping out the butter was called buttermilk. This was poured into a jar and placed in the icebox or refrigerator. Buttermilk was mainly used was for cornbread. Cornbread covered in buttermilk was the typical Sunday evening meal. Often I watched Mom go to the icebox and pour herself a big glass of buttermilk, tip it up, and drink it down. She claimed it was good for digestion. I had to mix buttermilk with something else to hide the taste. I could not drink it straight.

A churn tragedy averted....

A long time after I left home, I received a panic call from Mom. She had dropped her paddle churn on the floor and broken the glass jar. She had searched everywhere around home and couldn't find a replacement. She asked me, "Do you have time to look around Roanoke to see if you can find me a new jar? I am sure there are some old farmers around Roanoke who still churn butter."

Of course, I said I would help her if I could. I called around and asked all of my friends' mothers and grandmothers if there might be a store in Roanoke that would carry a paddle churn. They all recommended that I go to Agnew Seeds in the Roanoke City Market. Sure enough, they had a replacement jar for Mom's paddle churn. This happened in the late 1980s. The joy and relief in her voice when I told her I had a replacement made all the effort worthwhile. Some of my professor colleagues at Radford University were also relieved, because they had become quite fond of Mom's homemade butter, as well as her cottage cheese.

Another milk product that made Mom popular with Uncle Rob and her brother, Uncle Charlie was "clabber." Clabber is non-pasteurized milk that is allowed to sour and thicken or curdle naturally. After Mom skimmed the cream off her sweet milk, she took a shallow serving dish and filled it with the partially skimmed milk. She placed the dish on the back of the stove and kept it warm until it began to sour. It turned into a thick, custard-like substance.

I remember watching Uncle Rob take the serving dish to the kitchen table. He shook a lot of pepper on top of it, and ate the clabber with a tablespoon, all the while exclaiming that Mom made the best "clabber" he had ever eaten. He claimed it helped his "ulcers" and made him feel better so he could go back to work at his saw mill. That was all he had to say to make sure Mom kept a frequent supply of "clabber" on the back of her wood stove. When Uncle Charlie drove in from Pennsylvania with a load of coal, he stopped in to see us and enjoyed Mom's clabber as much as Uncle Rob did.

Sometimes Mom turned her milk into cottage cheese, which was one of my favorite milk dishes. Her cottage cheese was known far and wide as the best. It always turned out with a slightly gritty texture very different from the slimy cottage cheese that you purchase in a grocery store. Sometimes I ate her cottage cheese plain with just a sprinkling of black pepper on it. At other times I mixed it with Grandma Molly's homemade apple butter and enjoyed it with a side dish of pinto beans and ham.

When I walked in from school on cold winter days and saw a small white cotton flour sack hanging on the clothesline, I knew we were having cottage cheese for supper. Mom put her sour milk in a clean cotton sack and hung it on the clothesline. The sack swung in the breezes as the whey slowly dripped into a dishpan placed on the ground below. In the summer, she hung the sack from a hook on the enclosed back porch so bugs and flies couldn't get to it.

The whey looked like green water. It was a great addition to the hog slop or you could drink it for extra nourishment. Remember Little Miss Muffet? She ate her curds and then drank her whey.

___

Cottage Cheese Recipe.....

Put a gallon of partially skimmed raw milk into a crock. In the summer, set the crock of milk on a side table in the warm kitchen and let it sour slowly. In the winter, set the crock of milk on the back of the wood stove where it will just stay warm and sour slowly. It takes about eight hours if the milk is cold.

When the milk turns to "clabber," put it in a pan and heat it over a low fire until it curdles. Pour the curdled milk through a bleached white flour sack and drain the whey off the curds.

Place the drained curds back into a pan and squeeze to work out the remaining whey. The more the curds are squeezed, the smaller they become so gauge the amount of squeezing based on how small you want the curds. While mixing, sprinkle in salt to taste.

Add some sweet or sour cream to make the cottage cheese as creamy as you want it. Pack into containers and keep cold in the refrigerator until used. Cottage cheese keeps up to two weeks in the refrigerator.

___

It was not uncommon for Mom to experiment with ideas for recipes that came to her. One of these was a treat she called "stovetop cheese." When she made this recipe, it never lasted long enough to be chilled or stored; therefore, we never knew how it would keep. Mom would be working quietly in the kitchen and suddenly call us to come; much as an old hen called her baby chicks after she had scratched up some bugs to share with them. Mom would open a box of saltine crackers, and we all stood around the stove and ate until the "stove-top cheese" was gone.

Stove-Top Cheese Recipe...

Ingredients

1 gallon of clabbered milk	1 egg
Salt to taste	¼ teaspoon soda

Heat the clabbered milk until medium warm. Strain the milk through a clean white flour sack so as to remove as much whey as possible. Mix cheese curd, egg, salt, and soda. Use a double boiler and heat the mixture while stirring. Stir until smooth and totally blended. Eat warm or pour into a container and chill.

Mom cooked many of her vegetables with milk because Ole Jerse gave so much. We often had creamed peas, corn, potatoes, and butter beans. Most of her desserts called for milk, and we ate whipped cream on all of them.

One of the favorite foods in Hopkins Gap, and especially in my family, was gravy made with milk. This dish was just a basic food to which the cooks added some type of meat for flavoring. The type of meat was often determined by the season of the year. In the fall hog-butchering season, the meat was fresh sausage or drippings from fresh tenderloin that had been rolled in flour, with salt and pepper and fried in hog lard. During the late winter, spring, and summer Mom used canned pork sausage or canned tenderloin to make gravy. In late fall hunting season, milk gravy was flavored with the drippings from fried venison steak which had been prepared similarly to the fresh pork tenderloin. In winter squirrel season, the milk gravy was flavored with the broth from boiling the squirrels.

Mom's Milk Gravy Recipe....

¼ cup drippings from frying some type of meat
¼ cup of plain flour
2 cups of whole milk
2 cups of water
Salt and pepper to taste

After frying meat, pour out all but about ¼ cup of drippings.

Turn the heat to low. Add the flour to the drippings and stir to make a smooth paste. Cook the paste, stirring constantly, until the mixture begins to bubble and turns a golden brown.

Mix the milk and water and add to the skillet. Return to heat and cook, stirring constantly, until the mixture begins to thicken and bubble. Add salt and pepper to taste and serve immediately.

Thanks to Ole Jerse and Mom's other cows, she "had her own milk" most of her adult life. Since she was so creative and resourceful with her own milk, she hated the "store bought" milk. She found that it had been processed so much that it limited the ways it could be used in cooking and feeding our family.

Bread: the Staff of Life

Bread was indeed the "staff of life" in Hopkins Gap homes. No meal was complete without it. It was the cooks' responsibility to make the bread and bring it to the table with the rest of the meal. There were four types of bread commonly made in Hopkins Gap:

light bread, fried bread, warm bread, and corn bread.

Light Bread. Light bread is leavened bread made with wheat flour. While the rest of the country simply calls it bread, southerners and Appalachian mountaineers and specifically Hopkins Gap folks, call it "light bread." Contrary to what northern folks might think, light bread is not another title for white bread. Light refers not to the color of the bread but to the yeast that "lightens" it. Light bread can be made with whole wheat or white flour.

Light bread is not easy to make. It takes nearly a whole day to make a batch. Mom and Aunt Ethel were known for many of their dishes, but making perfect loaves of light bread was among their most appreciated cooking talents. Mom always baked her bread for the week on Tuesdays. It became a tradition at my house to have hot light rolls and a fresh pot of pinto beans on Tuesday evenings. Those days were special because the aroma coming from the kitchen greeted us as we came up the hill from the school bus. It seemed the smell of light bread and pinto beans traveled further than any other smell.

Mom taught Larry's wife, Hilda how to make light bread and hot light bread rolls. Hilda is the youngest woman I know who still makes light bread every week, and her bread is just as good as Mom's because she learned at Mom's elbow. Hilda shared her recipe with me recently and allowed me to take pictures of each step as she baked her bread for the coming week.

Light Bread Recipe...

(Single batch = 4 loaves and a pan of 18 rolls).

Fill a big pan with sifted flour (approximately eight pounds). Scrape the flour to the sides leaving a hole covered with a thin layer of flour in the middle. Add:

¼ cup of hog lard

1 tablespoon of salt

¼ cup of sugar
2 tablespoons of yeast (soaked in warm water)
4 cups of warm water

Grease hands with hog lard and work the dough (see photos) until outside of the dough ball is not sticky.

Grease a clean pan with hog lard. Lift the dough ball into the air and drop upside down in the clean pan.

Let the dough ball rise to twice its size. Knead out the air and let it rise again to double its size.

Knead the dough again and pull off pieces large enough to shape into loaves. Place the loaves into single pans or one pan that will hold all four. Pull off pieces and shape the rolls. For the rolls, tightly pack them, sides touching, into a pan. This will help hold their shape.

Place loaves and rolls in the oven at 350 degrees and bake until golden brown. Approximately 1 hour.

Hilda starts her baking by first measuring flour into a large bread-mixing pan. She then measures lard and puts it into a hole in the middle of the flour. Next, she adds in the salt and water.

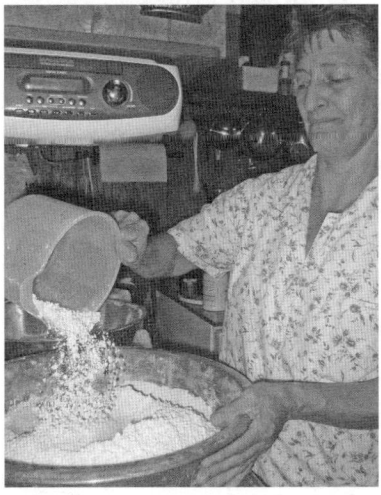

With all the ingredients in her pan, Hilda uses her hands to stir the flour, lard, salt, and water together. As her hands move, the flour from the sides of the pan gradually mixes into the pool of ingredients.

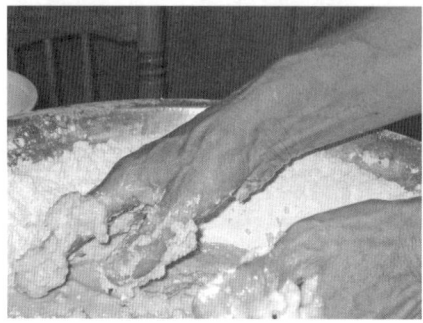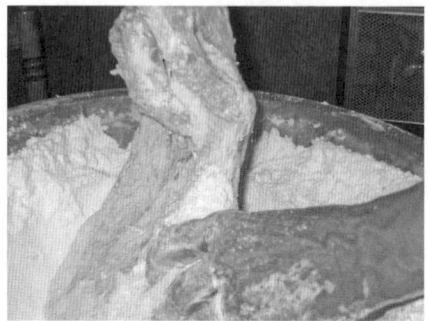

As the ingredients start to become dough, she pulls and tugs at it, all the while working in more flour. The ball of dough grows larger as Hilda pulls at it and kneads it with her knuckles. She explained the importance of kneading and letting the bread rise, "Kneadin' and lettin' the dough rise are the keys to how smooth your bread is, how it holds together, and how porous it is. These steps are important in how you feel about the results. I love to knead bread. It kinda affects me like milking a cow. I get my rest. It is calming and very peaceful. I feel like I am getting' something done that is worth doing and there is no way to hurry with it." I asked Hilda, "How do you know when you have kneaded long enough?" She answered, "You have to knead until the dough itself tells you it's done. I learned by experience. I knead until the dough stops getting holes in it and feels really smooth."

Once the dough is no longer sticky, it is ready to put aside to rise. Hilda lifts the ball of dough out of the flour pan, tosses it into the air, and places it upside down in a clean pan that has been greased with hog lard. The bread pan is placed in a warm place usually on the kitchen counter near the warmth of the stove. Hilda explained, "For a good rising of your dough, you need a really warm kitchen. That's no problem in the summer time because we don't have air

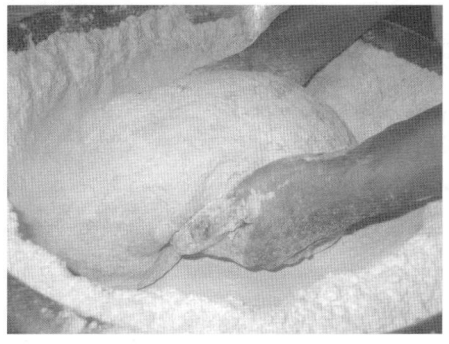

conditioning. In the winter I set it close to the wood stove that we heat the enclosed porch with."

The dough rises under Hilda's watchful eye. When it rises to about twice its original size, she kneads the bread again to remove some of the air. She sets the dough aside to rise again. One the dough has risen the second time, she begins to shape her loaves and her smaller rolls from the dough. She gets about four loaves and a pan of eighteen rolls from a batch of dough this size.

The loaves and the rolls are placed in the warm spot again, until they rise to the desirable size. Then they are placed in the oven to bake. Soon the house smells like a bakery and all is well. The bread comes out of the oven a golden brown.

Hilda then takes a brush and dips it into the lard bucket. She brushes the top of the bread so that the crust will stay soft. By the time supper is ready, the bread is cool enough to slice. However, the family usually chooses to eat the light rolls first while they are warm. They save the loaf bread for the up-coming meals.

While Hilda was baking her bread, she gossiped about how Grandma Molly and Aunt Lena never had fresh light bread. She said, "Grandma Molly and Lena made another batch of light bread as soon they had eat two or three loaves of the previous batch. That way they never enjoyed fresh bread right out of the oven. I don't do that. Bread is always the best right after it is out of the oven. My family really looks forward to eating supper the day I bake."

Light bread with apple butter and milk was one of our favorite everyday desserts. Sometimes before bed, Dad would slice a "chunk of bread" as Mom called it, from a loaf, put it in a plate, smear it with roughly four heaping tablespoons of apple butter or sometimes fresh strawberry jam, and pour milk over it. He ate it as if the dish was going to run away—fast and furious—grinning and smacking his mouth until it was all gone. Of course, all of us kids had to do the same thing. Mom bitched and yelled: "Norman, it's like takin' your dick out in a whorehouse; everybody wants some when they see it. Damn it!!! I will have a mess of dirty dishes to get up to in the morning." Dad just kept on slurping as she fussed.

Bread and milk as medicine.....

Light bread also had medicinal uses. It was not uncommon for Hopkins Gap children to have boils, and I was no exception. The pain of a boil is something I will never forget. It was not unusual for me to get sick and vomit from the pain. Mom treated my boils by making a poultice with a small piece of light bread, soaked in milk. She put the bread in a small pan with some milk and heated it on the wood stove. While the bread was boiling hot, she placed it directly on the boil and wrapped a clean white cloth around it to hold it in place. This treatment was applied just before bedtime. The hot bread scalding the boil made me scream with pain. It was nearly unbearable, and Mom often found a blister on my skin around the boil in the morning; however, the boil had come to a head and opened during the night. The awful pain of the boil was gone, and the pain of the blister was bearable until it healed.

Fried Bread. Some of my best memories were coming home from school to a treat of fried bread and apple butter. This treat was best when Mom was using her wood cook stove for baking. After the bread dough rose the first time, Mom pinched off pieces of dough. She used her rolling pin and rolled them out into round or oblong shapes leaving them about one inch thick. She rubbed them with a little lard and put them directly on the stovetop. As they turned a golden brown on the outside, the heat partially baked the dough inside of them. When they were done, we cut the ends open and put apple butter inside (similar to a pita pocket today). Hot bread, plus warm apple butter, and a glass of Ole Jerse's milk from the refrigerator added up to "hog heaven."

Warm Bread. Warm bread served the same purpose as the family pie. It was a way to feed the family fresh hot bread, without the cook having to work at bread making while she was busy with other chores. Warm bread was quick and easy and could be served at every meal, including breakfast. It was a quick substitute for light bread. It was especially delicious with pinto beans and gravy. Warm bread is served in a large flat cake and each family member breaks off whatever size portion they want.

Warm Bread Recipe...

Ingredients
1 tablespoon of active dry yeast
2 tablespoons warm water
5 cups sifted all-purpose flour
¼ cup sugar
2 teaspoons of baking powder
1 teaspoon salt
1 cup of lard
2 cups of buttermilk

In a medium bowl dissolve the yeast in the warm water and set aside.

In a large bowl, sift together flour, sugar, baking powder, and salt. Using your fingers, stir in the lard until the mixture resembles very coarse cornmeal.

Add buttermilk to the yeast water, stir briefly, and add to the flour mixture. Stir until the mixture is just moistened. Turn the dough onto a greased and floured baking pan. Sprinkle the top lightly with flour, and knead by poking the knuckles of both hands into the top while flattening the dough into the corners of the pan.

Bake in a preheated oven for 15 to 20 minutes or until golden brown. Serve warm.

Buttermilk Biscuits Recipe...

Ingredients

2 cups flour
½ teaspoon soda
1 cup buttermilk

2 tablespoons hog lard
½ teaspoon salt
½ teaspoon baking powder

Mix flour, salt, and baking powder. Sift into a large mixing bowl. Put lard into the flour mixture and, with your hands, work it gently into the flour. Add soda to the buttermilk and stir until it starts to bubble. Add mixture to flour, gradually working it into stiff dough. Turn dough onto floured tabletop and knead softly until smooth. Roll out to about ¼ inch thick. Cut into biscuits and bake at 400 degrees on a greased cookie sheet for about 12 to 15 minutes or until golden brown.

Corn Bread. I have never heard anybody from Hopkins Gap or my immediate family say, "I don't like cornbread." Quite likely at one time, it was the main bread served in Hopkins Gap. Dad told me that in the early days, "Everybody had a corn patch or shared corn that was planted in 'high-top patches' on the mountains, and just about every body had a corn crib. The corncrib was a storage area with cracks between the boards so air could circulate through

the corn. When the corn was harvested, some was stored in the corncrib for the pigs and chickens. The men carried the remaining corn on their back across Little North Mountain to have it ground into meal at Stultz's Mill. Mr. Stultz ground their corn into meal between two large stones. The process

Stultz's Mill shortly before it burned. (1972)

took two days; and the men would sleep on piles of sacks in the mill, so that they could carry their corn meal back home the next day.

My family ate corn bread as a Sunday evening treat after the huge Sunday dinners we ate in Hopkins Gap. Mom would bake cornbread and Dad and we children would all crumble it up in a bowl of cold sweet milk. We ate it with a spoon like soup. Mom, who favored buttermilk, crumbled her corn meal into a bowl of

Great Aunt Millie and Uncle Joe Morris's corncrib where they stored corn and hung their stuffed sausage by wrapping it around poles high in the crib.

buttermilk. In the spring, we ate corn bread with the first batch of creasy greens. Mom always put a lot of water on her creasy greens when she cooked them. The water mixed with the juice from the greens, the hog lard, and the seasonings, and we called it "pot likker." My favorite thing to do with corn bread was to crumble it into a bowl of creasy greens "pot likker" and eat it like soup.

Old Timey Buttermilk Corn Bread Recipe...
Ingredients
1¾ cup corn meal
1 cup buttermilk
2 tablespoons of melted hog lard

Preheat the oven to 475 degrees. Put two tablespoons of hog lard in an eight-inch iron skillet and place it in the oven to heat to melt. Put the corn meal into a mixing bowl and slowly add the cup of buttermilk while stirring. The batter should be thin enough to pour, and if not, add extra buttermilk as needed. Remove the skillet with the hot lard from the oven, and while it is still very hot, pour the batter into it. The batter should sound like it is frying when poured into the skillet. Put the batter-filled skillet back into the oven and bake at 475 degrees for about 25 minutes, or until golden brown.

When the corn bread came out of the oven, Mom turned the iron skillet upside down and dumped it on a large round plate. We each broke off a piece with our hands. Corn bread was never cut. Mom told me that it was bad luck to cut corn bread. She said, "You have to break it with your hands just like Jesus did at the last supper, or you will have bad luck."

Over time, the cooks in Hopkins Gap adopted wheat flour and old timey buttermilk corn bread was replaced by a lighter, tastier corn bread, with wheat flour, eggs, baking powder, and soda.

Buttermilk Corn Bread Recipe....

Ingredients
3 tablespoons wheat flour
1¼ cups cornmeal
1 teaspoon of salt
¾ teaspoon baking powder
1 cup buttermilk
2 small eggs
2 tablespoons hog lard
½ teaspoon soda

Mix cornmeal, flour, baking powder, and salt. Beat the eggs and add the buttermilk. Melt the hog lard and add to the liquid mix. Cut the liquid into the dry ingredients. Add soda dissolved in a tablespoon of water.

Pour into a hot, greased, cast iron skillet, or pan, and bake at 425 degrees for 25 minutes or until golden brown.

By the time I arrived on this earth, the old timey buttermilk corn bread recipe had been "fancied up" to an even tastier version that includes sugar and sweet milk. This is the recipe I use when I get homesick for corn bread and soupy pinto beans. I still use a cast iron skillet to make my corn bread.

Sweet Corn Bread Recipe....

Ingredients
1 cup of unbleached all-purpose flour
1 cup cornmeal
2 tablespoons sugar
2 teaspoons of baking powder
¾ teaspoon salt
1 cup milk
1/3 cup canola oil
1 large egg, beaten slightly

Preheat the oven to 425 degrees. Grease an 8-inch cast iron skillet with butter or nonstick cooking spray. Sift the dry ingredients into a mixing bowl. Form a well in the dry mixture and add the milk, canola oil, and egg. Stir just until everything is combined. The batter will be slightly lumpy. Pour the batter into the greased skillet and bake for approximately 25 minutes, until the corn bread starts to brown around the edges. Insert a fork or knife in the middle. If it comes out clean, the bread is done.

Chickens and Eggs

A hen house and a flock of chickens were two essential parts of every homestead in Hopkins Gap. Chickens served the Hopkins Gap family in many ways. Fried chicken was the favorite dish; second only to pork. Mom and Aunt Ethel could fry chicken that practically melted in your mouth and deserved a write-up in the local newspaper. Fried chicken was almost always served for Sunday dinner, as a treat and a break from the pork dishes eaten all week long.

On Saturday, the cooks in Hopkins Gap would spend most of the day cleaning the chickens. Sometimes, Mom would catch the chickens late on Friday evening, after they had gone to roost in the hen house. Chickens were easy to catch after sundown when they were asleep. Mom would just walk quietly into the hen house and pick three or four chickens off the slanted roost by wrapping her hand around their legs. Because they were asleep, they went along quietly, with little flopping, and were placed in a chicken coop. The next morning she had them close at hand for killing and cleaning.

When I was old enough, I was recruited to help with this smelly job. After breakfast on Saturday mornings, when the dishes were washed and put away, Mom would take me with her to the woodpile where she had penned the chickens in the coop. One by one she took them out of the coop and had me hold them by the head, while she held their feet. We laid their neck across a block of wood and she chopped off their heads. When she let go of their feet, the chickens would flop around the yard flinging blood everywhere. Mom always told me this was a good thing so that the chicken would "bleed out good" and taste better for Sunday dinner. The first time I experienced the chicken slaughter and watched how they flopped around, I was upset because those particular chickens had been scratching around the yard where we played. Sometimes I had found their hidden nests and watched as their babies hatched and followed them around the yard also.

Until I understood the place of chickens in the whole scheme of my family's life, I felt sorry for them when Mom whacked off their heads. I felt each chicken's humiliation as it jumped around, spewing blood everywhere. When I first started helping, I cried for the chickens until Mom warned me, "Stop crying. They die harder if you feel sorry for 'em." She always put the strangest twist on those kinds of events. After a few experiences, and taking Mom's warnings and explanations to heart, I soon began to chop off the chickens' heads myself. When I got a bit older, I asked Mom if I could target practice with Dad's .22 rifle by shooting the chickens in the head while they walked around the yard. She said, "Yes, but as soon as they fall over, chop their heads off so they can bleed out." I was a good shot.

The next step, after the headless chickens had stopped jumping around the yard, was a short trip to the washhouse, where Mom had an iron kettle filled with boiling water. She poured some boiling water out into a tub, dipped the dead chicken in the scalding water, and held it there for a period of time. Then she handed me a scalded chicken and told me to start pulling out the feathers.

Once the chicken was bare of its big feathers, Mom put a pile of newspapers into another metal tub and set the papers on fire. She then grabbed the plucked chicken by the feet and waved it through the flames. She burned off what she called the "pin feathers," which were too small to pluck.

The washhouse would become filled with the most putrid smell—the steam from the boiling water smelled like chicken shit and wet chicken feathers. The chicken was now ready to "gut." Mom started by removing the chicken's rectum, then reached up inside with her hand and pulled out the guts. This part of the process only added to the awful smell that was already wafting through the washhouse. Mom always saved the chicken's heart, gizzard, and liver to be cooked and added to the gravy for flavor and texture. She carefully removed these parts and showed them to me. The liver was tiny, but Mom skillfully felt around until she found the gall and removed it. She held the gizzard in the palm of her left hand. Using a sharp knife, she split it open and showed me the inside. It was filled with gravel, bits of weed, bugs, and some chicken feed. The lining was filled with ridges. Mom explained that the chicken gizzard was the same as a human stomach. The ridges worked like a grinder to prepare the food to enter the small intestine. She very carefully picked at the edge of the gizzard lining with all its contents and pulled it out of the gizzard. The lining was thrown outside for the cats to eat.

Once the guts were out and gone, Mom would cut the chicken into parts—first the legs came off, then the wings. The legs were cut into two sections—the drumstick and the thigh. Each wing was tucked into a compact piece. Then she used a large butchering knife and split the breast into two pieces. The back was separated out and divided into two pieces—one section contained the ribs and the other piece was the lower back which had some delicious meat around the back bone. Mom left the piece that held the tail feathers but was careful to remove the oil glands just to the front of the tailpiece. She explained that the chickens kept their feathers clean and shiny by squeezing oil out of that gland with their beaks when they were preening their feathers. I appreciated this part of my education; whenever I saw a chicken picking at the spot in front of their tails I knew exactly what they were doing.

When Mom finished she had two piles of chicken pieces. The heart, ribs, liver, and neck went into a cook pot to make stock for chicken gravy. The legs, thighs, breast, wings, and lower back went into a large pan of salted water and set on the back porch cabinet until ready to cook. I asked her why she did that and she answered, "The salt takes the bloody taste out of the meat and makes the chicken taste good."

When Aunt Ethel or Mom put a huge platter of fried chicken on the Sunday dinner table, I knew exactly what they had been doing for the past two days. I could even conjure up the sights and smells with which the various stages of preparation had poisoned the air and nostrils of those who were involved. Today, when I hear the statement, "You are jumping around like a chicken with its head cut off" I have no problem putting the whole image together in my mind.

Fried Chicken Recipe...

Cut your chickens up into pieces—legs, thighs, wings, and breast (split in two pieces). Boil the backs, necks, gizzards, livers, and hearts in salt water and use the stock for chicken gravy.

Mix the following ingredients together for each pound of chicken.

¼ cup flour
½ teaspoon of salt
¼ teaspoon pepper
1 teaspoon paprika

Put the dry ingredients in a deep plate and roll the chicken pieces in it.

Drop chicken pieces into a hot cast iron skillet with about ¾ inch of hot hog lard. Turn pieces to brown evenly. Once the pieces are browned, cover the pan and reduce heat. Fry slowly until tender—30 to 45 minutes, depending on the size of the chicken pieces. Turn the pieces often; trying not to pierce the chicken with the fork or to shake off the browned flour coating.

Since Mom and Aunt Ethel didn't waste anything, they slid the pan where they had fried the chicken in back onto the hot stove and made gravy with the drippings.

Fried Chicken Gravy Recipe...

Ingredients
Drippings from pan fried chicken
2 tablespoons of flour
1 cup of chicken broth with boiled chicken giblets cut up in it
2 cups of milk
Salt and pepper to taste

Heat the dripping from the pan-fried chicken. Add flour and stir until the flour is brown. Remove the pan from the heat. In a separate container, mix the chicken broth with giblets and the milk. Pour the mixture into the pan with the brown flour and return the pan to the hot burner. Stir continuously until the gravy just starts to bubble, then season to taste with salt and pepper. Remove from the stove, pour into a dish, and serve.

Chickens, along with their by-products, served many useful purposes in the early days of Hopkins Gap. Chicken feathers were sometimes used to stuff the bedding that folks slept on every night. A main ingredient in many of Mom and Aunt Ethel's recipes was eggs. Free-ranging chickens kept down insects that threatened the garden; although the chickens themselves were also a threat to the garden. They would dig up freshly-planted seeds or peck at the tender leaves of baby plants. Later in the summer, when the tomatoes were ripening, they would peck holes in them. On the positive side, they pecked at weeds that otherwise grew in the yard and farm lots. The roosters crowed at the same time every morning to awaken the woman of the house so she could make a fire in the wood stove for warmth and for cooking the morning meal. These are some of the reasons every homestead in Hopkins Gap valued their flock of chickens and provided a hen house for the chickens' safety and the owners' convenience.

The hen house was usually built between the main house and the barn and was fairly small--no more than six feet high on the front wall and about five feet high on the back wall. A sloping tin or tarpaper roof kept out the rain. Typically, there was a row of small windows across the front of the building to provide fresh air for the hens. Where the wall met the floor, square holes were cut out for the chickens to go into and out of the hen house. Our hen house was built on a slope, and the chicken doors had little ramps attached to the bottom so the chickens could walk right out onto the ground without having to jump down. Little strips of wood were nailed across the ramp to serve as treads for the chickens' feet. These ramps were lifted up at night to keep out the predators. This was a job for my brother, Larry, and me, as we got old enough. The job was passed on down to my sister, my brother born after her, and so on, until the baby of the family was given this responsibility.

Mom stressed the importance of keeping the hen house safe from predators. "If foxes get all my hens, then we won't have eggs to eat. I will not be able to make egg custard, egg custard pies, and banana cakes," she said as she showed each one of us how to unhook the ramps and close them for the night. She opened the ramps in the morning when she fed the hens.

We had about fifteen hens and one or two roosters at a time. There were Bantam hens and roosters that we called "Banties," Rhode Island Reds, and White Leghorns. The Bantams were very small and weighed one or two pounds. They laid smaller eggs; mostly light brown in color. Banties tended to be a little wild, but throwing table scraps in the chicken house where they roosted at night could control them. The scraps reminded them of their home and where they were supposed to lay their eggs. The banty roosters tended to be mean and dangerous to little children because of the long, sharp spurs on the back of their feet. One of our banty roosters didn't like Larry up until he was twelve years old. Every time he could get to Larry, he ran up and flopped at him, leaving puncture wounds in his legs where he got him with the spurs. After one of the more serious attacks, the rooster ended up on the Sunday dinner table.

The Rhode Island Reds laid large brown eggs, and the leghorns laid large white eggs. Occasionally we got an egg with two yolks—a double egg. Mom made us take turns eating the egg so we didn't fight over the double yolk. I always liked when it was my turn to eat the double egg, even though Mom would warn my sister and I that "we might have twin babies when we got married because we ate the double egg."

Dad built roosts in the hen house for the chickens to sit on at night. The roosts consisted of boards nailed at a slant from ceiling to floor. Smaller boards were nailed across the slanted boards, providing a nice perch at different heights for the chickens. Chickens, being easy prey for skunks, foxes, and other predators, prefer to be off the ground at night. They tend to tuck their heads under their wing, and apparently, sleep very soundly. Sitting high on a roost or in a tree causes the predator to have to jump or climb to get to them. This provides noises to awaken the chickens, and they can escape by flying away.

A row of small wooden boxes had been built against the back wall of the hen house. The hens were supposed to lay their eggs in these boxes. Some of the hens were uncooperative and laid their eggs back in a corner under the roosts. Since chickens don't seem to stop pooping while they sleep, the child who had to collect the eggs from under the roosts usually came out with chicken poop smeared on various pieces of clothing and always on the shoes or bare feet. I recall coming out from under the roost with one egg and three bare toes with black chicken poop oozing out from between them. I soon learned how to use a weed to get rid of most of the poop. I wrapped my toes around the stalk and pulled upward so the leaves could whisk away most of the slimy poop. This procedure at least got me to the cistern where I could pump some water over my feet to remove the stain and smell.

The chickens usually stopped laying eggs in the fall. Mom called this "molting." Molting started gradually as the days began to grow shorter. The supply of eggs would slowly decline until the hens were in full molt, which lasted through the fall months.

Mom explained, "It is when the chicken takes a rest from layin' eggs. Part of it is replacing their old, worn out feathers. They also make another egg sac full of eggs of all sizes so they can lay again after they are rested up. I'll show you sometime when I cook an old hen for Sunday dinner."

The chickens were free to roam wherever they wanted to go. They often crossed the dirt road that passed our house in their quest for bugs and grass they thought might be greener on the other side. Surely enough, not long after the discussion of the egg sac, a car hit one of our hens and killed her. Mom didn't waste anything, so she cleaned the chicken and cooked the parts that weren't damaged by the car. While she was cleaning the chicken, she opened up the egg sac and showed it to me. She said, "A hen holds about two dozen eggs in all sizes; from tiny ones about the size of your little finger tip up to the one she will lay the next day." The eggs were lined up and had varying degrees of hardness to their shells. The eggs that were in line to be laid over the next few days were the regular size of that hen's egg, but they had a soft shell. I was amazed at how the chicken was able to harden the shell in one day before the egg came out.

As the weather turned colder, Mom tacked plastic over the hen house windows to keep out the cold. When January rolled around she started preparing the hen house for the next egg-laying cycle. She cleaned out the old nests and put in fresh straw to catch the eggs as the chicken laid them. She started feeding her hens table scraps mixed with laying mash and water or whey from when she made cottage cheese.

As the laying season got closer, Mom placed a pan of crushed oyster shells in the hen house. She told me, "Chickens need to eat oyster shells so the shells on their eggs will be hard. Otherwise they'll lay eggs with brittle shells, and I can't use them. They usually step on brittle-shelled eggs and mash them up. Then they start to eat their own eggs to get more of what they need to make hard shells. Some old hens, once they get a taste of the egg, break good eggs and eat them too. No choice after that except to have the old hen for Sunday dinner." Other folks handled the problem of hens eating their own eggs by saving eggshells, crushing them up, and browning them on the wood stove. The shells were then fed back to the laying hens.

By mid January, Mom's hens were singing and their combs were getting bright red. All chickens have a jagged piece of tough flesh on top of their heads called a comb. The color of the comb often indicates if a chicken is healthy. Just before the hens start a new season of laying eggs, the combs turn a bright, healthy red. By the third week in January, Mom was often gathering one or two eggs a day. Before long, she would have too many eggs for us to eat or for her to use in her cooking. She would pass the word along and folks were soon stopping in to buy the extra eggs by the dozen.

Hens that laid eggs for the first time were called pullets. Mom knew exactly when they were going to start laying. She would say, "Look at that pullet. She is broad across the behind just like a pregnant woman, and her comb is red. That means her egg sac is filling up." Then Mom would wait until the pullet was on the roost asleep or sneak up behind her when she was eating and catch her. With the pullet's head tucked under her arm, Mom would see if her index finger and her middle finger would fit side by side between the bones in the chicken's rear end. She explained to me she put my fingers between the bones, "When both fingers fit in the place between the bones, she'll be laying her first egg in a day or so." Pullet eggs were very small at first, and then grew larger as the pullet matured into a hen. Mom sold the pullet eggs for twenty-five cents a dozen and the hen eggs for fifty cents a dozen.

I used to love to sneak into the hen house and watch the chickens lay their eggs. I felt kind of guilty because it was a rather private act; however, I enjoyed peeping up over the nest and watching. I had an intense desire to see the egg come out. I patiently waited for a hen to stop scratching in the yard and head for the hen house. She would be singing and clucking like she was not going to get on the nest, but I waited around until she jumped up and got settled in the straw. The hen began laying by puffing her body up, and her comb turned very red as she squeezed and squeezed. I was very impressed with the effort it required from the hen. Finally, I saw the tip of the egg pushing out of her rear end. The hen squeaked as she pushed the egg out bit by bit. After some really hard squeezing, a wet egg would roll out into the straw. The hen would always turn around and look at it, move it around with her beak, and then jump off the nest cackling as loud as she could, as if to say, "Whew, I'm glad that's over for today."

When spring arrived, some of the hens, just like all other farm animals, wanted to have babies. They would sneak under the barn or under the hay in the milking barn and "steal" a nest. We always wanted some hens to hatch their eggs because that was how we replaced the older hens and roosters. Mom allowed certain hens to have a nest in the chicken house because she knew that those particular chickens had been good mothers. Gathering eggs when the hen wanted to hatch some babies was not easy. Because she wanted to keep her eggs, the hen would peck your fingers with her beak. Sometimes this brought blood. My sister, Brenda, came up with a solution for pecking hens. She reached in first and grabbed the comb so the chicken couldn't peck her. One time she grabbed a little too hard, and the hen's comb came off in her hand. She ran to the house with the comb between her fingers screaming, "Mom, Mom, I killed my chicken." The chicken was fine, lived a long life, and laid many eggs with no comb on top of her head.

Biography of Speck: Larry's Banty hen ....

Mom worried when the hens "sneaked" a nest because often the nest would be raided by a black snake or a skunk. The eggs would be lost as well as the future replacement chickens. Mom avoided hen's stealing nests in a couple of ways. She allowed each of us kids to have a chicken hen of our own. She told us, "Now you keep an eye on your hen and listen for her to cackle when she lays an egg. If you don't see her for a day or so, you'll have to find her nest and take the eggs away." Each of us named our chicken and guarded her as much as possible, so that she didn't end up on the Sunday dinner table. My brother, Larry, was particularly fond of his banty hen, and took especially good care of her. He said, "Uncle Shirl gave me my banty hen when she was about one year old. I named her Speck. She was a really good settin' hen and took good

Larry at age four, a few years before he became responsible for his Banty hen, Speck.

care of her peepies. I saw her jump from the ground onto one of Mom's cow's back and flop her good when she shook her head at the peepies." In those days, the cows and chickens shared the barnyard, and the setting hens loved to take their little chicks into the barnyard so they could scratch up the manure and find insects. The cows seemed to enjoy peace and quiet in the barnyard. A chicken was noisy enough with the crowing, cackling, and scratching; but a hen with a dozen or so chicks was too much and the cows would seem to fight back.

Larry took extra special care of Speck for many years even after she was too old to lay eggs. She was on the wood yard one day sitting on a block of wood when she suddenly fell over, dead as a doornail. Larry was very upset and picked up her body to see if something or someone had hurt her. She was not wounded or bleeding. Mom figured up that Speck was close to fourteen years old and simply had died of old age.

When Larry established his own home, his yard was always the home to Banty hens and roosters. He recently told me, "I love to watch Banty hens take care of their peepies. Not too long ago, one of Hilda's dogs was messin' around some peepies. The mother hen jumped on the dog's back and rode him all the way to the house and under the deck. She was peckin' his head all the way."

Larry didn't just love Banties; he found a nest filled with wild turkey eggs one spring, and discovered that the hen had been killed not far from her nest. He took the eggs home, incubated them, and raised the little turkeys. He maintained a small flock of wild turkeys for many years. As he neared the end of his life, he gave his last turkey hen to a life-long friend, Simon Frye. Two days before Larry died, he told his wife, Hilda, "Mom and Ruby came to my room last night and told me that my wild turkeys deserved to be free. I want you to take them to the mountains and let them go." (Mom has been gone since 2001, and Cousin Ruby has been dead for two years).

Another way that Mom knew when a hen had "stolen" a nest was that each hen had a unique egg—size, shape, and color. Thus she knew which hens were laying eggs in the hen house and which ones weren't. When Mom missed a certain hen, we all had to hunt for the "stolen" nest. Once we found it, Mom taught us to take all the eggs and leave just one "nest egg" as she called it.

"By doin' that," she said, "the hen will go back everyday and lay a new egg, and we'll take that one too. That way she'll keep on layin'. If we can't find her nest and she lays it full of eggs, she'll stop layin' and set on them until they hatch." With as many hens as we had, sometimes gathering eggs in the spring was like following a road map. Blackie would be nesting under the foundation of the old barn; Old Cluck was under the hay in the milking barn; and another hen would have her nest in a barrel by the fence. Nearly every summer, at least one hen would show up one day with a dozen or so little peepies following behind her. Even Mom had to smile because the little ones were so cute. I enjoyed watching the hen scratch in the dirt and call the babies to come and eat the insects she had uncovered for them.

When Mom broke our hens' eggs into her cake batter or to fry, the yolks were dark orange because our hens ran free in the sunshine. They supplemented their hot table scraps, cracked corn, and oyster shells with grass and insects they scratched out of the dirt. They absolutely loved the wood yard because sow bugs, grub worms, and many other types of insects lived under the wood chips.

Pickled Eggs

It was traditional in Hopkins Gap to prepare a big pot of pickled eggs to eat on Easter. The hens were in the spring peak of egg laying, so there was no shortage of eggs. All winter Mom served pickled beets as a condiment at every meal. She saved all the juice in a jar in the refrigerator. About a week before Easter, she hard-boiled several dozen eggs, peeled them, and put them in the pickled beet juice. What a treat this was on Easter morning. The whites of the eggs had turned a beautiful purplish red from the beet juice, and the flavor was a combination of vinegar, sugar, spices and egg—a taste all its own.

It was expected that pickled eggs would serve as a snack until they were all gone. I loved them so much that several times I asked, "Mom, "Why don't we have pickled eggs all the time?" Her answer was always the same, "Pickled eggs are for Easter." Obviously the reason for pickled eggs on Easter, if there ever was one, had been lost over time. I now think that we had pickled eggs at Easter because there was an abundance of eggs with the hens in the peak of their laying season.

Pickled Eggs Recipe…
Ingredients (for those cooks who do not have pickled beet juice).
1 (14 ounce) can of red beets
¼ cup brown sugar
½ cup white vinegar
½ cup cold water
½ teaspoon of salt
4 whole cloves
1 small cinnamon stick
6 hard-boiled eggs

Pour the beet juice into a cook pot. Stir in the sugar, vinegar, water, salt, cloves, and the cinnamon stick. Place the pot over medium heat for 6 to 8 minutes, stirring occasionally. Place the beets into the liquid mixture and let it cook for an additional 2 or 3 minutes to allow the beets to color the liquid. Remove the egg shells and place the hard boiled eggs in a container with a tight-fitting lid. Strain the beets out of the liquid, and pour the liquid over the eggs. Close the lid on the container and place it in the refrigerator for at least 24 hours before eating. The flavors from the liquid and the color from the beets will permeate the egg whites for a delightful and colorful treat.

Mom had many recipes in her head that we enjoyed when there was an abundance of eggs. During the spring months, when egg laying peaked, she made egg custard, egg custard pies, banana pudding, and deviled eggs. I have included some of her favorite dessert recipes here.

Egg Custard Recipe...
Ingredients

4 eggs	¼ teaspoon salt
½ cup sugar	1 teaspoon vanilla
Sprinkle of nutmeg	3 cups milk, scalded

Beat eggs well. Add sugar, salt, and vanilla. Stir well. While stirring, add milk to mixture. Stir until the custard thickens. Pour into a dish and place in the refrigerator to cool. As it cools, it will thicken more. Serve in small dishes with fresh baked cookies.

When I call to request a visit with Aunt Ethel and Uncle Shirley, she always asks me what kind of pie I would like her to make for me. After fifty years she certainly knows that I will always say egg custard pie. Mom knew and Aunt Ethel still knows how to make the best egg custard pie. Recently Aunt Ethel allowed me to photograph the steps.

Old-Fashioned Egg Custard Pie Recipe with Mom Shifflett's Pie Crust Recipe...

Ingredients for Egg Custard Filling

6 whole eggs	2 cups milk, scalded
1 cup sugar	1 teaspoon vanilla
Dash of salt	¼ teaspoon nutmeg

Mix all ingredients in a deep mixing bowl and beat until sugar is dissolved.

Pour into unbaked pie shell. Bake at 350 degrees in preheated oven for 45 minutes until custard is set. Cool before serving.

Ingredients for Pie Crust

1 teaspoon salt	1¼ cup hog lard
½ cup water	1 egg
1 teaspoon vinegar	bowl of flour

In a small dish, beat egg, add water and vinegar and stir with a fork. Put lard in the bowl of flour and work with one hand while slowly pouring in the liquid mixture. Form a clump and fold over. Work with fingers until when you poke the dough with your finger, the hole closes up. Shape the clump of dough into a round flat ball, and roll with rolling pen until large enough to cover a pie plate.

Aunt Ethel prepares her pie dough, rolls it out flat, and with both hands, she places it over an ovenproof glass pie plate. Then she tucks it carefully into the grooves of the plate and trims off the excess dough with the palms of her hands.

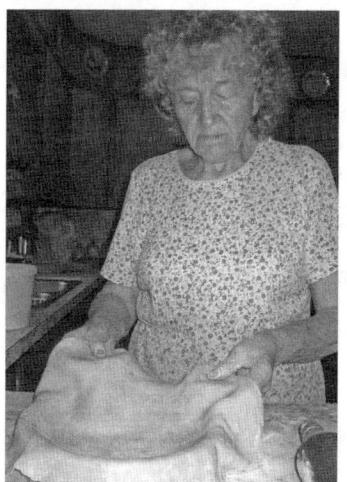

(1)

(2)

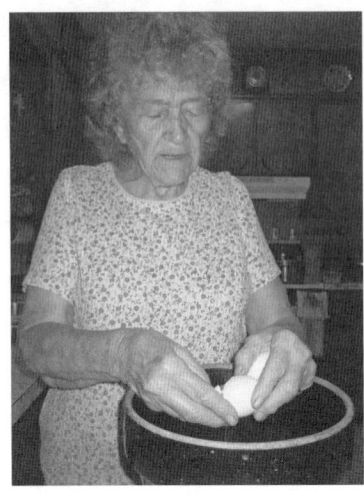

(3)

(4)

(5)

Aunt Ethel breaks her eggs into a large bowl and adds her sugar. She makes her milk very hot and adds it to the mixture. Finally, she pours the egg custard mixture into the unbaked pie shell and sprinkles the top with nutmeg. She told me how to determine when the pie is baked. "You open the oven door and reach in and shake the pie plate. If the custard don't separate, the pie is ready to take out of the oven." When the pie was brown on top, Aunt Ethel let me test it for doneness. Following are some other favorite dessert recipes from Mom and Aunt Ethel.

Banana Pudding Recipe...

Ingredients

1/3 cup all purpose flour	¾ cup sugar
A dash of salt	4 eggs, separated, at room temperature

| 2 cups milk | 1 teaspoon vanilla extract |
| Vanilla wafers | 6 bananas, medium size, fully ripe |

Combine ½ cup sugar, flour and salt in top of double boiler. Stir in egg yolks and milk. Stir well. Cook uncovered over boiling water. Stir constantly until mixture thickens. Reduce heat. Cook for 5 minutes, stirring occasionally. Remove from heat. Add vanilla. Spread a small amount of mixture on the bottom of a 1½ quart baking dish. Cover with a layer of vanilla wafers, then a layer of sliced bananas. Pour a layer of custard over the bananas. Continue to layer the wafers, bananas and custard until you have 3 layers, with the custard on top. In a separate bowl, beat egg whites, gradually adding the remaining ¼ cup sugar. Beat until stiff peaks form. Spoon the beaten egg whites on top of the pudding, spreading to cover surface and edges. Bake at 425 degrees for 5 minutes or until the peaks turn a light, golden brown. Chill. Place banana slices and wafers upright around the edge of the dish before serving.

Bread Pudding Recipe....

Ingredients

Day old bread	3 eggs
1 cup sugar	2 cups whole milk
½ cup raisins	1 tablespoon vanilla
Nutmeg	

Break bread into small pieces and place in a baking dish. Beat the eggs and add sugar. Beat in the milk and add the vanilla. Stir in the raisins. Pour mixture over the bread and press down with the back of a fork. Add milk if needed to completely soak the bread. Sprinkle nutmeg over the top. Let stand for 30 minutes to 45 minutes. Bake at 350-degrees for about one hour until lightly brown. Serve hot.

Butter Scotch Pie Recipe...

Ingredients

1 cup brown sugar	1/3 cup all-purpose flour
1 cup white sugar	4 egg yolks
3 tablespoons butter	baked pie shell
4 cups milk	½ teaspoon vanilla
4 egg whites	¼ cup white sugar

Combine first six ingredients in a double boiler and stir continuously over medium heat until thick. Remove from heat. Add vanilla, and when cooled, pour into crust. In a separate bowl, beat egg whites, gradually adding ¼ cup sugar. Beat until stiff peaks form. Spoon the beaten egg whites on top of the butter scotch pudding. Spread to cover surface and edges. Bake at 425 degrees for 5 minutes or until the peaks turn a light, golden brown. Chill in refrigerator and serve.

Lemon Meringue Pie Recipe....

Ingredients

1 cup plus 3 tablespoons sugar	1 tablespoon grated lemon rind
3 tablespoons corn starch	¼ teaspoon cream of tartar
3 egg yolks	2 cups cold water
3 egg whites	baked pie crust
¼ cup fresh lemon juice	½ cup powdered sugar
1 teaspoon vanilla flavoring	

Mix sugar with cornstarch. Add cold water to make a thick paste. Add egg yolks. Beat the mixture with a wire whisk. Cook in a double boiler over medium heat 20 to 30 minutes until thick. Pour filling into the pie shell. Beat egg whites until foamy. Add cream of tarter and vanilla. Add powdered sugar, one tablespoon at a time. Once sugar has been added, keep beating the meringue until it forms small peaks. Spoon the meringue onto the pie. Sprinkle with granulated sugar. Brown the meringue in a 350-degree oven for about fifteen minutes or until just brown.

Deviled Eggs Recipe...

Ingredients
12 hard-boiled eggs
1 cup mayonnaise
1 teaspoon mustard, prepared
1 teaspoon salt
2 tablespoons paprika

Remove shells from the eggs, cut them in half, and remove the yolks. Mash yolks with a fork and then add the rest of the ingredients. Mix well until moist. Spoon about 1-2 tablespoons of the filling into the egg white halves. Sprinkle with paprika. Cover and chill for at least an hour before serving.

Prune Cake with Buttermilk Icing Recipe...

Cake Ingredients

1 cup uncooked prunes, pitted and chopped	1 cup chopped nuts
	1 teaspoon soda
1 teaspoon nutmeg	1 teaspoon cinnamon
1 teaspoon allspice	2 cups flour
1 cup lard	1½ cups sugar
½ teaspoon vanilla	3 eggs well beaten
A dash of salt	1 cup buttermilk

Preheat oven to 350 degrees. Sift together soda, nutmeg, cinnamon, allspice, and flour. Add lard, sugar, vanilla. Beat well. Add eggs and salt. Beat well. Add buttermilk and beat well. Fold in prunes and nuts. Mix well. Put in cake pans lined with wax paper. Do not grease the pan. Bake the cake for 1 hour, or until it is done.

Icing Ingredients

1 cup sugar	½ cup buttermilk
2 tablespoons white corn syrup	½ teaspoon vanilla
¼ cup butter	½ teaspoon soda

Boil all ingredients until mixture forms a soft ball. Boil 1 minute more. Pour on hot cake.

After many years of having her own free-range chickens and a bountiful supply of eggs, Dad convinced Mom that he was paying more for chicken feed than it would cost if she bought eggs when she bought her other grocery staples. Reluctantly, she killed off her old hens for Sunday dinners and let Dad tear the chicken house down so he would have a good place to put his scalding pan when hog butchering time rolled around. We all missed those fresh eggs with the orange yolks that stood up in the frying pan as if to say "good morning." I know Dad missed the fresh eggs too, but he would never admit it.

Chapter 5

Late Winter and Early Spring Foods

Those who contemplate the beauty of the earth find reserves of strength that will endure as long as life lasts. There is something infinitely healing in the repeated refrains of nature— the assurance that dawn comes after night, and spring after winter.
—*Rachel Carson*

Winters were harsh when I was a child; and our house was cold and drafty. We had a coal stove in the living room and the wood cook stove in the kitchen. The windows were so loose that the wind whistled around the sashes and shook the curtains on the inside of the house. Mom stuffed old rags around the sashes, and the rags didn't stay in place because of the harsh winds. She fussed all winter, "The wind blows everyday here on this hill. I can't stand it much longer."

Fifty years later, Mom was still stuffing rags around the windows every fall. She was right about the wind. It blew all night every night getting under the tin roof and bouncing it up and down. It felt like the house was falling in. My sister and I awoke in the morning with frost in our nostrils. We jumped out from under four large comforters into a freezing room and dashed down the steps to hover near the wood stove in the kitchen.

I wished for a warm house where I could be in any room at any time of the year. In the spring and summer, I spent a lot of time in the upstairs rooms. I wrote little poems and short stories at a make-shift desk and fantasized that I lived in a big house with heat in every room. I longed for privacy that was not possible in the cold winter months. Mom, Dad and five children were all confined to either the kitchen or the living room for the four cold months of the year. We were separated only at night by a mad dash into the cold stairway and a quick dive under three or four heavy comforters.

We had snows that lasted for days and drifted high enough to cover the fence posts. Schools were closed for a week at a time. The road past our house was one of the last to be cleared because it was a gravel road, narrow, and only a mile long. The sides of the road were lined with outcroppings of limestone rock. The road crew knew they would inevitably break a snowplow on those rocks. The snow-clogged road affected only two families, but those two families were severely affected. My dad had to get to work. He would walk the mile-long road, climbing over snow drifts to catch a ride to his job at the feed mill in Harrisonburg. Our neighbors, Lloyd and Fannie Jane Myers, were dairy farmers, and when the milk tanker could not get in to collect their milk, they poured out hundreds of gallons of milk each day. These facts did not bring the snowplow any sooner until the workers were ready to face the hazards of the jutting limestone on the banks of our road.

One of the things we did for fun during those long days at home was to make "snow cream." Mom put on her boots and headed up over the hill where there were no cows, sheep, or horses. There she would gather a bucket of clean, fresh-fallen snow and rush home to make snow cream. Even though it was cold outside, the icy treat was readily eaten because it was not often that we got a taste of real ice cream.

Snow Cream Recipe...

Ingredients
Fresh fallen snow
Vanilla flavoring
Sweet cream
Sugar

Dip fresh fallen snow into a bowl, add very cold sweet cream and stir in a drop or two of vanilla flavoring and two teaspoons of sugar. Stir and eat quickly before it melts.

The worst snow we had was in March 1964. It snowed for three days and then the wind blew for another three days. All the cars were totally covered, with only the tips of the radio aerials sticking above the snow. There was a foot or more of snow blocking the front door of the house. From that point, the snow got deeper until it reached thirteen feet high across the road. We could not open the front door. The back door was also blocked by drifts, and Mom had to help me out of a window, so that I could move enough snow from the back door for her to get to the barn to milk the cows. We had seventeen cats at that time. They all lived at the barn. The temperature dropped below zero and froze eleven of the cats. When the snow melted, we found them at different points along the path between the barn and the house.

We were basically trapped in the house for a week, except to tend the chickens and the cows. Even my dad couldn't make it to work for two days. We did a lot of eating during this week. Mom was always prepared, so some of her best cooking was done in these situations. She went to the cellar and came back with cans of puddin' from November's hog butchering. She fried it down with onions, made a pan of fried potatoes, a pot of pinto beans, and cornbread.

This was our supper several evenings. For breakfast we had corn cakes and syrup, eggs, and sausage gravy.

Corn Cakes Recipe...

Ingredients

1 cup corn meal	1½ cups boiling water
¼ cup butter	1½ cups buttermilk
2 egg yolks, separated	1 cup flour
1½ teaspoons baking powder	¼ teaspoon baking soda
½ teaspoon salt	2 egg whites
2 tablespoons lard	

Mix cornmeal, butter, egg yolks, water, and buttermilk. Blend dry ingredients with cornmeal mixture. Beat the two egg whites and fold into the batter. Put some of the lard into a hot iron skillet. Drop the cornmeal batter into the hot grease and fry until crispy brown. Turn once and fry the other side. Serve with warm maple syrup.

In spite of the good food and Mom's cooking, we anxiously awaited the coming of spring. As the time drew near, each of us watched for signs. For Mom, it was the robins that told her spring was coming. She excitedly told us, "I saw a robin today. It was in the garden hopping around lookin' for worms. When it stopped, it turned its head to the side listenin' for worms under the ground." We all got excited but often that robin sighting would be followed by another snowstorm.

A definite harbinger of the coming spring was the appearance of various greens in the fields and along the roadways. Mom and Aunt Ethel were firm believers in the purgative powers of these early wild greens to cleanse a body of winter's excesses.

Creasy Greens

Hopkins Gap families survived the cold, dark winters because they knew they could look forward to "creasy greens" served with ham potpie or just about any other food. Creasy greens were the favorite dish the first time we ate them each spring. Mom threw creasy greens in a pot and cooked them. After they boiled, filling the house with a sharp but pleasant smell, similar to Brussels sprouts, she "fried them down" in an iron skillet with about a half-inch of melted hog lard. "This'll loosen you up," she told us. For sure, the next day we made lots of trips to the "two holer" in the back yard.

Very often Mom had already gathered creasy greens with Aunt Ethel and Uncle Shirley before the last snowstorm of winter. Creasy greens grew wild in Hopkins Gap and in the cornfields surrounding Hopkins Gap. They were the first edible green plant to signal the coming of the spring season, and were abundant in late February and early March. Their flavor was best while the plants were young and tender. By the end of March, the plants displayed a bright yellow sea of flowers and were too bitter and tough to eat. The blooms gave away the location of the next year's plants. We would be driving along a road and Mom would point out a field of yellow blooms. She would say, "Norman, let's remember this place for next year. It will be full of creasy greens. I'll have to tell Ethel and Shirl."

Mom and Aunt Ethel brought home bushels and bushels of creasy greens. While they were cutting them, they took the time to field clean the greens; which meant they removed as much dirt and dry leaves as possible. After Mom got her share of greens home, she washed them several times; but the first washing was the most interesting. She had an old wringer washing machine that she had purchased when she was first married. Mom filled the washing machine with cold water and would dump the creasy greens into the water one bushel at a time. She then started the machine and literally laundered the greens. The dasher moved the greens back and forth through the cold water just the way that it had once moved our dirty clothes. The only difference was that she didn't put lye soap in with the greens, and she didn't run them through the ringer to squeeze out the water.

Mom removed the creasy greens from the washing machine a small batch at a time and rinsed them again in a bucket of clean water. The final washing was done in a big dishpan in the kitchen. The first batch of greens was put into a large cook pot and boiled for supper on the day they were gathered. Mom didn't waste any time getting a dish of creasy greens on the supper table for us to eat.

Creasy Greens Recipe...

Depending on the size of the family, gather 1 to 2 gallons of creasy greens. Pick over the greens to remove dry leaves and shake out as much sand as possible. Wash and rinse three times. Parboil the greens in a large cook pot until tender, about one hour. Test level of tenderness by sticking a fork in them. Drain the broth from the greens and add ham or beef broth for flavor. The broth should be just below the top of the greens in the pot. Bring to a slow boil for 15 minutes, until flavor penetrates the greens, and then season to taste with salt and pepper. Serve with a teaspoon of vinegar per serving.

Weed Greens

"What?" I said to Mom the first spring I was old enough to process the words "weed greens." She went into her teaching mode and said, "Yes, I said weed greens. Now go with me to gather some for supper." She took a bucket off the porch, put the bail across her arm, picked up a paring knife, and off we went toward the road. I followed her wondering what she would find along the road. To my surprise she leaned over and cut some dandelion leaves just peeping through the ground. Not too far down the road, she found some "rock" lettuce and added those leaves to her bucket. She started to describe all the things we could anticipate in the spring and the upcoming summer, fall, and winter seasons.

Mom had hope in her voice as she said, "These early greens are prettier than I have ever seen them—so green and tender—I bet we have a good garden this summer." She told me a story that I had already heard many times about her Mom, my Grandma Mary Lamb Morris. She said, "Mom died when I was five years old, but I remember her gathering weed greens for us. She took me with her. I guess that's when I started wanting to learn about cookin'."

Mom continued, "Your grandma pointed out everything to me before she cut it to put in her basket. It took a long time to find enough weed greens for our big family. We still had about eight kids at home out of eighteen." Then Mom would turn her attention back to gathering greens and say, "I wish I had a little water cress from Muddy Creek to add to this mess of greens. Water cress is really good for ya." If I had more time, we'd go over the hill and get some." If we had extra time, she and I would make the trek over the hill to Muddy Creek.

As we walked along the fencerows and over the hill to Muddy Creek, she would continue talking, "Spring is a good time because everything is coming out. It's a good time for a body to be cleanin' and freshenin' everything and that goes for us too," she said as she picked some plantain, wild strawberry leaves, tiny blackberry leaves, polk shoots, and the tips of lambs quarter. She went on to say, "These weed greens will clean us out and get rid of the winter fat. We've been eatin' a lot of meat, pinto beans and bread, and we need a good cleanin' out."

When we got home Mom carefully washed the weeds and put them in a pot of water to boil. When they had boiled long enough, she drained the greens and put them into a large iron skillet with about a half-inch of hog lard. She "fried them down" as she called it and served them with fried potatoes and pinto beans. I must say they were appetizing. You could eat weed greens any time in the early spring, but it was traditional to serve on the Thursday before Easter for their best effect as an intestinal cleanser and harbinger of general good health. This day was referred to in many cultures as "Green" Thursday. When I was growing up, the cooks never mentioned Green Thursday. This part of the cultural tradition had been lost. They did, however, continue to cook "weed" greens around Easter.

Water Cress

Watercress grows in March, in cold, deep springs. When I was growing up next door to Pop and Minnie May, she would take me with her down the hill and through the pastures to a large spring, that was boxed in with concrete. It was just over the fence from her land, but we could reach through and collect watercress. The water was very cold as I pulled at the cress. Minnie told me to get some for Mom so she could add it to her weed greens. Minnie always made watercress soup.

Watercress Soup Recipe…

Ingredients
1 large onion, chopped
1½ lb. potatoes, cubed
2 tablespoons flour

6 cups soup chicken stock
1 large bunch of watercress

Wash watercress. Hold back about a third of the watercress leaves. Place potatoes, onion, and remaining watercress plus stems into a large cook pot.

Cook until the vegetables are soft and then sieve. Add a little flour for thickening and when thickened add the remaining watercress leaves, chopped. Simmer 5 minutes more before serving. The chicken stock can be replaced with 3 cups of water and 3 cups of milk.

Wild Turkey

Wild turkey is another sought after delicacy in early April. At this time, turkeys are mating, and a skillful hunter, using a turkey caller, can fool a male turkey. The tom will puff his feathers out and often walk right up close to the hunter and sacrifice himself to the supper table. The meat, especially the breast, is moist and tastes very different from domesticated turkey.

Uncle Shirley's son, Butch, poses after a very successful spring hunt. He called this "tom" turkey with a turkey caller and got him close enough for a deadly shot.

Roasted Wild Turkey Recipe...

Ingredients

1 wild turkey	butter
Salt and pepper	simple stuffing
Chicken stock	

Stuff the turkey and rub well with butter, salt and pepper. Place it on a rack in a roasting pan. Roast in a 325 degree oven and allow 25 minutes per pound of turkey. Baste turkey often with equal amounts of butter and chicken stock.

Dandelions

Folks in Hopkins Gap did not despise dandelions like modern gardeners do. They saw dandelions as one more gift from Mother Nature, and a wonderful way to get some fresh greens into their diets after a long hard winter of bread, meat and canned vegetables. Dandelion greens taste like chicory and endive, with an intense heartiness, overlaying a bitter tinge. Modern folks avoid bitter flavors because they've grown accustomed to sweet and salty processed food. Folks in Hopkins Gap thought there was a good bitterness and a bad bitterness; and prepared just right and served with fried potatoes, dandelion greens were an example of a good bitterness and a real delicacy in the spring.

Mom and Aunt Ethel and the other cooks in Hopkins Gap gathered dandelion greens in early spring, before the blooms appeared. "That's when they're the tenderest and not so bitter," Mom told me. "You can gather them again after the first frost in the fall, and boiling them will get a lot of the bitterness out of them."

Dandelion Greens Recipe...

Gather about 1 gallon of young dandelion greens (before they bloom)
Wash three times in tub of cold water to remove all grit and sand
Drain and put in a large cooking pot. Cover with boiling water.
Add 1 lb. of salt pork
Add two tablespoons of salt

Boil for 1½ hours and then drain. Add more boiling water.
Cook 2 hours until tender. Drain well again.
Serve as is or fry with hog lard in an iron skillet for 10 minutes.

Dandelion greens were used as a salad with bacon grease. A favorite recipe was called "wilted dandelion salad."

Wilted Dandelion Salad Recipe...

Ingredients
5 cups torn dandelion greens (about 1 lb.)
3 or 4 strips of home-cured side meat (middlin)
2 tablespoons of apple cider vinegar
1½ tablespoons of sugar
1 tablespoon of prepared mustard
1 small onion chopped fine

Rinse greens several times, discard stems, drain and place in a large bowl.

In a skillet, cook the side meat over medium-high heat until brown and crisp.

Drain meat on towel, reserving two teaspoons of the pan drippings in the skillet.

Crumble the side meat into small pieces. In a small bowl, place vinegar, sugar, mustard, and onion—mix well. Pour this mixture into the skillet with the reserved drippings and cook over medium-high heat, stirring constantly, for 2 minutes.

Quickly pour the dressing over the greens, add the crumbled side meat, toss to mix, and serve immediately.

Dandelion wine and green cherries....

Once the cooks had gathered the young leaves of the dandelion for delicious salads, the remaining plants produced their yellow blossoms. For those folks in Hopkins Gap who enjoyed a sip or two of good homemade wine, it was time to benefit once more from the dandelion plant. Mom and Dad had too much work to do to gather dandelion blooms for wine; however, my brothers, John and Larry, and a friend, James Hartman had just entered their teenage years. They decided a little wine making and sipping might add some spark to their summer days after school closed.

On one of our trips to Hopkins Gap after church on Sunday, they found Charley Conley. Charley gladly shared his ancient recipe with them.

The boys gathered dandelion blooms in Aunt Goldie's bluegrass field over the next two days. They were far more diligent about this wine making project than they had ever been about their chores. They pooled their money and rode their bicycles about two miles to Bridges Service Station and Grocery to buy sugar. The next step was to locate a five-gallon crock. They found one in the basement of a neighbor, and "borrowed" it without permission. They mixed all the ingredients and set the crock in a corner of Aunt Goldie's bluegrass field that was overgrown with blackberry briars and locust bushes. They often visited their wine to make sure it was okay and carefully marked the time until it was ready to sample.

As time passed, the boys decided to experiment with a little moonshine on the day the wine was ready to drink. John made an agreement with Cousin Herman to buy a pint of Hopkins Gap moonshine to start their day of experimenting with alcohol. Herman dutifully carried the moonshine on the school bus to school where John paid him a dollar and a quarter.

Finally, the day arrived. Larry, John, and James Hartman got on their bicycles and rode down to the Hirsch farm where they snuck into the haunted barn to drink their moonshine. They drank the pint, and then decided to fish for a while along Muddy Creek. Muddy Creek, which ran through the old Hirsch farm, got its name because it flooded easily and spread a wide stream of muddy water through the fields. When it was not flooding, the creek was narrow enough at most places to jump across. It was a slow day for fish, so the boys rode up to the bluegrass field, opened the crock of wine, and tasted it. Larry said, "It tasted mighty fine, so we sat around and drank quite a bit of it."

John said, "After we finished drinking the wine, we were cravin' cigarettes and somethin' to eat. We got on our bicycles and rode to

Bridges Station." Larry added the next part of the story, "On the way we spotted a couple of cherry trees just loaded with green cherries. We sampled a few and thought they were ripe enough to eat some." They spent some time climbing around in the cherry trees and filled their stomachs with green cherries. The desire to end their meal with a cigarette drove them to again mount their bicycles and ride on to Bridges Station.

John on his bicycle.

Both John and Larry said they don't remember much about the time they spent at the store. However, they do remember that James Hartman got cramps in his stomach. Larry said, "All of a sudden James bent over double. His face was white as a sheet and he looked scared. He made a mad dash across the store parking lot. The last thing I remember is hearing the toilet door slam shut. There was an outside one-holer attached to the end of the storage shed."

The boys left the store and returned to Muddy Creek. Larry told me what happened, "We found a soft grassy spot by the creek and sat down. The sun was shining warm on us. All of a sudden, James Hartman made a strange noise like a half whimper and passed out on the grass. He started to sweat and the drops on his forehead were as big as my thumb. Me and John laid down and fell asleep. We slept a long time and when we woke up, the sun was hot. We decided to go swimmin' in a water hole down the creek. We took our clothes off and jumped in the cold water. We laid around in the water for a while and sobered up. A snappin' turtle started bitin' my ass, so we got out of the river and went home."

When the boys returned to Bridges Station a week or so later, the store owner, Paul Bowman said, "John, Larry, James have you puked up any toilets lately?" The boys, of course, denied any part in pukin' up the toilet; mainly because they didn't remember if they had or not. The storeowner then blamed Sheldon Hartman, James' older brother, who got drunk on a regular basis. The only question the storeowner never got an answer to was why Sheldon would have been eating so many green cherries.

When I asked John what happened to the rest of the wine, he told me, "We still had a lot left, so we wanted to share it with some other guys. We told Kenny Dean about the wine and where it was. He got together with another guy, Wendell Henkel, and they stole the wine. I saw them carrying it out of the bushes while I was groundhog huntin'. I aimed my .22 rifle on the crock and was going to shoot it while they were carrying it away. I didn't shoot because I was scared the bullet might glance off the crock and hit one of them. Wendell Henkel claims he don't remember stealing our wine. One of these days I am gonna' ask him what he did with that sauerkraut jar we made the wine in."

John didn't run into Kenny Dean. I ran into him one evening this spring when I was in Harrisonburg. I asked him what Wendell did with the sauerkraut jar after he finished with the dandelion wine. Kenny said, "Wendell gave that jar back to Larry and John." Now I was really confused, so I called John and asked him if Wendell returned the jar. He said, "You know, there is a sauerkraut jar in Larry's living room that looks a lot like the one we had. I am gonna take a closer look and ask Larry if Wendell did return it." So the story of the dandelion wine continues to unwind as I attempt to uncover the facts, while writing about a time long ago when memories have faded.

Dandelion Wine Recipe...

Gather 2 gallons of dandelion bloom pods and put them into a five-gallon crock.
Add one cake of yeast and 10 pounds of sugar.
Fill the crock with fresh water allowing 2-3 inches at the top of the

jar for fermentation.

Cover the crock with a clean cloth, fasten it down with elastic, and let it set for two weeks.

At the end of two weeks, remove the cloth and sift out the bloom that will be on top of the liquid.

Cover with cloth again and let set for three weeks.

At the end of three weeks, the wine is ready to drink.

Besides the many and varied wild greens Mother Nature offered, there were numerous other wild foods that she provided in the early spring. Mom's expertise in locating these edibles was passed to her children. We delighted in gathering these foods and seeing them on the supper table.

White Suckers from Muddy Creek

School let out for our spring break around mid-March. My brothers and I used this time to fish for white suckers, a type of mullet, in Muddy creek. We waited until the sun warmed up and melted the frost from the broom sage in the fields and then headed toward the two farms across the road from our house. Muddy Creek wound its way through both of these farms. One farm belonged to Roy Long and the other was the old, abandoned Hirsch farm.

The old Hirsch farm...

The Hirsch farm had an interesting history, and one that fascinated us. There was a two-story brick house and a huge barn. The farm was abandoned. Larry, John, and I wanted to explore the inside of the house. When we first forced the front door open, a flock of pigeons took off through a hole in the roof. We found the floors and stairs about six inches deep with pigeon droppings. Once the sounds of pigeon wings had drifted away, the house was eerily quiet. We just stared in awe as we teased each other about ghosts because of the story that Mom had told us about the family that who once lived there. Their name was Whetsel.

Mom seemed to love to tell the story, "One day Mr. Whetsel found out that his wife was running around with a man whose last name was Boykin. Mr. Boykin lived at the top of the hill on the farm that Goldie and Rob later bought. When Mr. Whetsel found out what was going on, he took his gun and went up the hill. Mr. Whetsel shot through the front door window and killed Mr. Boykin as he ran up the stairs to get away from him. Another man ran out the back door and came face to face with Mr. Whetsel at the front yard gate. Mr. Whetsel shot him. He then went back down the hill to his house after the shooting, and before the sheriff arrived to arrest him, Mr. Whetsel went out to the huge barn and hung himself." She continued, "They say the rope is still hanging from the rafters where the sheriff cut him down. I don't know myself, because I would be afraid to go near the place."

As Larry, John, and I stood in the foyer the first and only time we opened the door of the house, we speculated about where Mr. Whetsel's ghost might hang out, "Would his ghost hang around in the house or would it stay out in the barn where he killed himself?" Because we couldn't really answer that question, we never ventured beyond the front door. We were too scared to go into the barn, but we peeped through the cracks in the barn doors to see if we could see the rope. We never saw it, but we returned every spring to peep through the cracks and try to catch a glimpse of it.

We started fishing for white suckers at the edge of Roy Long's farm and worked our way along the creek to the Hirsch farm. We got down into the water and reached our hands back under the banks until we found some white suckers. We stuck our fingers in the gills, pulled the fish out, and threw them on the banks of the creek. Sometimes we saw a bunch of fish just resting in a shallow pool. I had my brothers to chase them back down the creek to a shallow riffle in the creek, were I would be standing ready to hit the fish in the head with a stick as they came across the rocks. On occasion, my cousin Randy would go with us. He tied a metal spike to the end of a pole and taught us how to spear the fish.

Mom was delighted to get the fish we brought home. She cleaned them, dipped them in corn meal, and fried them for supper. The fish were filled with bones, but were a welcome treat after a long winter of hog meat. She was always proud of us when we brought in food for the family, and would brag to my dad and uncles about our efforts.

Sassafras Tea

Just before the sap started running in the trees, Aunt Goldie would come to our house and get me to go with her to hunt for red and yellow sassafras roots. We trudged along the dirt roads, and she pointed out the small sassafras trees. The roots were easy to get to because they grew on the banks of the road. All we had to do was dig back under the bank, expose the roots, and cut some. She always put the dirt back over the roots while saying, "We need to cover these roots so the tree won't die. We'll need some more sassafras tea next spring." She took the roots home, cleaned them, and scraped the bark from the roots in order to brew the tea. I remember the tea smelled very good and tasted delicious.

Aunt Goldie suffered from high blood pressure; so every spring she drank yellow sassafras tea made from the sap-filled root bark of the small tree. "Yellow sassafras tea lowers your blood pressure," she told me. We gathered red sassafras roots, scraped the bark off, and made tea for me because I had anemia, which Mom and Aunt Goldie called "low blood."

Sassafras Tea Recipe...

Dig and wash the roots of the red sassafras or yellow sassafras tree. Peel the bark off the roots. Do this early in the spring before the sap begins to rise from the roots into the tree. Boil a few pieces of the root bark. Let simmer for 10 minutes. Cover, remove from the heat and let steep for 5 minutes. Strain and sweeten with sugar or honey if desired. Serve hot.

Morels or "Toadstools"

In late April, it was time to hunt morels. I have heard them called many different, names including hickory chickens, because they taste like chicken and are found under hickory trees (p. 91) Farr. Other names include dog peckers, pinecones, spring mushrooms, and molly moochers (p. 107) Sohn. In Hopkins Gap we always called them "toadstools." Cousin Randy taught me about toadstools.

Morels or "toadstools" as we called them in Hopkins Gap, are hard to see in the leaves and underbrush.

We hunted for them in old apple orchards. The amazing thing about toadstools was that you would see one and if you were not careful, you would step on five getting to that one. Randy taught me to stand just under the outer limbs of an apple tree and scan the ground beneath the tree. He said, "When you spot a toadstool, don't just run under the tree and grab it. Just stand for a minute or two and look all around, and always watch exactly where you put your feet when you are lookin' around. I have wasted far too many toadstools by bein' in a hurry to grab the first one I saw."

After Randy learned to drive a car, we rode around on the back roads by old apple orchards. He could spot clumps of toadstools from the car, and would slam on the brakes, and climb across fences to get them. We came home many times with two grocery bags full. After Randy died, I taught my brother, Warnie where to look for toadstools. He knows the best places to look now and occasionally he will remember who taught him how to find them and shares his toadstools. Sometimes he will reveal where he found them to his immediate family members.

Morels have a very unique taste; an interesting combination of smoke, dirt, and walnuts. I have never experienced anything even similar to their taste. They grow in varying sizes and look like a human brain on a stem. Toadstools are delicious any way they are prepared; but I think their flavor is at its best when they are fried. Some years they are scarcer than other years. If that is the case, then I definitely recommend them fried. If toadstools are abundant, then there are at least two other recipes that are worth the effort to prepare.

Fried Morel Recipe...

Ingredients

Morels

Salt

2 eggs

¼ cup hog lard

½ cup milk

¾ cup flour

¼ teaspoon pepper

Cut toadstools in half, wash thoroughly and soak in salt water, in the refrigerator, for several hours or overnight. Rinse and drain just before cooking. Lightly beat two eggs in a shallow bowl and add ½ cup of milk. Prepare flour, salt and pepper in another shallow dish. Heat an iron skillet with about ½ inch of hog lard. The lard must be very hot but not to the point of smoking. Dip the morel halves in the egg/milk wash, and then dip them into the seasoned flour. Drop them into the hot grease. Let them brown and then turn only once to brown the other side. Use the left over grease to make toadstool gravy following the milk gravy recipe on page 115.

Morel Soup Recipe...

Ingredients
14 ounces small morels
¼ cup sweet butter
2 finely chopped shallots
1 quart chicken stock
1¼ cups heavy cream
6 egg yolks
Salt and freshly ground black pepper

Fry one half of the morels in half of the butter for 4 minutes over medium heat. Set them aside, leaving excess butter in the pan. Finely chop the remaining morels, and fry in the rest of the butter along with the shallots. Add chicken stock and bring to a boil. Remove from the heat, pour in the cream and whisk in the egg yolks. Add a dash of salt and pepper. Return to the heat and slowly bring back up the temperature, whisking continuously. When it begins to thicken, the soup is ready to serve.

There's never been an April that rolled around during my sixty-five years when I did not think about toadstools. I yearn to go exploring under old apple trees for these delicacies of Appalachia. In the past few years, I have noticed how folks guard their toadstool locations. I called a woman who is known for finding a lot of toadstools every spring. I said, "Would you tell me where I can find some morels?" Her response was so typically Appalachian, "You can find some in my refrigerator. I'd be glad to give you a mess, and I'll tell you the kind of places to look, but I won't tell you where you where I find mine." So, I am still yearning for toadstools every spring, and have yet to locate a secret patch of my own.

Morels with Sour Creamed Potatoes Recipe...

Ingredients
2 medium potatoes, peeled and cut into one inch squares
1 medium-sized onion, sliced
½ cup chopped green pepper
1 tablespoon minced fresh parsley
2 tablespoons butter or bacon fat
2 cups morels, chopped
1 cup sour cream
Freshly ground black pepper
Salt

Simmer potatoes in water until tender; drain. In a large skillet, sauté onion, pepper, and parsley in butter until tender. Add morels and sauté until all liquid has evaporated. Add potatoes and heat through. Before serving, stir in sour cream, heat well, and season to taste. Serves 4.

Wild Asparagus and Country Ham

The Appalachian Mountain winds and breezes help to scatter the seeds of wild asparagus. This delicacy is not found in the mountain hollows and gaps, but is abundant in the foothills. Because Dad and Mom moved just outside Hopkins Gap and raised us in the foothills, we enjoyed wild asparagus every year, right around my birthday in early May.

Shenandoah Valley farmers and gardeners planted asparagus years ago. They always left a few plants to branch out, grow tall, and drop their seeds to replenish the patch. Breezes and birds picked up some of those seeds. Since fences were sometimes the first barrier met by the seeds as the breeze carried them along, and since birds often sit on fences to rest and relieve their bowels, many asparagus seeds ended up along fencerows. Nowadays, many fencerows around my home are great places to hunt wild asparagus.

Over time, I have learned to drive slowly along country roads and spot asparagus stalks. Whenever I see one stalk and stop to pick it, I usually find as many as five or ten more. Wild asparagus grows in various sizes based on the age of the plants. The older plants have larger diameters. Very old plants send up the most sought after (and most expensive) white asparagus stalks.

It has been a rare year when I didn't take off a day from work and drive to West Virginia, to gather wild asparagus. I had a map in my memory that led me to the oldest asparagus patches growing along fencerows on public property. I often take my friends with me to hunt asparagus and fool them about how well I can see. I drive along slowly and pretend to spot a stalk, but it is really a patch that I remember from previous years. We get out of the car and I show them a stalk of asparagus. They look at me in amazement. In reality, once you know where an asparagus patch is located, you can almost bet your life you will find stalks in the same spot year after year. I have often returned from Pendleton County with a half bushel of delicious wild asparagus. The flavor of wild asparagus is much stronger and richer than the stalks you buy in a grocery store.

When Mom and Dad were still living, I would pack my lunch and travel from my home in Salem, Virginia, to Pendleton County, West Virginia, to gather asparagus. By mid-afternoon, when I had finished visiting each asparagus patch on my mental map, I would turn my car toward Hopkins Gap. I usually arrived home just in time to share my bounty at suppertime. Dad would go out to his meat house and bring in a six-month old ham. He said, "This asparagus is a good excuse to cut one of my hams to see if it is curing right." Well, his hams were always good. He cut a few slices right out of the best side of the ham, and Mom fried each of us a big slab in her iron skillet. She boiled the crisp asparagus shoots just long enough to get them hot and a little tender. She always had a pan of fried potatoes for supper, because Dad required them. The ham was just beginning to taste salty after six months. It was still very red on the inside and tender. Wild asparagus, six-month old country ham, and a dish of fried potatoes made a feast for the gods.

Eventually, there were enough signs around the home place that we knew spring had arrived. We had gathered and eaten our creasy greens and canned the excess for the fall and winter. Mom, Aunt Goldie, and Aunt Ethel had gathered dandelion and cooked big pots of weed greens. We had struggled with many, many bones as we ate the spring treat of white suckers. Easter had come and gone with my favorite—pickled eggs. In late April, we had gathered and eaten all the "toadstools" we could find, and around my birthday, in May, we had enjoyed wild asparagus with six month old country ham and fried potatoes.

Dad had planted his potatoes; the ewes on John I. Myers' farm had begun lambing; the "sheep rains," a cold rainy spell after which farmers could shear their sheep, had come. Since these rains coincided with my birthday, I fussed and fretted because of my cold and wet birthday. In my sixty-five years, I can still count on one hand the warm sunny birthdays I have enjoyed. Mom listened to me fuss. She often said, "We need these rains. The blackberries are bloomin'; and if the vines don't get any rain while they're bloomin', we won't have any berries to pick this summer." One year she had my full attention when she pointed out, "I just used the last jar of blackberries in a family pie last week." My mind went back to that pie and how luscious it had tasted with fresh cream from Ole Jerse. I knew I wanted that mouth-watering experience again and immediately stopped complaining about the cold rain.

Just after the "sheep rains," John I. Myers' sheep would appear on the green hillside without their wooly coats. Each ewe had at least one lamb by her side, butting at the full teat with its long tail wagging. When we saw our first bumblebee around May 10, it was the final sign that spring had arrived, and Mom would let us put our shoes away and go barefoot for the summer.

Chapter 6

Spring Gardening and Wild Foods

To create a garden is to search for a better world.
In our effort to improve on nature, we are guided
by a vision of paradise. Whether the result is a
horticultural masterpiece or only a modest
vegetable patch, it is based on the expectation
of a glorious future. This hope for the future
is at the heart of all gardening.

—*Marina Schinz*

Gardening

The first settlers in Hopkins Gap gardened as a part of subsistence living. As the years passed by, the roads improved and food was available at grocery stores; however, the folks continued to plant big gardens every spring and summer. I overheard numerous discussions between Mom and Dad about gardening in the later years of their life. They debated whether the hard work, buying the seeds, fighting the insects, and canning, was paying off for them, when they simply could go to the store and buy their food. These same discussions occurred between Aunt Ethel and Uncle Shirley; and, I am sure, between other married couples in Hopkins Gap. But when spring rolled around, the debate was forgotten and, once again, the garden was planted.

During my lifetime, I have come to the conclusion that gardening is about much more than the food it produces. When I plant my green beans in a raised garden that is about eight feet long and four feet wide, it is not about feeding myself all winter. It is about being able to share them with my guests and a feeling of pride when I tell them, "These are for you—fresh from my garden." This year I was able to brag when I served fresh green beans on June 26, just five days later than the June 21st date when my Grandma Mary and Mom liked to serve their first green beans.

When I enter my tiny garden, it is about continuity. I garden because my parents gardened before me, and they gardened because their parents did before them. Mom and Dad's parents gardened because they had to in order to feed their large families in a time when grocery stores were few and far between. They faithfully followed the signs of the moon and the zodiac when they planted various vegetables. They practiced rituals to get rid of pests such as cutworms that destroyed their plants. Mom and Dad mouthed the lore of the "up and down" signs of the moon and the zodiac signs, but they gardened without religiously following the signs. My generation has forgotten the signs of the moon and the correct times to plant, to harvest, and to process.

No matter what the reasons, Hopkins Gap folks continue to garden. Perhaps it is the pride of seeing their hard work come to fruition or because they know their mom and dad would want them to keep the tradition alive. It could be simply the desire for the fresh taste of a ripe, homegrown tomato that is still warm from the sun. I like to think that the reason is the values shared with us by our parents and grandparents—traditional Appalachian values that keep us plowing, planting, and harvesting.

Dad's Early Spring Garden

Early in the spring, my dad would come home with a hundred pound sack of seed potatoes. "St. Patrick's Day is comin' up. We need to get the garden plowed for my potato patch," he said. As soon as the ground was dry enough from the winter snows and early spring rains, Mom made the arrangements with Wayne Hartman to bring his tractor and plow the garden. If there had been a lot of snow and spring rain, the ground was often not ready to be plowed until late April or early May. Mom was careful not to let Wayne take his tractor in the garden until the soil was dry even though Dad pressured her to get it plowed and ready for planting. After so much aggravation, she yelled at him, "Damn it, Norman, the garden will be hard as a rock this summer if he plows it while it's wet." She always won that argument.

Spring gardening started when Dad planted his potatoes. My dad loved potatoes. He had them for every meal of his life except breakfast, and he would have eaten them then but Mom wouldn't fix them for him. They argued a lot throughout their long marriage, much of the time about potatoes. Some folks used their left over potatoes which were sprouting in the cellar to start the new patch. Old potatoes can be used as seed because you plant potatoes to grow potatoes, and desperate families have been known to plant potato peelings and have gotten a fine crop. Dad, however, never took a chance on his potato crop, and he always bought new seed potatoes. He argued with Mom when she suggested he might save some money by using last year's potatoes for seed, "Myrt, I think I should get seed potatoes so I can be sure I get enough for the year. Those old potatoes are worn out and won't give me a good crop." Seed potatoes were one of the things he was always willing to spend money on.

Do potatoes have eyes....?

After supper Dad would sit on the back porch and begin to cut his seed potatoes in pieces. I watched him and thought it was magical how he searched over each potato and then made a cut in it to remove a chunk. He turned the potato over and over studying it again before he made the next cut. I asked him, "Why do you do it like that?" His answer only confused me more, "Each piece has to have a live eye in it so it can grow." I looked and looked for "eyes." I picked up a piece he had just cut—there was no "eye." I picked up a whole potato—there was no "eye" in it either. I asked him if I could cut some potatoes. His response was even more mystifying. "I am afraid you won't leave an eye in each piece. You have to leave at least one good eye so the potato will grow." My respect for Dad went out the roof because he could see things in a potato that I couldn't see. It was several years before I figured out that the "eye" was actually a bud that would grow in the soil, warmed by sunshine and watered by the spring rains.

Once the garden was plowed and harrowed, Dad dug rows across the potato patch. He tried a variety of ways to get his rows opened up for the seed potatoes including hooking up Larry and me to the plow. Of course, we were too little to pull the plow through the damp and heavy soil. Then he tried to hook the car up to the plow by running chains through the garden fence and bringing the car into the pasture behind the garden. He drove the car and had Larry and me try to hold the plow in the soil to make a row. This attempt failed, because we could not hold the plow in the soil far enough to dig a row. Year after year he tried different ways to make his potato rows. When it was time to harvest the potatoes, he tried some of the same ways to plow them out of the dirt but always ended up digging them out with a hoe. Finally, several years before he died, he bought a little tractor. He used it to make his potato rows, but he still had to harvest them with a hoe.

When the rows were dug, the whole family got involved in planting the potatoes. Dad let Larry and I drop the pieces of seed potato into the rows. He went ahead of us to spread lime in each row. Mom helped us after she finished her evening milking. By dark, we had about twenty-five rows of potatoes planted and covered. We all stayed out of the potato patch for two weeks. At the end of that time, Dad would sneak up to the garden fence to see if his potatoes were peeping through the dirt. He had to sneak because Mom yelled at him about going in the garden and tracking mud in the house.

As soon as Dad saw a few potato plants breaking through the soil, he started watching for potato bugs. He walked up and down the rows with a tin can with some kerosene in the bottom. He dropped all the potato bugs he found into the can and later set it on fire. He had a gleeful look on his face as the bugs popped open in the inferno. He absolutely hated potato bugs.

When all the potatoes had grown enough so that he could see the rows, Dad would be out there digging around the plants. I know this was a time of meditation for him because I could stand at the fence and tell him supper was ready several times before he would look up. He was in his potato patch from the moment he got home from work, until dark, with only a quick break for supper.

Mom's Early Spring Garden

After we got the potatoes in the ground, we moved to the side of the garden nearest the road and started to plant Mom's garden. She was responsible for early spring crops like spring onions, peas, lettuce, kale and mustard greens, radishes, and red beets. Mom planned a trip with Aunt Goldie to Wetzel Seed Co., in Harrisonburg to pick up some onion sets, lettuce, kale, red beets, and mustard seed. Those vegetables were her responsibility, while Dad always took care of the potatoes. Dad and all of us children helped get her seeds in the ground, but it was understood that Dad would spend his time in the potato patch, while Mom took care of her side of the garden.

Usually the first vegetables to peep through the ground were onions and lettuce. As soon as the leaves were big enough to pinch off, Mom was in the garden with a bucket gathering lettuce for a dish of spring onions and wilted lettuce for supper.

Wilted Lettuce Salad Recipe...

Ingredients
5 cups torn lettuce (about 1 lb.)
3 or 4 strips of home-cured side meat (middlin)
2 tablespoons of apple cider vinegar
1 ½ tablespoons of sugar
1 tablespoon of prepared mustard
1 small onion chopped fine

Rinse lettuce several times, discard stems, drain and place in a large bowl.

In a skillet, cook the side meat over medium-high heat until brown and crisp.

Drain on towel, reserving two teaspoons of the pan drippings in the skillet.

Crumble the side meat into small pieces. In a small bowl, place vinegar, sugar, mustard, and onion—mix well. Pour this mixture into the skillet with the reserved drippings and cook over medium-high heat, stirring constantly, for 2 minutes.

Quickly pour the dressing over the lettuce, add the crumbled side meat, toss to mix, and serve immediately.

As the onions matured, Mom pulled them and cleaned them. She left some of the green tops on them and served them in a condiment dish. We all loved them with butter bread. We held the onion in one hand and a folded piece of butter bread in the other. After a big bite of onion, we chased it with a bite of butter bread and a swig of sweet milk. That was some fine eating. For dinner on butter-making days, Mom often made herself a sliced onion and fresh butter sandwich on homemade light bread.

The next vegetable from the early spring garden was mustard greens, mixed with kale and beet tops. Mom cooked these greens together. She said, "Mustard tastes too strong by itself and so does kale. The beet tops kinda' sweeten the pot." She knew what she was talking about, because we couldn't get enough of her greens. She washed them several times and then picked up each individual leaf and checked both sides for bugs and dirt. I asked her, "Mom, that sure takes a lot of time to look at each leaf. Don't you think you got all the bugs off when you washed them?" She answered, "I don't care how long it takes. The last thing I want is to see a worm or a bug floating in the broth when I dip these greens up for supper. That's why I don't buy canned greens. I know they don't half clean the greens." Mom went on to share horror stories, "I heard that somebody bought a can of spinach, and after they ate half of it, they found a worm." That message was planted in my head, so that even today when I buy a bag of spinach at the store that claims it has been pre-washed, I say to myself, "I know they didn't clean it like Mom did." I always give my greens an extra washing or two before I cook them. I appreciated Mom's extra effort because I loved to crumble corn bread in the juice left by the greens after they had been cooked with a ham hock, and the last thing I wanted to see was a worm in the "pot likker."

Mustard, Kale, and Beet Top Greens Recipe...

Ingredients

Mustard greens	1 four inch square block of salt pork
Kale	water to partially cover greens
Beet tops	salt and pepper to taste
Vinegar	

Pick equal amounts of mustard greens, kale, and beet tops.

Look over each leaf for bugs and rinse two or three times. Put in large cook pot and pour water to about three-fourths the depth of the greens. Place salt pork on top of the greens, add pepper and boil until done, approximately 3 hours. Check the water level often. You should be able to see the water bubbling up through the greens. When done, sample for salt taste and add salt if needed. Serve with a teaspoon of vinegar poured over each serving, as desired.

Mom and Aunt Ethel's Late Spring Garden

After May 10, when the danger of frost had passed, Mom and Aunt Ethel started their late spring gardens. Uncle Shirley loved to garden. He and Aunt Ethel got their garden "in," as they called it and then came across the mountain to help Mom plant. Some vegetables grew better across the mountain in Hopkins Gap, and some grew better in Mom's garden just outside the mountains. By planting both gardens, with whatever grew better in each one, the two families had more to eat in the summer, fall, and winter seasons. Mom, Dad, Aunt Ethel and Uncle Shirley shared in that way for many years. After Dad died, Uncle Shirley and Aunt Ethel stopped planting a whole garden at their home. Instead, they shared the work of planting Mom's garden, helped with the processing, and took a portion of the produce home for their labor.

Soon after May 10, green beans, sweet potatoes, beets, cabbage, corn, cucumbers, squash, and tomatoes were planted within a few days time. Once the garden was "in," they constantly wished for the right amount of rain to produce a bountiful crop. Dad had already been watching how the spring storms came across the mountains while his potato patch was in bloom. If they made it over the Allegheny Mountains to the west of our house, then we got a good amount of rain. Dad told me, "If the storms move north along the Allegheny Mountains, then the pattern is set for a dry summer."

Planting Sweet potatoes

American Indians were growing sweet potatoes as far back as we have records. There are many varieties of sweet potatoes but all can be categorized as orange-fleshed, white fleshed or light yellow fleshed. Mom considered the very light yellow fleshed sweet potatoes to be the oldest variety and the best. Just as Dad took great pride in his Irish potatoes, Mom took an equal amount of pride in her sweet potatoes.

Mom started her sweet potatoes from plants called "slips." If she wanted to plant just a few sweet potatoes, she started her own "slips" by placing a sweet potato in a dish of shallow water with the buds up and above the water. She sat the dish in the windows of her enclosed back porch. Soon she had young vines climbing across the window sills. When Mom wanted a lot of sweet potatoes, she would ask Aunt Goldie to drive her to Whetsel's Seed Store where she would purchase the old-timey yellow-fleshed "slips."

Once Mom's "slips," were ready, the hard work began. She picked the best spot in the garden and dug two trenches about eight inches deep and five feet apart across the garden from fence to fence. She piled the dirt from the trenches along the edges. She took the wheel barrow and headed up the hill to the hog pen. She explained to me as we walked along the path, "Hog manure is the best. It stinks to high heaven, but it grows some fine sweet taters."

When we got back to the garden, Mom filled her trenches with about six inches of hog manure. After several trips we had the trenches ready for the next step. She took a shovel and put dirt on top of the hog manure in the trenches until they were level with the ground again. The next step was very hard work. She dug along side each trench and piled that dirt on top of the trench. She called this "making a ridge." Finally, after several hours of digging and shoveling, she took the yard rake and smoothed the sides of the ridges until she had two perfect "ridges" about fifteen inches high. She said as she stood back and admired her work, "It's time to put the 'slips' into the ridges." She took a broom stick, walked along each ridge, and poked a four inch hole in the very top about fifteen inches apart. She told me, "You can help me by taking the slips and dropping one in each of these holes and press the dirt around them real easy with your hands."

While I was putting the "slips" into the holes, Mom explained, "These slips will grow down through the loose dirt in the ridge, and when their roots hit that hog manure, you will be able to watch them grow." I asked her, "Where will the sweet potatoes grow?" She answered, "We dig them out of the ground right where we put the hog manure." I grimaced and asked, "But won't the potatoes taste like hog manure?" Her answer was something that I always remembered, and to this day I use it in trying to understand many aspects of everyday life.

She said, "Peg, how many times do I have to remind you that just about everything good comes out of something bad? Just like me heatin' the chicken slop on the stove in the winter. I know that smells awful in the house with the doors and windows shut; but look what comes later if you take the time to heat the slop. My hens are healthier and happier, so I get more eggs to eat and use in my cookin'." I looked at her and she must have thought I needed another example, so she went on to say, "You've seen me clean the manure out of hog guts when we butcher. I take those same guts and stuff

This is Mom's light yellow-fleshed sweet potato ridges (1994). She planted two ridges across the garden between her pole beans on the right, and her half runner beans on the left. In the background is the hog pen, a fair distance from the house, with the two holer outhouse that Dad moved next to the hog pen to store his hog feed after we got the indoor toilet in 1969.

sausage in them, and we eat it all winter. So just about everything that's good starts with something we think is bad."

It wasn't long after that day of planting that Mom's sweet potato ridges were covered with beautiful lush vines. The vines spread across the space between the ridges and beyond the ridges on both sides. Mom pointed out another important lesson to me, "You see those sweet potato vines? They are so thick that weeds can't grow where they are. That saves me a lot of time because I don't have to weed that whole section of garden."

Wild Strawberry Season

Oh, those beautiful days in mid-May on a hillside filled with wild strawberries! The vegetables were barely in the ground and beginning to sprout, when it was time to pick wild strawberries. Mom, Aunt Goldie, and Aunt Ethel knew where all the good patches were located. Arrangements were made for a truck, usually Uncle Shirley's because Aunt Goldie was working. The cooks packed lunch for everybody. They gathered up buckets and containers, large and small. All the pre-school aged children that were available were loaded onto the back of the truck, and off we went to pick strawberries.

"Strawberry hill," as we called it was not too far from our house. It was also an apple orchard, but wild strawberries had been planted there by means of bird droppings. Strawberry plants replenish themselves year after year by sending out "runners" from the main plant that will attach to the ground and bear strawberries the following year. Wild strawberries are smaller than store-bought ones, but they are sweeter and tend to have a stronger flavor. They are red all the way through the fruit, whereas cultivated strawberries tend to be a lighter color on the inside. Mom said, "I wouldn't trade wild strawberries any day for tame strawberries. Tame strawberries have a lot less flavor than wild ones."

We must have looked like a family of slow moving bears as we stooped and crawled up the hill on our hands and knees while parting the grass and weeds to find the bright red berries. I would get really tired and hot with the sun pounding down on my back and begin to complain. Close to lunch time, I occasionally slipped a ripe berry in my mouth. Mom caught me. She reminded me that I shouldn't eat while I picked, "We will make strawberry short cake out of these berries. I'll whip some of Ole Jerse's cream to eat on top of them. She asked, "You do want some strawberry jam for next winter, don't you?"

Well of course I wanted strawberry jam the next winter. I thought that was a dumb question. Mom then came up with another strategy to make me stop eating the berries. She said, "I'll bet you can fill your bucket before I get mine full. Here, let me see how many you have. Okay, it's about the same as I have. Let's race to see who can pick fastest."

Lunch time was wonderful with sandwiches and cold lemonade, but eating didn't seem to help me. I just got more tired. By three o'clock we left strawberry hill because Mom and the other cooks had to start supper. I gladly jumped on the back of the truck, thinking the day was over. Mom put the strawberries in a cool place when we got home. While she was cooking supper, she reminded me, "We have to cap the strawberries after supper. We can't leave them over night because they will get too mushy." I thought to myself, "I can't help with the capping. I will die of boredom and I am too tired." But, I did help with the berries into the evening hours until they were cleaned and ready to be processed into preserves the next day. Mom kept her promise. The very next day she whipped up a strawberry short cake for supper; and sure enough, she served it with fresh whipped cream on top. Mom never baked a family pie with strawberries. She said they were too mushy.

Wild Strawberry Shortcake Recipe...

Ingredients

Shortcake	Strawberry Filling
1½ cups flour	wild strawberries
½ teaspoon salt	¾ cup sugar
3 tablespoons baking powder	1 pint cream, whipped
3 tablespoons butter	
2 tablespoons sugar	
3 tablespoons cream	
1 egg, beaten	

Mix flour, salt, baking powder, 2 tablespoons sugar and sift into a large mixing bowl. Add butter and mix well. Add egg and 3 tablespoons cream. Knead gently and spread dough in bottom of a rectangular baking pan. Bake in a 400 degree oven until light brown—about 15 to 20 minutes. Cap and clean the strawberries. Cut the shortcake into two layers and remove the top. Spread strawberries over the bottom layer and sprinkle with ¾ cup sugar. Add top layer and cover with strawberries. Cut and serve with whipped cream on top.

Strawberry Jelly Rolls Recipe...

Ingredients
3 eggs
1 cup granulated sugar
3 tablespoons cold water
1 cup flour
1 teaspoon baking powder
1/3 teaspoon salt
Homemade strawberry jelly

Beat eggs and sugar until thick. Add water, then flour, baking powder and salt, sifted together. Line cookie sheet with wax paper and rub with lard. Sprinkle with flour and shake until evenly covered. Pour batter onto lined and floured cookie sheet. Bake at 425 degrees for 12 to 15 minutes. Turn onto cloth on which you have sifted confectioners' sugar. Trim edges and spread with strawberry jelly and roll in cloth. Slice into servings.

Using the recipes found on boxes of Sure-Jell, Mom made a lot of strawberry jam for eating mixed with cottage cheese, on peanut butter sandwiches, and with left-over warm bread. She poured it into pint jars and let it cool. Before she took it to the cellar, she sealed the top of the jam with paraffin wax, then placed lids on the jars. When we opened it to eat, we used our fingers to push down on the layer of wax to break the seal. I always enjoyed licking the jam off the back of the wax before putting it in a shoe box to save for the next jam making day. Mom washed the wax and melted it again so she didn't have to buy more.

Cherry Season

By mid-June, strawberry season ended just as the sweet cherries began to ripen. There were all types of cherry trees in and around Hopkins Gap—sweet red cherries, sweet black cherries, sour red cherries, and yellow wax cherries. Although Mom could not drive a car, she was the organizer of the cherry pickins' and reminded us as June rolled around that we had to go pick cherries. She made arrangements with someone who had a truck and a ladder—sometimes Uncle Jim or Uncle Shirley, and she certainly knew there were plenty of good climbers and pickers among all of my first cousins.

We all looked forward to cherry season, as it was the first opportunity to experience fresh fruit in a warm family pie. We had enjoyed family pie all winter, but it was made from canned fruit (or frozen fruit in later years after Mom got her freezer). It always tasted scrumptious, but not the same as when it was made at the end of a day of gathering fresh fruit.

Cherry pickin' and not grinnin'.…

Several summers, Mom had some trouble organizing the trips because it was especially difficult to find a person who could drive a truck to carry the ladder. When this happened, she would be furious that she had never learned to drive and would curse my Dad because he didn't have the patience to teach her. The fact is Mom didn't have the patience to go through the process of learning to drive. She wanted to get behind the steering wheel and take off driving without learning.

Dad was afraid to take Mom on the road to teach her to drive, so he took the car into the pasture where Mom would have wide open spaces to practice driving. Sometimes a few of us kids went along for the ride. She could not get her hands and feet coordinated to push in the clutch, change gears, and steer the car at the same time. She often looked down to make sure her feet were hitting the right pedals. She stomped on the accelerator and, without paying attention to the steering of the car, headed for a rock, a cow, a fence, a tree or whatever dangerous barrier there was without realizing she could turn the steering wheel and miss it.

We went bouncing across the pasture with Dad screaming, "Myrt! Myrt! You're gonna hit something." She yelled back, "How in the hell am I gonna learn to drive with you yellin' at me?" She remained on her course toward destruction until Dad jerked the steering wheel to the right or left to avoid a collision. We must have made a hilarious picture to anyone watching. The old car lurched, sped up, lurched again, spun out and threw grass behind us. The cows headed for the corner of the field and stood watching until the driving lesson was over. We did not dare laugh from the back seat while Mom was driving, so we held it in until we were out of the car and out of sight of Mom and Dad. Then we all rolled around in the pasture field and laughed until we were sick to our stomachs.

Mom was very stubborn and didn't want anybody telling her how to do something. When Dad tried to help her learn to drive, she got mad because that was him telling her what to do—a forbidden thing in their marriage. As with most instructions—she called them "orders"—"I don't take orders from no man," she said. So, when he told her to turn the wheel right, she turned it left or didn't turn it at all. Please realize I am not poking fun at Mom, just explaining how head strong she was. I often wonder what she could have accomplished if she had learned to drive a car. Because she didn't learn, she had to depend on other people to drive her where she needed to go. For an independent woman like Mom, this was a lifelong source of frustration.

After each attempt to learn to drive, Mom and Dad would not speak for a week. These times were always difficult for me as a child because I thought they would never get over being mad at each other. I simply hurt all over when there was tension in our home. It brought out the "diplomat" in me, so I would devise ways to force them to talk to each other until one of my strategies made them laugh at the same time. That seemed to work. They would start talking again, and I would breathe a sigh of relief.

As I grew older, I often told them to go get a divorce if they couldn't speak to each other. That statement at least got my Mom to yell at me, "I married him for better or worse—sometimes its better but right now its worse!!!! Get the hell out of here and shut up." It seemed to me that she got rid of her anger by yelling at me, so by the evening, when Dad came home from work, she was speaking to him again.

Cherry Seeding

By early afternoon on cherry picking day, we arrived home with buckets and buckets of cherries. Plans had been made the day before with several generations of women in Hopkins Gap to gather at a designated house to seed cherries all afternoon. In the earlier days, the cherry seeding was held on the back porch at Uncle Shirley and Aunt Ethel's house. The morning sun had gone across the house leaving the porch nice and shady. Grandma Molly and her daughters, Aunt Vernie, and Aunt Pauline came down the road to help. Aunt Vernie's daughter, Ethel was always there. Ginny Riggleman, and her daughter, Millie Morris, came up the road to help. On at least two occasions, Mom caught a ride across the mountain and helped with the seeding.

Cherry seedin' and birthin' babies, and the bonds of friendship....

Food and food events were embedded in family history. I remember being with a group of Hopkins Gap women including Grandma Molly—the central figure in all food preparation events—Mom, Aunt Vernie Conley, Aunt Pauline Shifflett, Aunt Millie Morris, Ginny Riggleman and others at Uncle Shirley's and Aunt Ethel's house on the bank of the Shoemaker River. The women were seeding cherries that had been picked earlier that morning. Each woman was dressed in her traditional homemade bonnet, apron, and dress. Some of the older women—Grandma Molly, Aunt Millie, and Ginny—wore cotton stockings tied up with strings to cover their legs. They sat in a semi-circle facing toward the road.

Birds sang in the trees along Shoemaker River, against the background of music from the river as it splashed over rocks and into silvery pools, on its way down through Hopkins Gap. An occasional honey bee, attracted by the sweet smell of cherries, would drift around the women and briefly land on the edge of their pans. No one seemed to be scared they might be stung. The older children, including me, played with the younger ones in the yard under the watchful eyes of the cherry seeders. The freshly picked cherries sat soaking in a washing tub of water.

Each of the women had a pan of cherries on their lap and used both hands to seed. The right hand reached in for several cherries, and while they mashed the seeds out of the fruit, the left hand was picking up several more cherries. When the pan was empty, the cherry seeds were dumped into a bucket, and each woman refilled her pan from the washing tub.

As the morning wore on, their fingers turned from a light brown to a dark brown from the cherry juice. It took days for the stain to wear off Mom's hands and from under her fingernails. She apologized for her stained hands when our neighbor, Fannie Jane Myers, who often dropped in without notice, caught her with her hands kneading a pan of bread dough. She would say to Fannie Jane, "I know you think my hands are filthy, but I have been seeding cherries." Fannie Jane smiled, as she assured Mom, "I know you are a clean cook. I wouldn't be afraid to eat your light bread or anything you cook."

Uncle Shirley had arranged for the cherry seeders to come to his house on one occasion because Ethel was in the hospital with a new baby and could not help with the seeding and canning. In the middle of the afternoon, Shirley drove into the back yard with Aunt Ethel in the passenger seat. She had a new baby boy in her arms. He parked near the back steps so Ethel didn't have to walk very far to get into the house. One of the women went to the car and took the new baby from Ethel's arms and showed her around to the circle of women who had gathered to catch their first glimpse of the newest Hopkins Gap citizen, Sammy. Ethel went inside the house and lay on the bed. The cherry seeders went back to work and before the day was over, the cherries were canned and ready to go into Ethel's cellar, and there was a beautiful golden brown family pie in the oven for Uncle Shirley's family.

Exactly one year and one day later, the same women were sitting on Shirley and Ethel's back porch. They were dressed in the same style of clothing, sharing stories, and seeding cherries that Uncle Shirley and others had picked early that morning. At just about the same time of day, Uncle Shirley drove his car into the back yard and parked near the steps. Aunt Ethel was holding a new baby girl, Bonnie. One of the women walked over to the car and took the baby out of Ethel's arms and showed it around the circle. Aunt Ethel went in the house and lay across the bed. Needless to say, the women went back to seeding cherries and history had repeated itself down to the smallest detail. Aunt Ethel has two children born, in cherry season, one year and one day apart.

Mom often reminded me of this event. She treated it as if that was how it was supposed to be. She said, "We helped each other out like that. Ethel would have done the same for us and often did." Until the end of her life, Mom would arrive home from grocery shopping and find her house sparkling clean, her breakfast dishes washed, and a pot of coffee on the stove. Aunt Ethel and Uncle Shirley had dropped by on their way home from the grocery store in Harrisonburg. Aunt Ethel recently told me how she knew Mom wasn't home. She said, "Your mom always propped her walking stick against the mail box by the road when somebody drove her into town. Me and Shirl would drive by and see her walking stick, and we knew she wasn't home. We always went on in the house. While Shirl took a nap on your daddy's recliner, I cleaned your mom's house and washed her dishes. Then I made a fresh pot of coffee for her when she come in. Sometimes we stayed until she got home so we could all drink coffee and visit. Other times me and Shirl had to go on home."

I was sometimes the one who drove Mom to the grocery store. We would walk into the house with the groceries and smell fresh coffee. Mom said with a big smile, "Ethel and Shirl were here." As she put her groceries away, she talked about what a good friend Ethel was to her. "She would do anything for me, and I would do whatever I could for her." When she finished with her groceries, she walked to the phone and called Aunt Ethel. She said, "The good fairy was at my house today, and I thank her very much."

Steamed Cherry Dumplings Recipe...

Ingredients

Dumplings	*Cherry Sauce*
1 cup sifted flour	½ gallon fresh picked,
1½ teaspoons baking powder	seeded cherries
½ teaspoon salt	¼ cup water
¼ cup sugar	2 tablespoons butter
2 tablespoons butter	
½ teaspoon vanilla	
½ cup milk	

Mix cherries, water, and 2 tablespoons of butter in a 3 ½ quart saucepan.

Boil for 5 minutes. To make dumplings: mix together flour, baking powder, salt, sugar and cut in butter. Add vanilla to milk and mix with flour mixture, just enough to moisten all dry ingredients. Drop dumplings by teaspoonful onto the hot sauce. Boil uncovered for 5 minutes. Cover and steam gently for 30-35 minutes or until dumplings are no longer moist on top. Serve dumplings warm with cherry sauce.

Mom often strayed from her traditional pies and cakes for desserts. She began to explore recipes she found on cereal boxes. Kellogg's cornflakes were always a big hit. Dad ate them as a bedtime snack; we children enjoyed them for breakfast sometimes. It was on a Kellogg's box that Mom found the recipe for our favorite cookies. When we arrived home from school one afternoon, we smelled a different but mouth-watering aroma coming out the kitchen door to meet us. Mom had baked cherry winks and had them covered with a dish towel and cooling in a basket on the cabinet. We asked, "What is that smell?" She lifted the towel. Later on, she laughed as she told us, "All of you had eyes like saucers when you saw the cherry winks."

They were the most beautiful cookies I had ever seen. Mom said, "Wash your hands and you can have one or two to hold you until supper." She poured each of us a glass of Ole Jerse's milk to go with them.

Cherry Winks Recipe...

Ingredients

1 1/3 cup of crushed corn flakes	2 eggs
2¼ cup flour	2 tablespoons milk
2 teaspoons baking powder	1 teaspoon vanilla
½ teaspoon salt	1 cup chopped walnuts
¾ cup butter (soft)	½ cup chopped cherres
1 cup sugar	15 quartered cherries ("winks")

Beat butter and sugar until light and fluffy. Add eggs and beat well.

Stir in milk and vanilla. Add flour mixture. Mix well, stir in nuts and cherries.

Using teaspoon, shape into balls and roll in the crushed cornflake crumbs.

Place one cherry "wink" into the middle of the ball.

Place on a lightly greased cookie sheet. Bake at 375 degrees for 10 minutes until light brown.

Kissin' up with cherry winks....

My brother John was very fond of his third grade teacher so he took her a few cherry winks every time Mom made them. He recently told me, "I got a lot of mileage and special pats on the back from that teacher, so I took cherry winks to my fourth and fifth grade teachers.

They liked them a lot, and they seemed to like me better because I brought them cookies.

"When I started the sixth grade, I was disappointed because my teacher was a man—Charles Garber. I didn't feel that it was proper for a boy to be takin' cookies to a man teacher, so I didn't." I asked John, "Did you get treated any differently in the sixth grade?" He said, "Yes I did. Mr. Garber put me and Herman and Bobby Caldwell in a row of desks by the window. He called it his 'Alcatraz Row.'"

"Since I didn't feel I could take cookies to Mr. Garber, I figured out another way to get on his good side. Most of the boys had baseball gloves, and I didn't have one. Mr. Garber took us out at recess and batted baseballs to us. Every ball that came to me, I caught with my bare hands. Other boys who had gloves were missing the balls that went to them. When we got back to the room, he bragged about me catching all his fly balls with my bare hands."

Cherry Winks became a family favorite. We begged Mom to make them as long as she could cook. After her stroke, she taught her granddaughter, Paula, how to make cherry winks.

Cherry Pudding Cake Recipe…

Ingredients

3 cups fresh pitted cherries	1 cup flour
1 teaspoon baking powder	salt to taste
1 ½ cups sugar	½ cup milk
3 tablespoons butter	1 teaspoon vanilla extract
1 tablespoon cornstarch	1 cup boiling water

Place fruit in the bottom of a buttered 9 inch square baking dish. Combine flour, baking powder, salt and half the sugar in a mixing bowl. Add milk, butter and vanilla. Mix until smooth. Spread batter over fruit. Mix remaining sugar and cornstarch and sprinkle over batter. Pour boiling water over the mixture. Bake 45 minutes at 350 degrees or until tester comes out clean.

Cherry season ended by mid-June and brought the Hopkins Gap cooks right up to the beginning of summer. The vegetables that were planted after May 10 had been growing in the warm garden soil. The families had worked hard keeping the weeds out of the plants. Hopefully there had been enough rain and the vegetables were growing. The busiest season of the year was approaching for the cooks.

Chapter 7

Summer's Garden and Nature's Bounty

Then followed that beautiful season... Summer....
Filled was the air with a dreamy and magical light;
and the landscape
Lay as if new created in all the freshness of childhood.
—*Henry Wadsworth Longfellow*

The summer season was the most challenging for the Hopkins Gap families because that was when most of the food for the upcoming winter was picked, processed, and stored, so the family would have enough to eat through the cold months. As the vegetable plants and fruit trees produced their crops, the cooks, and all the children they could enlist to help, had to deal with this produce immediately. Vegetables that are too old and fruit that is too ripe are worthless.

Before the days of freezers, all fruits and vegetables were canned. The women stayed busy canning green beans, pickled beets, cucumber pickles, corn, tomatoes and other produce they grew in their gardens. As each summer season rolled around, they did the same thing.

Hopkins Gap cooks used three methods of canning. Some vegetables and fruits were cleaned and prepared on the stove. While boiling hot, they were packed into glass jars and covered with lids.

The lids were screwed on the can as tight as the cook could get them. The vegetables in the jar contracted as they cooled causing the jar to seal. The cook knew when the jars were sealed because they each made a little popping noise.

Some foods required the "water bath" method of canning. The glass jars were packed with the vegetable or fruit; the lids were screwed on but not fully tightened. The jars were then placed in a large boiler pot that was filled with water as high as the "shoulders" of the jars. The jars were boiled in the water for an amount of time determined by which vegetable or fruit was being canned. For example, jars of peaches were boiled for ten to fifteen minutes, while green beans were boiled for three hours. The jars were carefully removed from the "water bath," the lids turned tight, and set where they could cool. Again, as each jar sealed, there was the telltale sign of the lids popping.

In the last fifteen years of her life, Mom used a pressure cooker. This manner of canning requires turning the can lids tight and placing the jars in two to three inches of water, covering them, and cooking them under pressure for a certain amount of time. After Mom started using the pressure cooker, she didn't worry as much about her vegetables spoiling. Pressure canning was especially good for low-acid foods such as corn and meat.

Cooks like Mom, Aunt Ethel, and Aunt Goldie had to be aware of when each vegetable or fruit came into season, how long they could wait for processing, and how to do the processing when the time came. I know that Mom calculated how much sugar, salt, pickling spice, canning jars, and canning tops and rings she would need. When she did her canning on the wood stove, she made sure there was plenty of wood to keep a fire. After she moved

This copper boiler is like the one that Mom used for canning. (Courtesy of Maynard Keeling Jones)

her canning to the butchering building, I gave her a small propane gas stove so she wouldn't get so hot when she canned. She always checked the gas tank to make sure she didn't run out of gas in the middle of water bathing some vegetable or fruit. Aunt Ethel often came to our house to can her fruits and vegetables after we set up the gas stove. Having the canning stove in the butchering building kept most of the canning mess out of the kitchen.

Mom always had a plan for preserving and canning that stretched out for several weeks ahead. It was similar to watching a highly sequenced activity such as building a house. Although Mom canned many and various fruits and vegetables, I am going to share her preparations and recipes for some of our family favorites.

Green Beans

The summer vegetables matured beginning with green beans in mid to late June. Green beans are also called bush beans or snap beans, because you really can and should hear them snap when you are preparing them to cook—the fresher the bean, the sharper the snap. If possible, we snapped beans as soon as they were picked. Snap into about one inch lengths. Mom taught us not to cut green beans because a cut through the small kernels would cause pieces to fall out of the pod. Hogs love to eat the tips that come off each end of the bean.

Green beans by June 21...

One memory that Mom had of her mother, Mary Lamb Morris, was that she always set a goal to serve fresh green beans from her garden by the first day of summer. Of course, Mom set the same goal. It was not easy to get beans to grow and produce unless spring came early and the garden soil warmed up nicely. But Mom had ways of making the ground warmer when she was trying to meet her goal. I remember only one time during my years at home when Mom actually achieved the goal set by her mother. Mom contributed a huge pot of fresh green beans for Sunday dinner on a June 21st at Aunt Ethel's house. She was very proud as folks dipped into her delicious green beans with comments such as, "Myrt, how did you get beans this early. Mine are just starting to bloom."

After receiving all the positive comments about what a good gardener she must be, Mom confessed that she had spread black plastic between her bean rows so that the heat from the sun made the ground warmer than it otherwise would have been. Her creative solution to meeting her goal became a common practice by Hopkins Gap gardeners.

Bush beans are one of the easiest vegetables to grow even in poor soil. The plants bear in approximately sixty days from planting and continue to bear for four or five weeks. The secret for longer bearing is to pick every three days and pick all the mature beans on the vines at each picking. Bean vines are very fragile, so they pull up or bruise easily and must be treated with kid gloves while picking. Also, bush beans must be watered if the season is dry.

Mom always picked her beans early in the morning or late in the afternoon. These times of day were kinder to the picker and the bean-picking was just as easy. When we grew old enough to help with the bean picking, we didn't want to get out of bed early because, afterall, it was our summer break.

Mom came to the bottom of the stairs and yelled up at us, "Get out of bed before the sun sours your guts! The beans need to be picked before the sun gets too high in the sky."

Green beans were cooked in a variety of ways. Sometimes Mom put new potatoes in with the beans near the end of cooking time. She occasionally added corn or onions. The recipe given here is the way she typically cooked green beans.

Green Beans Recipe....
Ingredients
Approximately 3 lbs. of green beans, fresh from the garden.
1 medium onion, diced
¼ lb of salt pork, cut into small pieces
Salt and pepper to taste
Water

Snap the beans, clean and put in large cook pot.
Add salt pork pieces and onion to the top of the beans.
Add water to about ½ the depth of the beans.
Cook slowly, on low heat, approximately two hours.
Add water as needed.
Serve with fresh cole slaw and fried potatoes.
Serves 7 with a few beans left over for the next day's lunch.

Hay Beans

Mom's favorite beans to plant were Half Runners because they matured early and satisfied our hunger for fresh green beans. She used these green beans to dry for winter "hay beans," as we called them. Other Appalachian areas call them "shucky beans" or "leather britches." After we ate what we wanted of the fresh Half Runners, Mom dried what was left in the garden on the exhausted vines. This was one of my earliest contributions to the winter's food supply. Mom strung the beans and broke off the ends. She got a large needle and threaded it with twine string she saved from her cow feed bags. She showed me how to stick the needle through the bean and pull the thread through. Bean after bean went on the string until we had about a dozen ten foot long strings of beans.

Mom went up in the attic and strung two wires from the across the joists, and she opened a little vent at each end of the attic. We took the beans up into the attic and hung them over the wires. The heat in the attic, combined with the bit of fresh air, dried the beans to perfection. By August, Mom took the beans down and put them in paper bags for storage. What a wonderful treat they were in the winter months.

Hay Beans Recipe...

Ingredients
Salt pork—about 3 to 4 ozs.
3 to 4 cups of dried hay beans
½ teaspoon of salt
¼ teaspoon of pepper
Water, as needed

Wash the beans and throw away any that are black or look bad. Put in pot, cover with water and soak overnight.

Cut the hard skin off the salt pork and cut it into ¼ inch pieces. In a cook pot, fry the salt pork until it is brown. Add the beans, salt, and pepper.

Cover with water and simmer 2 to 6 hours, adding water as needed.

Cooking time depends on the size, level of maturity, and variety of the hay beans. Use low heat and cover the pot.

When the beans are tender (mash a bean kernel to check), remove the lid, increase the heat to medium, and continue to cook until the water has thickened.

The pot likker is full of flavor and tastes great served over corn bread or light bread crusts.

Old Timey Pole Beans

Toward the end of June, Mom and Dad joined forces to plant old timey pole beans. Grandma Molly had handed down her pole bean seed to them, and Mom and Dad saved some seeds each year for the next summer. The best thing about pole beans was their long production season of about six weeks. This allowed picking and canning over a longer period of time. Dad planted fence posts across the middle of the garden and nailed up fencing wire for the beans to climb on. The structure became a permanent fixture in the garden.

Pole beans were Mom's and Dad's favorite beans for canning. They let them mature on the vine until just before they became too tough to eat. The bean pods were filled with fully-matured bean kernels. In the canning process, some of the pods broke open and the kernels came loose in the jar. These jars of beans were a beautiful sight on the shelves in the cellar.

Dad picked the pole beans as they matured, and Mom canned them for the winter. She always canned about twenty pints for me to enjoy over the coming year. After Mom and Dad got all the beans they needed for winter, Mom called my brothers and sisters and told them to pick all the beans they wanted. When there were beans still left on the vines, she called Aunt Ethel and Uncle Shirley. They came and picked pole beans for their family.

I still have a few pints of pole beans in my closet from Mom's and Dad's 1993 garden. While I want to eat them, I feel as if the beans keep me connected somehow to Mom and Dad since they are both gone now. I look at the jars and know that their hands planted, picked, and canned those beans while they were thinking of me living so far from home. They always wanted me to return home and never acknowledged that I might have made a permanent residence away from them.

Blackberry Season

As late June and July rolled around, family pie was made first with low blackberries, commonly known as dew berries, then high blackberries, and later, peaches in August. Low blackberries were in season around mid July. They grew low to the ground in pasture fields. While the green beans were being canned, all of us children and Dad were out picking dewberries and blackberries. Mom canned and froze blackberries at night after we were all in bed and asleep. Picking them included a lot of suffering. First of all, you had to stoop over to pick them and second, they grew under the mid-July sun which beat down on your back mercilessly as you picked them.

In the earlier days before suntans were popular, Mom forced us to wear long sleeves so we didn't get sun-burned. If we did get sunburned, the cure was worse than the burn. Mom would find a fresh cow pile, dip a flat stick into it, and rub it on our arms. Then she wrapped our arms with clean white cloth to keep the cow manure against the sunburned skin. As a child, I thought the treatment really worked. As an adult, I think that probably we just quit complaining about sunburns after we had the treatment foisted upon us. I will never know the truth about cow manure for sunburn. I have to admit that suffering in a variety of ways was the name of the game before we could have family pie made from low blackberries.

Thinking back on the misery involved in picking the berries nearly erases the pleasure of placing a spoonful of low blackberry pie with fresh cream on it in my mouth. There were only two good things about low blackberries. They were smaller and sweeter than high blackberries, so they required less sugar for the family pie, and the berries grew on top of the bramble away from the merciless thorns.

High blackberries, on the other hand, presented a different dilemma of pain and joy. The joy of high blackberries included the fact that you could stand up straight to pick them because they grew on high brambles that often reached above my head; however, the best and largest clumps always grew in the shadiest and deepest recesses of the thorny bushes.

High blackberry briars were even more difficult to pick through than low blackberry briars and there were more of them. Wearing gloves to pick them simply added yet another layer of clothing for the sharp thorns to catch on to, so I always picked without gloves knowing that that evening and the next day would be spent with

Mom squeezing and picking briars out of my fingers with a sharp needle.

After I picked all the blackberries that Mom needed, I sold them to the neighbors for one dollar a gallon. It hurt me to spend those blackberry dollars, because the pain and effort to earn them remained fresh in my memory for months after blackberry season was over.

Blackberry pickin' and ants in the pants...

When my nieces, Angie and Paula, grew up enough to hang out with me, they always wanted me to give them spending money. I told them that I knew how they could earn some money with the investment of a little bit of work. They were excited at the prospect of earning money and eager to begin. They thought it was the coolest thing, that Aunt Peggy would show them how to work and earn money. I took them to the high blackberry patches one hot July day to pick berries. As with everything I did with them, I played the clown. When I got hung up in a blackberry briar I would say, "Oh my God, ohhh lordy, oh Jesus, oh God help me" over and over until I untangled myself. They laughed so hard they forgot the briars were sticking them too, and even forgot the hot sun.

I always warned my nieces to watch where they were placing their feet as they walked around and into the tall brambles. "There could be snakes, ant hills, and stinging insects in here," I told them. "They like blackberries just like we do." As they spied yet another large clump of berries deeper in the vines, they forgot my warning just as I knew they would.

Angie was reaching high into the briars to fill her bucket with juicy blackberries. Not watching her feet, she stepped on an ant hill. I heard her yelling and looked around. The ants were crawling up her legs and had already reached her underpants. She was jumping up and down, scratching, and clawing at her body, but the ants had taken over the territory. Before I could get to her to help, she had stripped her clothes off and was standing in the blackberry patch stark naked. It was a "sight for sore eyes," as Mom would have said—a young developing girl standing in the woods stark naked. Paula and I helped her shake the ants out of her clothing. She dressed again, and we continued to pick blackberries all the while avoiding the ant hill and watching for others. I teased Angie the rest of the day. I asked her, "What if Bill Ralston had walked up on you standing there naked?" She was always quick with retorts to my teasing. She said, "I would have asked him to help me get the ants out of my clothes. Afterwards I probably would have been embarrassed."

I took Angie and Paula around to the neighbors to help them sell their berries, but by this time I was much smarter than I was as a child. Instead of telling the neighbors how much I wanted for the berries, I let them look at the juicy and shiny blackberries and have one or two to taste. They always said, "Oh my, they are so beautiful and sweet too. How much do you want for them?" My response after getting smarter with age was, "How much are they worth to you?" By letting the customer set the price, my nieces got four dollars a gallon for their high blackberries. Pretty soon, they were taking orders for more blackberries as the word spread about how big and sweet their berries were and how good they were in pies. By the end of each summer, for several years, my nieces had earned enough to buy many of the things girls want for the beginning of school in the fall.

We ate a lot of family pies during the summer while Mom was so busy with the garden. None tasted better than the ones made with fresh blackberries. Other ways that Mom fixed blackberries included putting sugar on them, and letting them set in the refrigerator for a day. She placed a dish on the table, and we dipped them into a saucer and poured cream over them.

Mom also canned blackberries for making pies in the winter season. She made blackberry jam the same way she made strawberry jam. We especially enjoyed blackberry jam mixed with cottage cheese, on peanut butter sandwiches, and on left-over warm bread. I enjoyed crumbling up my cornbread, dipping a few spoonfuls of blackberry jam on top, and eating it with milk.

Blackberry Dumplings Recipe...

Ingredients

Dumpling Dough
3½ cups self-rising flour
½ cup buttermilk
1 cup hog lard
2 cups water

Blackberries
1 quart berries
1¼ cups sugar
2 cups water

For dumplings, sift flour into a mixing bowl. Make a hole in the middle. Mix in buttermilk and lard. Work gently with fingers until a ball of dough appears. Knead dough gently. Place berries, sugar, and water in a pan. Bring to a boil. Pinch off pieces of dough and drop into the boiling fruit. Cover and simmer until dough is cooked. Dough will be floating on top of the berries when the mixture is done.

Wild Mushrooms

If there was adequate rain during the month of July, the mountains in Hopkins gap provided a bountiful supply of wild mushrooms. The first to arrive were called yellow mushrooms, and could be identified as edible by their smell and the consistency of the sticky, milk-like juice that dripped from them when they were broken off the stems.

Before the yellow mushrooms stopped growing, dark brown "leatherbacks" appeared along with them. The "leatherbacks" looked dry on top and were lined just like leather. They grew as large as a dinner plate when the season was good. Depending on the size of

Earnest Morris and Layton Lam display strings of "leatherbacks" they gathered in the mountains of Hopkins Gap. Earnest's baby son, Wayne, is examining his dad's collection for the day. (Picture courtesy of Mary Morris Turner)

the crop, folks just fried them and enjoyed them as a meat substitute. When the crop was abundant, they were canned so that they could be enjoyed throughout the winter.

Fried Mushrooms Recipe...

Ingredients

Wild mushrooms	2 cups flour
Salt	pepper
1 cup lard	

Clean the mushrooms and remove the caps. Split the large caps into four pieces to prevent curling up in the frying pan. Split the stems long ways to help with frying. Soak mushrooms and stems in salt water to remove any dirt hidden in the undersides of the caps. Refrigerate during soaking. Mix salt, pepper, and flour in a dish. Dip mushroom pieces into the mixture to cover both sides. Put lard in a skillet as needed starting with about ¼ inch. Heat until near smoking then put the mushroom pieces in the hot grease. Fry crispy brown on both sides, turning only once. Place on a dish towel or paper towel to drain excess grease. Serve hot.

Canned Mushrooms Recipe...

Ingredients
Wild mushrooms   salt
Water

Clean the mushrooms and split the larger ones in quarters. Pack into wide-mouth quart-size canning jars. Add a teaspoon of salt to each jar and fill with water to cover the mushrooms. Place lids on the jars and place in a water bath. Boil for 10 minutes. Remove the jars and turn the lids tight for sealing.

Peaches

The women of Hopkins Gap spent a good number of days in late July and early August canning peaches. In the early years of my childhood, Aunt Goldie had her own peach trees. Her peach trees shared the orchard with the apple trees. The peach trees were closest to the house, and included both cling and free-stone peaches. The names of the peach trees had long been lost. We just knew them by their taste and color. We called them the "yellow-fleshy peach trees," the "hard peach trees," the "early white peach trees," and the "cling peach trees." Cling peaches were mouth-watering in flavor, but the seeds would not come out of the peach. The cooks used these peaches for pickling.

Pickled Peaches Recipe...

Ingredients
1 gallons ripe cling peaches   6 cinnamon sticks
3 lbs. white sugar   whole cloves
3 cups cider vinegar

Peaches should be solid and just ripe. Boil a pan of water and pour over the peaches. Let them set for a few minutes until the skins slip off the peaches in your hands. Do not remove the peach seed. Pour off the hot water and replace with cold water. Skin the peaches and set aside. Combine the sugar, vinegar, and cinnamon sticks in a large cooking pot. Boil slowly for ½ hour. Dip a few peaches at a time into the hot mixture and cook them until tender but not too soft. Lift the peaches out of the mixture and pack them into hot quart or pint jars, tossing in a few whole cloves. Fill jars with the boiling syrupy mixture. Screw on the tops and seal.

Some peaches, when split open, released the large seed very easily with the use of a knife under the edge. These were known as freestone peaches. Mom liked to can these peaches to serve in the winter and to make winter pies.

Aunt Goldie's peach trees did not supply enough peaches for her family and our family, so Mom usually bought about five bushels from peach farmers near Broadway, Virginia. Uncle Shirley used his truck to haul peaches for both Mom and Aunt Ethel.

When the peaches arrived Mom sorted them according to level of ripeness. She placed the ripe peaches in a washing tub of cold water. This removed any dirt and most of the peach fuzz so that she didn't itch while she was canning them. She placed a pan in her lap and put about eight clean peaces in the pan and began processing them. She split each peach in half before peeling it. The large seed stuck in one half or the other until she used the edge of her knife to remove the seed, and then she peeled the halves. The halves were neatly packed into small-mouth quart canning jars. Mom mixed sugar and water to make syrup which she poured over the peaches in the jars before putting the lids on and processing them in her copper boiler.

Little hands make great peach packers...

One of the most meaningful times I spent with Mom was when she was canning peaches. When I was about eight years old, she called me into the kitchen. She took a small-mouth canning jar and asked me if I could stick my hand down in it. My little hand slid right down into the jar. She smiled and said, "You can be my little peach packer. My hands are too big to stack the peaches in the jars like I want them. You can help me make the peaches look good on the cellar shelf and make the work go faster." Because she was so encouraging, and bragged about how good I was at it, I packed and packed peaches for her for four or five years until my hands grew too large to fit into the jars. When she brought a can of peaches up from the cellar, she showed me how pretty they looked in the jar because they were so neatly stacked. I took great pride in my work and was very appreciative of Mom bragging about me to Aunt Goldie and Aunt Ethel.

Mom let her peelings drop into the pan on her lap and saved them to make peach jelly. She took the clean peelings and put them on the stove to boil in water. The juice from the peelings turned a nice color similar to the sunny side of the peach. It was usually a bright red-orange color. She made peach jelly using the recipe from a Sure-Jell box.

On those busy peach canning days, we knew we would have a fresh peach family pie, and over the next several days we were sure to have whirligigs made from fresh peaches.

Peach Whirligigs Recipe...

Ingredients

Dough	*Filling*
2 cups unsifted flour	5 large fresh peaches
2½ teaspoons baking powder	2 cups water
½ teaspoon salt	1½ cups sugar
½ teaspoon baking soda	3 tablespoons cornstarch
1/3 cup lard	¼ cup melted butter
¾ cup of buttermilk	¼ cup sugar
	1 teaspoon ground cinnamon
	Chopped walnuts or pecans
	(optional)

Peel, pit, and slice peaches. In a saucepan, over medium heat, combine peaches, water, sugar, and cornstarch. Cook while stirring constantly. Bring to a boil for one minute. Lower heat and keep warm. In a large mixing bowl, mix flour, baking powder, salt, baking soda, buttermilk and lard. Work with fingers to make soft dough. Using a floured surface, knead the dough about 8 times. Roll the dough into a 9-inch square. Rub butter on the square of dough. Combine ¼ cup sugar with cinnamon (and nuts if using them) and sprinkle on top of the buttered dough. Pour hot peach mixture in the bottom of a 8 x 8 baking dish. Roll dough into a log. Cut the log into 1½ slices. Place slices on top of the peach mixture. Bake for 20 to 25 minutes in 425 degree oven.

Peach Jam Recipe...

Ingredients

5 cups ripe fresh peaches	2 tablespoons fresh lemon juice
1¾ ounces powdered fruit pectin	3½ cups sugar
1 teaspoon butter, melted	

Peel, pit, and chop the peaches very fine. In a large cook pot, combine the peaches and lemon juice. In a small bowl combine the pectin and ¼ cup of the sugar and mix well. Stir into the peach mixture along with the butter. Over medium to high heat, bring the peach mixture to a full boil, stirring constantly. Stir in the remaining 3 ¼ cups sugar, return the mixture to a full boil, and cook for 1 minute, stirring constantly. Remove from heat and skim off any foam. Ladle the jam at once into hot, sterilized pint jars. Leave ½ inch space at the top of each jar. Wipe the jar rims with a clean, damp cloth. Fit the jars with hot lids, and tightly screw on the metal rings. Process in a bath of boiling water for 5 minutes (water should cover the jars about 1 inch), cool on a wire rack, and store in a cool, dry place.

The peach tree and the tragic childhood of my wayward sister...

My sister Brenda was the proverbial "accident waiting to happen." By the time she was fifteen months old, her curiosity was getting her into serious trouble. Her first life-threatening incident occurred when she dragged a chair up to the kitchen stove, climbed up, and spilled a pot of boiling ham broth down the front of her clothes. She fell off the chair into the hot ham broth, and Mom found her sliding on her stomach in the hot grease and screaming for her life. She had third degree burns on her stomach and hands. She carries the scars to this day.

Brenda at about the age when she ate the light bulb.

Another time, she got in the closet and found a light bulb. Obviously she thought it was a toy, so she took it to the stair steps. She crawled up the stairs to roll the light bulb down the steps. Of course, the bulb shattered into a million tiny pieces. When Mom found her that time, she was picking up the pieces and putting them in her mouth. Needless to say, her tongue was bleeding. Mom nicknamed her "Nosey" after the light bulb incident.

Shortly after that, she wiggled her way behind the wood stove where Mom kept a tin can of kerosene to help start the morning fires. Brenda spilled most of the kerosene on the floor then turned up the can and took a big swallow that was still in the can. She lost her breath from the fumes. Mom heard her struggling for her breath, and grabbed her up. Brenda came down with pneumonia shortly after the kerosene incident. Mom and I often wondered if the kerosene was the cause.

As do most kids when they are growing up, we all loved to climb trees, especially when there was a tempting ripe apple or peach at the very top. Brenda was about three years old, which means I was six years old, and we were playing in Aunt Goldie's peach orchard. Mom and Goldie had picked most of the peaches and were peeling and canning them on Aunt Goldie's back porch shaded by the huge Bartlett pear tree.

The chicken house blocked Mom and Goldie's view of the peach orchard, and I decided that Brenda and I would take advantage of being out of sight. We looked around in the trees for stray peaches. Brenda saw a really pretty peach hanging on a tree. It was a beautiful red and yellow as it waved just a little in the summer breeze. It seemed to be saying, "Come and get me. I am ripe and juicy." Before I could stop her, Brenda was climbing the peach tree and heading to the top for the delicious looking peach.

I climbed up behind her to try to stop her because I had already learned the hard way that it is much easier to climb up a tree than it is to get down. For once Brenda listened to me and turned to come down out of the tree. Suddenly she realized she was stuck and couldn't get down. Her little leg which had stretched enough to get up on a higher limb no longer reached where she needed to step. I tried to talk her down and gave her my hand, but she was afraid and started to cry. I came up with the idea of having her jump out of the tree and break her fall by landing on my back. She said she would try. I bent over, and she let go of her limb and dropped on my back. I couldn't see what happened to her, but she landed on my back and rolled over on the ground screaming. It turned out she had diagonally split her leg bone below her right knee—a severe break.

Thank God Aunt Goldie could drive. We didn't have a phone to call Dad or the ambulance. Mom and Aunt Goldie carried Brenda to the car and made the long trip to Broadway to see Dr. Watson. He set the bone and put a huge plaster cast on her leg. He told Mom it had to stay on for eight weeks. We all laughed at Brenda when she came home. We told her that Dr. Watson had put her in that big cast to slow her down some. She stayed quiet for a day or so, but soon devised ways to travel around the house. She sat on her butt and slid around on the floor to get where she wanted to go. In a week or so, she had crushed the plaster cast in several places. By the third week, Brenda asked us to put her in our little red wagon and pull her around the yard. We turned her over a few times, and the cast was crushed in even more places.

Our house had a cement slab front porch that was level with the ground. When Dad came home from work he parked his car at the edge of the porch. One day we were playing on the cement slab when Cousin George drove up in Aunt Goldie's car. He had just turned old enough to get his drivers' license so he was full of himself behind the wheel. He ran in the house to get some cream so Aunt Goldie could make butter. He stayed a while, as George always did, because Mom probably offered him cookies or a piece of pie.

We continued to pull Brenda around in the wagon. We took her down around the house into the back yard and then back to the cement slab front porch. We pulled her all around Aunt Goldie's car. Mom and George came to the door. He got in the car and Mom handed him the jar of cream through the car window. He started the motor. At that moment, I realized that we had left the little red wagon with Brenda in it directly in front of Aunt Goldie's car.

George was so excited about driving that he didn't see us jumping up and down and yelling, "Stop. Brenda is in front of the car."

Mom ran toward the wagon, but it was too late. George hit the wagon, upset it, and Brenda was penned under it. The wagon wheels made such a noise as they scraped under the car that George finally realized he was running over something and slammed on the brake. Brenda survived. Luckily, she lost only the skin on the toes of her broken leg. Her cast was crushed even more than before. The wagon had turned on its side and sort of protected her small body. Needless to say, Larry and I got a good whipping for leaving Brenda in front of the car. Brenda continued to be accident prone with a few more broken bones and another serious bought with pneumonia. She survived, however, and is still with us today.

New Potatoes

Potatoes were harvested two different times at my home. By mid summer, the potato bin was empty and Mom was buying potatoes. She often commented how that was such a waste of money when we had new potatoes growing just under the dirt in the garden. The first harvest was done on the sly for special summer dishes; the second harvest was for the winter. New potatoes that Mom grubbed from Dad's potato patch, much to his dismay, were one of my favorite summer treats. Dad hated for Mom to start digging "his" potatoes before the vines died. He would say, as he put a huge bite of creamed new potatoes in his mouth at supper, "Damn it, Myrt. I don't want you grubbin' in my tater patch. We won't have enough taters for the winter. One of his major worries was whether or not he would harvest enough potatoes to last all winter.

Mom knew exactly how to grub for potatoes. She took her potato pan and went out to the garden in early August, before the potato vines fell over and turned brown. She used her strong fingers to move the dirt away from the roots of the potato plant. She stuck her finger in among the roots and "grubbed" until she found the small potatoes growing on the ends. She only took new potatoes the size of a ping pong ball. Mom knew that she shouldn't take all the potatoes on one plant. She showed me as she explained, "The best way to do it, without killing the plant and making your daddy mad, is to skip around the potato patch and pick and choose plants to grub around. I've grubbed a lot of times when he didn't even know it. New potatoes peel real easy. Most of the skin comes off when you wash them." Mom had several great recipes that called for new potatoes. They had a taste all their own.

Creamed New Potatoes Recipe...

Ingredients
10 or 12 new potatoes, about the size of ping-pong balls, grubbed
    from the potato patch
Water (amount determined by number of potatoes)
1 cup of milk
½ stick of butter (or two large tablespoons of homemade butter)
Salt to taste
½ teaspoon of pepper
1 tablespoon corn starch

Clean the potatoes and cut into quarters. Put butter into a cook pot and heat until melted. Add potatoes and just cover with water. Boil the potatoes until tender but still in whole pieces. Salt to taste and add pepper. Pour milk in a separate bowl and stir in corn starch. Pour this mixture slowly into the potatoes as they boil. The potato broth will thicken and have nice chunks of potato in it. Serve over sliced homemade light bread.

New Potato Bread
New potato bread was a slight variation on the recipe for creamed new potatoes. Mom made this recipe when she had some light bread crusts around that she didn't want to waste. She always

told us, "If you eat bread crusts, you'll grow up to be pretty." Even though such a promise was hard to resist, and her homemade bread crusts were delicious, we always wanted the soft bread. I figured I was young enough that I could start eating bread crusts a little later and still reap their benefits. Even today when I eat bread crusts, I can hear Mom's voice promising future beauty. My future is much shorter than it was in those days, and my beauty has remained elusive.

Just before serving the creamed new potatoes, Mom toasted the bread crusts she had on hand. When she still used her wood stove, she smeared them with butter and put them in the oven until they were crisp. Later on, she put them in the toaster without butter. When the crusts were toasted, Mom broke them into quarters and pushed them into the thick, boiling potatoes. She served the dish immediately while the toast was still somewhat crisp.

When I think of this recipe, I have flash backs to warm, late summer days before school started. I remember lying by the open window upstairs on my bed reading Zane Grey books. I would doze off to sleep, wake up, and then read some more. As I awoke from my naps, the various aromas of supper would visit my nose, as the smells left the kitchen and wafted in through the window. The smell of toasting bread crusts alerted me to new potato bread for supper.

Cucumbers

New potatoes were only one part of the bounty from the garden during the summer. Mom always planted a patch of cucumbers at the back corner of her side of the garden near the road. She guarded the patch as if her life depended on it. "I want a lot of pickles this year, and if I can I'd like to make some bread and butter pickles too," she said, as she warned Brenda and me not to go near the patch if we were "having a period."

One touch can kill...

One summer Mom's cucumber vines were thriving beautifully,

then suddenly one day they were wilted and dying. When she saw them, she said, "Well, I'll be damned. That woman who stopped in here yesterday to talk to me was having her period." Some extension agent had stopped on the road to ask directions while Mom was picking her cucumbers. She complimented Mom on her beautiful garden. The agent parked her car and was in the garden talking with Mom for half an hour.

Mom was suspicious of any female visitor who stopped in to buy milk, butter or cottage cheese. She always had her porch windows full of potted geraniums and other blooming flowers. As the buyers walked toward the kitchen door, they could not avoid seeing the elegant plants. They often asked for "slips" off of Mom's plants. Her answer was always, "If you ask for a slip and I give it to you, it won't grow. Sometime when you stop in to get your butter, you can just pick off a slip and don't tell me about it. Then it will grow for you. But, let me warn you. Don't touch my plants if you are having a period, because you will kill all of them."

Most customers just looked at Mom with the strangest expression on their faces. Then they asked, "What did you say?" That was all Mom needed to hear, and she would spend the next hour sharing horror stories about her dead cucumbers, house plants, and spoiled food—all killed by a woman "having her period."

One day I asked, "Mom, how do you know that women kill plants during their period? Her answer was very typical, "It says so in the Bible. It's because of Eve givin' in to the snake. God cursed her with a monthly period and made her dirty."

I heard this explanation so many times that when I got old enough, I searched the Bible for that story and many others that I was told were in the Holy Word. I didn't find them.

Mom picked over the cucumber patch every day so she could find the little cucumbers. She made the best little pickles I have ever eaten.

Cucumber Pickles Recipe...

Ingredients

Small cucumbers   salt

Vinegar   sugar

Pickling spices

Clean cucumbers and place in a large cook pot. Mix sugar, vinegar, salt, and pickling spices to taste. Pour mixture over pickles and bring to a boil. Reduce heat and simmer while packing the pickles into jars. When the jars are packed, bring mixture to boil once more and pour into the jars with the pickles. Put lids on the jars and let seal.

Bread and Butter Pickles Recipe...

Ingredients

About 30 medium sized cucumbers	8 large white onions
3 large sweet peppers	½ cup salt
5 cups apple cider vinegar	2 tablespoons mustard seed
1 teaspoon tumeric	½ teaspoon ground cloves

Clean the cucumbers and slice very thin crosswise. Slice onions and chop peppers; combine with the cucumbers and blend salt into the mixture. Cover with a clean white flour sack and let stand for 3 hours. The mixture will produce its own liquid. Drain the liquid from the cucumber mixture. Combine vinegar, sugar and spices in a large cooking pot. Bring to a boil and add the cucumber mixture. Heat until just about to boil, but do not boil. While hot, pack the pickles into jars, leaving ½ inch of space at the top of the jar. Remove air bubbles by running a table knife around the inside of the jars. Wipe the rims of the jars to remove any seeds. Turn on the lids and tighten. Water bath the jars for 10 minutes to seal the lids.

Mom didn't pick all the cucumbers while they were small; she had several ways that she served the larger ones. Sometimes she peeled them, quartered them, and served them as a condiment to compliment other things she had for supper. We ate them with our fingers and a sprinkling of salt on top. One of my favorite cucumber dishes was sour cream cucumbers. These were great with fried potatoes and pinto beans and a great way to use up the onions that were still taking up space in the garden.

Sour Cream Cucumbers Recipe...

Ingredients
3 or 4 large crisp cucumbers fresh from the garden
2 medium sized onions
1 cup of sour cream
1 and ½ tablespoons of vinegar
½ teaspoon of salt
2 tablespoons of sugar
Black pepper to taste

Peel the cucumbers and slice crossways, as thin as possible. Place them in a clear glass dish (The clear dish just lets you see how pretty they are. There's no special reason.)
Sprinkle salt over the slices. Set aside.
Peel the onions and slice them on top of the cucumber slices
Mix a dressing with the sour cream, vinegar, and sugar. Add black pepper to taste.
Pour the dressing over the sliced cucumbers and onions. Mix, chill, and serve.

Red Beets

A summer never passed that Mom didn't plant red beets. She claimed they were good for my "anemia" which I really don't think I ever had. She thought anemia caused me to take naps every afternoon in the summer. She didn't know that I rarely took naps; I read books instead. Pretending to be tired and needing a nap was the only way I could get away from the summer work for a short time.

Red beets matured at different intervals because of the way we planted them. We dug a deep row all the way across the garden to loosen the soil. Then we filled the row with softened soil and gently sprinkled seeds along the top. With our fingers we picked up soft soil and sprinkled on top of the seeds. The result was a very thick row of beets. As some of them matured we pulled them to eat, so the others would have room to grow. We wanted larger beets for pickling.

The first time I pulled beets for Mom to pickle she forgot to tell me not to cut the tops all the way down to the beets. I messed up about a half of a bushel before she caught me. "I thought you knew how to cut the tops off," she yelled, "Now these beets are going to bleed to death when I cook them." It was true. By the time those mangled beets were tender enough to pickle, their color was a light grayish red. I felt really bad about what I had done. I asked Mom if we cooked them with other beets, would their color come back. Her answer was, "No, the harm is done. Beets will not take in color after they've lost it. All the stuff that is good for you to eat is now in the water." I felt so bad that I offered to drink the water. Mom just glared at me. I learned my lesson with beets and have taught the same lesson to other people many times.

The best red beet recipes were made with the smallest and most tender beets. Sometimes Mom just boiled them and put them on the table so we could slice them and add salt and butter. We called these buttered beets. Another excellent recipe was for Harvard beets.

Harvard Beets Recipe...

Ingredients

3 cups cooked diced beets   1 teaspoon salt
½ cup sugar   ¼ cup vinegar
1 tablespoon cornstarch   ¼ cup water
2 tablespoons butter

Mix the sugar, salt and cornstarch. Add vinegar and water and stir until smooth. Boil for 5 minutes. Add beets to the hot sauce and let stand for 30 minutes. Just before serving, bring to a boil again and add butter.

Mom and Aunt Ethel joined forces every summer to can pickled beets. These were served as a condiment throughout the winter and were always requested by the head butchers on hog butchering day. The juice was saved to make pickled eggs for Easter.

Pickled Beets Recipe...

Ingredients

Beets   Vinegar
Sugar   Pickling spices
Water as needed

Gather beets from the garden. Wash and cut the plant tops off leaving about two inches on the beet. Boil the beets until tender; test tenderness by sticking one or two of them with a fork. Skins should slip off easily when tender. Skin the beets and cut into sizes appropriate for canning. Place beets in a large pan and cover with a mixture (amounts determined by taste) of sugar, vinegar, pickling spices, and water. Heat the mixture until near boiling. Take out the beet pieces and place in canning jars. Pour hot liquid over the beets. Place lids on the hot cans and seal.

Sweet Corn

While I absolutely loved to eat sweet corn, I resented its presence in the garden. To me, it grew too tall and blocked my view of the other vegetables. I always wanted Mom and Dad to plant it at the edge of the garden near the cow pasture so it wouldn't be so ugly when it started to dry up after producing the mouth-watering ears. My argument for planting in that space, I thought, was one of the best I had ever made up. I said to Dad, "When you cut the fodder in the fall, all you will have to do is throw it across the fence to the cows instead of dragging it all the way across the garden." They never followed my suggestion because that side of the garden was Dad's potato patch, and that was sacred ground. Each summer they planted the corn rows in the same spot where the early greens and onions had grown in the spring.

Every year I dreaded the day that school would start. The sweet corn blades rattling in the August breezes would remind me that the first day of school was rapidly approaching. My bedroom window opened out onto the garden right where the corn was planted; therefore, I could hear the corn calling me to the school house.

Mom didn't do much with sweet corn except to cook corn on the cob. She had a way of preparing it, so it was perfect every time.

Perfect Corn on the Cob Recipe...

Ingredients

Ears of sweet corn   Salt
Water   Butter

Bring a large pot of water to a rolling boil over high heat. Meantime, shuck and remove the silk. Drop 3 to 4 ears at a time into the boiling water so as to not cool the water. Leave the ears in the boiling water for 3 minutes. Remove, brush with butter, and sprinkle with salt. Serve.

Rug houses, corn silk cigars, and corn cob battles...

I think Mom gave us her old rag rugs and told us to go make something with them just to get us out of the house so she could get her work done. Whatever her reason, we did just that. We took the rugs and some sticks we found on the wood yard and headed for the orchard. We rigged a rectangular structure with the sticks and hung the rugs over it to make a shelter. The rugs had holes in them and we arranged the holes to work as windows so we could see out.

The Brown children lived across the road from the orchard, and they saw what we were doing with the rugs. They wanted to get in on the action, but we had other things in mind to do in our rug house. We had learned, on one of our many trips to Hopkins Gap to play with our cousins, that dried corn silk is fun to smoke. They showed us how to roll a stogie as large as a cigar using brown paper bags.

Little did we know that our rug house would not allow us to experiment with smoking without being seen. We had already tried smoking by stealing a pack of Dad's Lucky Strikes, but we made the mistake of taking our sister, Brenda, with us. We made her take a couple of puffs off a cigarette so she wouldn't rat on us. She coughed a while then ran straight to the house and told Mom. Mom came out on the front porch and saw a cloud of smoke rising in the air just over the hill. Needless to say, we all got a whipping except for Brenda.

As we sat in our rug house looking out the holes, we saw the Brown children come out of their house, cross the orchard, and disappear in the corn field. After a half hour or so, they came out with their arms loaded with ears of corn. As they passed our rug house, we went out and asked them what they were doing with the "field" corn. They said, "We're gonna cook it and eat it. That's all we have to eat." Just about that time, Larry noticed the dried corn silk at the end of the ears they were holding. I could almost see his mind working. Corn silk, rug house, brown paper.....Hmmmmm. He asked, "Can we have the silk off the corn? The Brown children answered, "We don't keep it. You can have it." We all helped Larry pull the silk off the corn, anticipating our first corn-silk cigarettes. One of us ran to the house and got a brown paper bag and some matches.

We crawled in our rug house, rolled our stogies, and lit up. The smoke started pouring out of the holes in the rug. Meanwhile the Brown children had gone into their house and cooked and eaten the stolen corn. We felt much empowered by our stogies, so when they came out again we yelled that we were going to tell the farmer they were stealing his corn. Suddenly heavy objects started landing on top of our rug house. When we rolled out, we saw a shower of heavy corn cobs that had been chewed on, flying across the fence at us. Mom heard all the yelling and came to the orchard. She found our stash of corn silk, partly smoked stogies, and other paraphernalia. She grabbed a switch and whipped Larry and me. Later, when she wasn't mad anymore she talked to us about the dangers of smoking corn silk. She said, "You can suck fire down your throat and into your lungs doin' that stuff. I never want to catch you again." We became even more interested in corn silk stogies, and we also became smarter. Mom never caught us again.

Tomatoes

Oh how I looked forward to fresh tomatoes, warmed from the sun, peeping through the green leaves of the plant. Mom had to force me to eat other food besides tomatoes. I lost so much weight every summer that she swore she could read the Bible through my ribs. Just before school started one summer, she asked Aunt Goldie to drive her and me to Broadway to see Dr. Watson. She worried that

I had worms or something worse since I weighed only seventy-five pounds soaking wet. The old doctor checked me over and laughed at her. "Let her eat as many tomatoes as she wants. This kid is as healthy as a horse," he told Mom. "She's letting her body tell her what she needs to eat. That's the way the cave men ate. When a fruit or vegetable came in season, they gorged themselves on it and then moved on to the next season. She'll fatten up when cold weather comes this fall." This speech still didn't get Mom off my back. She force-fed me a few fried potatoes with my supper of tomatoes, and of course, I did get some bread with my peanut butter and tomato sandwiches that I ate at dinner each day.

Mom did everything possible with her tomato crop. We ate sliced tomatoes every evening until she got tired of slicing them. The next stage was quartering them, and finally she just washed them, put them on the table in a dish with a sharp peeling knife.

The tomato season ends with the first heavy frost. When the nights became clear and cold, Mom gathered some green tomatoes and fried them. At that point, I knew Mom was sick and tired of tomatoes. Meanwhile she had canned a hundred quarts or more, made juice, tomato sauce, and tomato preserves.

Fried Green Tomatoes Recipe...

Ingredients
5 to 6 large green tomatoes	corn meal
1-2 eggs beaten	salt and pepper
Hog lard	

Remove the stem and blossom end. Cut crosswise into slices about ¼ inch thick. Sprinkle lightly with salt and pepper. Dip each slice into beaten egg and then into cornmeal making sure to coat both sides of each slice. In an iron skillet, heat about ½ inch of lard. Place the tomato slices in the fat and fry until brown. Turn and fry the other side until brown. Serve.

Canned Tomatoes Recipe...

Ingredients
Lots of medium ripe tomatoes
Salt and water

Pick and wash the tomatoes. Place them in a large dish pan. Boil water and pour over the tomatoes. Let them stand for a few minutes until the skins begin to come loose. Peel them, cut out any bad spots, and quarter them. Pack into quart jars. Put one teaspoon of salt in the jar; fill the jar with warm water. Place the lids on the jars but do not tighten. Place the jars in a canning boiler. Fill the boiler with water up to the shoulders of the jars. Bring the water to a boil and cook the jars for 30 minutes. Carefully remove the jars, tighten the lids, and let the jars cool. Store the jars in a cool dark cellar.

Tomato Juice Recipe...

Ingredients

4 gallons very ripe tomatoes	6-8 large sweet green peppers
6-8 large onions	1 large bunch celery
Salt	sugar

Wash the tomatoes and cut off stem end and bottom. Leave the skins on. Quarter the tomatoes into a large cook pot. Trim the peppers, remove the seeds and chop into the pot. Clean and quarter the onions. Clean the celery and pull off the strings. Do not throw away the leaf ends. Cut celery into 2 to 3 inch pieces. Add to the quartered tomatoes along with the leaf ends. Mix the contents of the pot. Add about 4 cups of water. Bring to a boil and stir the vegetables until they are boiling hard. Reduce heat and simmer until all ingredients are tender. Remove from the heat and force the mixture through a Foley food mill. Discard anything that does not go through the mill. Pour the juice into a large pot, bring to a boil, and pour it into quart jars. Add one teaspoon salt and one teaspoon sugar. Place lids and rings loosely on the jars. Water bath the juice for thirty minutes. Remove jars and cool. Store in a damp, cool cellar.

Tomato Sauce Recipe...

Ingredients

2 gallons ripe tomatoes	6 large sweet green peppers
6 large onions	2 tablespoons salt
1½ cups sugar	1½ cups brown sugar
1 cup of cider vinegar	2 tablespoons pickling spice (wrapped in a piece of white cloth and tied)

Peel and quarter the tomatoes, clean the peppers and chop the onions. In a large pot, mix and cook all the ingredients rapidly until the mixture is reduced to half. The cook must stay with the pot so the contents do not stick and burn. Lower the heat and simmer until thick. Pour into quart jars, loosely turn the lids. Process the jars in a water bath for fifteen minutes.

Tomato Preserves Recipe...

Ingredients

10 cups tomatoes quartered	4-5 pounds of sugar
Grated rind and juice of 3 lemons	2 tablespoons cinnamon

Scald, peel and quarter the tomatoes. Add sugar, cover with a clean cloth and let stand overnight at room temperature. The next morning, drain the juice into a large pan and bring to a boil. Boil rapidly until the juice spins a thread; that is, until a string of tomato juice clings to the spoon when you lift it from the boiling pot. Add the tomatoes, rind, lemon juice and cinnamon. Bring to boil again and boil until the preserves are thick and clear. Use the hot-water bath canning method to preserve in small glass jars.

During the winter, Mom used her canned tomatoes in several of our favorite dishes including her to-die-for vegetable soup. She added sausage meat balls to her tomato sauce for spaghetti. We drank the tomato juice with our meals or for a snack during the day.

Tomato Bread Recipe...

Ingredients

1 quart of canned tomatoes	homemade bread crusts
1 tablespoon sugar	1 tablespoon corn starch

Empty the tomatoes into a cook pot. Add sugar to taste. Bring to a boil. Mix corn starch with a small amount of water and pour mixture into the pot stirring until thick. Tear bread crusts into pieces and submerge in the tomato mixture.
Simmer until bread is soaked. Serve.

Tomatoes with Macaroni Recipe...

Ingredients

1 quart of canned tomatoes	1½ cups of elbow macaroni, dry
Salt and sugar	water

Put enough water in a cook pot to boil the macaroni until done.

Drain any excess water. Add the tomatoes to the macaroni. Add salt and sugar to taste. Bring to a boil for 4 to 5 minutes. Serve.

Vegetable Soup Recipe...

Ingredients. It is difficult to list the ingredients for Mom's soup because she just tossed in whatever she had available in the garden or in the refrigerator. For instance, if she had a few stalks of celery left over from another recipe, then the soup would have celery in it. If she had left over pinto beans, they went in the soup. Therefore, I am going to list the basic ingredients, and the cook can throw in whatever is available.

2 quarts canned tomatoes	Meat broth. (Could be broth from
Potatoes	boiled ham, backbone,
Salt and pepper to taste	occasional beef, boiled
4 large carrots	venison or pork shoulder.)
Corn	Green beans
	Sugar to taste

Bring the meat broth to a boil. Add canned tomatoes. Clean and chop carrots. Add carrots with any other slower cooking vegetables. Clean and toss in other available vegetables. Peel and cut potatoes into 1 inch squares. Add toward the end of cooking. When potatoes are tender, add salt, pepper, and sugar to taste. Serve.

Cabbage

By the first of August, one vegetable after another was ready to be picked and canned. Pole beans were ready and had to be picked off the vines about every three days. The red beets were being pickled about once a week as they matured. Often they had to be put off until the rush was over, but leaving them in the ground for a short while was not a problem. It was mainly the cabbage that had to be harvested when it was ready or the heads would burst open and waste. Before enough cabbage matured for sauerkraut making, Mom would cut a head and make a couple of great cabbage dishes.

Boiled Cabbage Recipe...

Ingredients
1 small head of cabbage   meat broth
Salt and pepper to taste   water

Split the cabbage heat and shred away from the core with a sharp knife while holding the cabbage on the edge. Toss the core in the slop bucket for the pigs. Place meat broth into a medium sized cook pot. Bring to a boil. Add water to dilute meat flavoring to taste. Put shredded cabbage in the broth. Boil until tender. Just before serving, add salt and pepper to taste.

Fried Cabbage Recipe...

Ingredients
1 small head of cabbage   ¼ cup of lard
Salt and pepper to taste   ¾ cup of water

Split the cabbage heat and shred away from the core with a sharp knife while holding the cabbage on the edge. Heat the lard in a cast iron skillet. Add the shredded cabbage. Sprinkle salt and pepper on top and pour water over the cabbage. Cover the pan and cook until the water has evaporated. Remove the lid and stir the cabbage until it begins to brown a little. Remove and serve.

Sauerkraut

Folks in Hopkins Gap made sauerkraut for more than 150 years, and they probably didn't understand many of the benefits. They only knew this was a good way to preserve their cabbage through the winter. Now it is commonly known that fresh, raw cabbage is very rich in vitamin C, and contains enough in one cup to supply a whole day's needs. Cooked cabbage and sauerkraut have about one-half of the RDA of vitamin C per cup, but who can stop eating after one cup of Hopkins Gap sauerkraut?

Sauerkraut is a self-fermented, cured product resulting from a summer of back-breaking work--planting, hoeing, replacing plants picked off by the blackbirds, and figuring out how to prevent cabbage worms destroying the crop. Spring had no sooner peeked around an April cloud than the cabbage butterflies would be drifting into the yard, then into the garden, searching out new cabbage plants in which to lay their eggs.

Many of the best gardeners had already prepared for their early arrival by planting a row of thyme about six inches from the cabbage plants. Cabbage butterflies hate thyme. As an extra measure of insurance, some folks threw dill seeds over the young cabbage heads. Cabbage butterflies just don't like a house with dill in it. Later on, in desperation, Mom used Seven dust on her cabbage.

Mom started her cabbage patches, as she called them, with plants that she bought at Whetsel Seed Company. She said, "I always get a big bunch, maybe fifty plants, because I had to replace so many that didn't survive the black birds pullin' 'em up or the rabbits chewin' 'em to pieces." (My brother, John, often helped Mom protect her cabbage plants. He stood at the upstairs window with his .22 rifle and shot the black birds and rabbits when they came in the garden to pull up or nibble on the cabbage plants.) "I kept the extras in a tin can with a little water in the bottom and used 'em along as I needed 'em. It all turned out pretty good because I had young cabbage growin' along as the first cabbage was ready to cut."

Mom planted her cabbages in long rows of fifteen plants

per row. She had a beautiful cabbage patch in the summer of 1994 just after my daddy died. As you can see in the picture, Mom spent most of her grieving time in the garden with her hoe and walking stick. There was not a weed to be found in her one-quarter acre garden.

Myrtle Shifflett (Mom) leaning on her walking stick as she surveyed her garden in 1994.

As the cabbage heads grew larger, Mom made frequent trips to the garden to watch for signs that the heads were tight enough to produce the most shredded cabbage. To maximize the amount of sauerkraut, it was necessary to catch the heads at the point when they were the most firm and just before they started exploding from the pressure, as cabbage grows from the inside of the head and puts pressure on the outer leaves. One important sign of ultimate firmness was when the cabbage head turned a whitish color and had a shiny appearance. Sometimes a tiny crack in the outer-most leaf indicated that an explosion was going to happen within the next day or so. To those who have taken excellent care of their cabbage patch, a cabbage head explosion is a sad

Mom's cabbage rows, summer 1994.

and sickening sound much like a muffled shot gun blast. It is sudden, unexpected, and leaves nothing but unsalvageable shreds of cabbage all around the original plant.

Most gardeners could predict the day to begin harvesting the cabbage. Mom said to me, "We'll have to start making kraut in a day or two." Before I was old enough to really know my mom, I prayed for rain thinking that she wouldn't go in the garden to cut the cabbage if it was raining. After observing her for several years, I recognized that rain would not stop her from cutting her cabbage when the time was right. She simply put on her boots and a long sleeved shirt, placed her military surplus hard hat on her head, and marched into the garden to cut the cabbage. She always called Aunt Ethel and Uncle Shirley to make arrangements for them to help. She said, "I just checked the cabbage heads, and they will be ready to cut by the end of the week. Which day can you all help me then?" Mom always knew that her daughter-in-law, Hilda, would help too. When the cabbage crop was bountiful, Aunt Ethel and Hilda each brought their own kraut jar. Mom shared her cabbage heads with them, knowing all the while that they would share with her when their cabbage was ready to cut.

In anticipation of the kraut cutting, the necessary tools were gathered from around the farm and brought to the wash house for cleaning. The tools included the ten gallon crock called the sauerkraut jar. It was a whitish color on the bottom with a thick brown colored stripe at the top. It had handles that were molded right into the sides of the crock. Some sauerkraut jars had wire handles that had been placed on the sides when the jar was made in the kiln. The sides and bottom of the sauerkraut jar were about one inch thick so that they could withstand a good pounding with the sauerkraut stumper.

The stumper was about four feet long and hand carved from a solid piece of poplar wood. The handle was carved so that it was easy to hold onto. The bottom of the stumper was left wide so it covered a lot of cabbage when it was pounded up and down in the sauerkraut jar. The ancient cabbage cutter and the kraut stumper were taken off the nails on which they hung since the previous summer, and the cob webs were dusted off. The sauerkraut jar and tools were given a good scrubbing with mild bleach water, then rinsed squeaky clean with cold water. The kraut cutters varied most in the number of blades. Some had two sharp blades embedded at an angle in solid walnut wood. Others had three blades. The three-bladed cutters made the kraut jar fill up fast. The last piece of equipment was a somewhat round, flat river rock from the Shoemaker River in Hopkins Gap.

In the summer of 1994, Aunt Ethel and Hilda each brought their kraut cutters, and with Mom's cutter, there were three people shredding kraut at the same time. The cabbage patch pictured previously produced seventy-five gallons of sauerkraut.

Early in the morning on kraut cutting day, Mom and I headed for the cabbage patch with a huge butchering knife. Mom walked up and down the cabbage rows looking for the firm heads that were close to exploding. Once she identified a head that was ready, she would lean over, bend the cabbage head to the side, and begin to cut through the stalk. The stalks tend to be tough, making the cutting a very difficult job. However, Mom had the strength to cut the cabbage head out of its bed of tough leaves because, at this point, she had been cutting cabbage and making kraut for more than fifty years. To her this was just another seasonal chore, among many, that comes from planting a garden and preserving its bounty. I never heard her complain about the hard work of gardening and canning. I did hear her complain if the summer was dry, and her garden didn't produce as much as she thought she needed to feed the family over the winter.

Once Mom had cut through the tough stalk, she stood up, and while holding the cabbage head in her left hand, she whacked off

Mom uses her walking stick to show me a cabbage head that is ready to harvest for sauerkraut

Mom removes the outer leaves so she can get to the tough cabbage stalk.

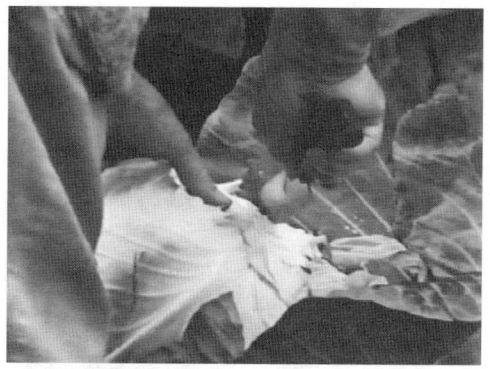 

Mom is making her final cut through the cabbage stalk.

This cabbage head weighed ten pounds. It was about the average size taken from Mom's cabbage patch in the summer of 1994.

the dirty outer leaves by hacking the knife into the base of the leaves near the stalk that she had just severed. The result was a nice round cabbage head with most of the garden dirt removed.

Mom carried the heads, one by one, and placed them in a large washing tub of cold water. By this time, Aunt Ethel, Uncle Shirley, and Hilda had arrived with some of Mom's grandchildren. My niece, Kathleen, also came to help. This made four generations working together to make sauerkraut out of Mom's beautiful cabbage heads.

After a careful washing, the cabbage heads were split into quarters. Three of us were sitting with the kraut cutters positioned between our knees as we waited for the first cabbage head quarters to be handed to us. We then rubbed the edge of the cabbage back and forth, with a lot of pressure, across the sharp blades. The shreds began to fall like snow into the kraut jars. The jars began to fill very rapidly.

Mom was supervising, so she watched as we cut. She stopped

us when the jars had about two inches of cabbage shreds in them. Taking a handful of salt from a large bag she kept at her side, she sprinkled it on top of the shredded cabbage. After the next two inches of cabbage, she added another handful of salt. Then she asked me to pick up the kraut stumper and begin to stump the cabbage down into the kraut jar. The reason the cabbage is stumped is to release the juice from the shredded cabbage so it can blend with the salt.

Mom said, "Now please be careful. Don't stump too hard. You might crack the jar." I stumped the shreds until the juice from the salt and cabbage mixture began to bubble up. At this point, Mom reached into the jar and put her fingers into the juice. She tasted the juice to see if it had the right amount of salt.

Mom tastes the cabbage juice to see if it has the right amount of salt. Uncle Shirley supervises in the background, while Aunt Ethel shreds cabbage into a dish pan.

After each layer and the subsequent stumping, she reached her fingers into the cabbage and tasted the juice that was by now higher than the shredded cabbage in the jar. She explained as she tasted, "The salt has to be just right. Too much will ruin the kraut and turn it slimy. Too little salt won't let the cabbage ferment and turn into sauerkraut."

We cut cabbage for several hours until we had three ten gallon jars nearly full. At one point, Hilda's kraut cutter was not cutting right. Mom examined the cutter and determined that one of the blades was loose. Uncle Shirley stepped up and said he could fix the problem. He hammered a small block of wood to the bottom side of the kraut cutter and stabilized the loose blade. Hilda went back to sliding the cabbage across the blades and all was well. The cabbage was turned over and over as it slid across the blades. All that was

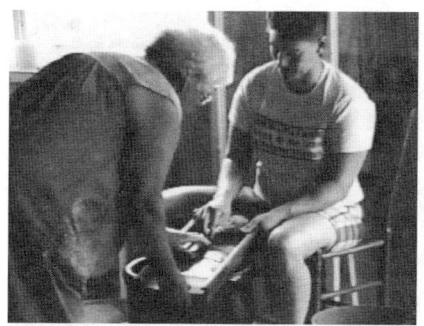

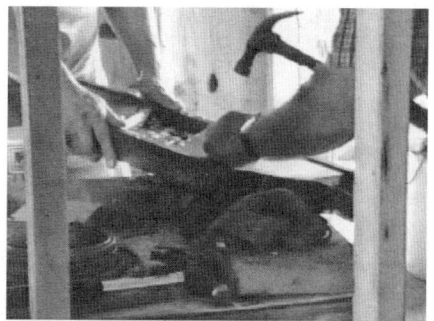

Mom examines Hilda's kraut cutter to see if she can figure out why it is not cutting as it should.

left was the bitter core of the cabbage head, which was fed to the hogs.

During a previous cabbage cutting experience, I learned that it was not a good time to let your mind wander, as one slip of the hand can result in fingertips in the sauerkraut.

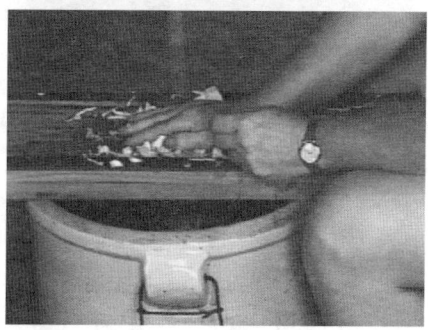

The author demonstrates the shredding of the loose leaves. On this particular occasion, there were no fingertips in the sauerkraut.

The most dangerous time was when all that was left of the cabbage head was the larger leaves that had been knocked loose by the cutter blades. Because nothing is wasted if it can be used, these leaves and pieces were carefully piled on the cutter, and, with the butt of the hand, were rubbed over the blades for shredding.

The cabbage heads were shredded until the kraut jars are filled to about three inches from the top. If more cabbage was needed to fill the jars, a trip back to the garden for a few more heads was made. On this day in 1994, several more heads of cabbage were needed to fill the jars. Mom and Uncle Shirley, along with two generations of young learners, went back into the garden to cut more cabbage heads.

After the kraut jars were filled, Mom went back to the garden

and brought in nine large cabbage leaves—three for each jar. She washed the leaves, and used them as a cover on top of the shredded cabbage.

The leaves serve as a barrier between the shredded cabbage and the weight that goes on top of the cabbage to hold it under the juice. Mom would tuck the edges of the leaves down the inside edges of the jar. The inside curved part of the leaf goes down over the contents of the jar and provides a canopy cover over the salted cabbage.

On top of the leaves, Mom placed a large round slab of wood cut especially for this purpose. On top of the wood she laid her heavy flat river rock. She explained that the weight of the rock would keep the salty cabbage juice covering the cabbage. This was necessary for the fermentation process and to prevent any uncovered cabbage from rotting and ruining the entire jar of sauerkraut.

A clean white cloth was then placed over top of the whole jar and held in place by a piece of elastic from the top of my dad's worn out jockey shorts. (Nothing was wasted if Mom could find a good use for it.) In later years, she added a sheet of plastic over the cloth to further protect the fermenting cabbage.

At the end of the long day's work, we had thirty gallons of

shredded cabbage on the way to becoming sauerkraut for the coming winter. Four generations of my family had been present to help, to learn, and to look forward to the variety of dishes that Mom, Hilda, and Aunt Ethel would cook and serve from our efforts on that cloudy, drizzly summer day in 1994.

During the next week or two, Mom visited the wash house to check on her fermenting cabbage. She found it bubbling out of the jars onto the plastic tarps she had placed under them. On about the ninth or tenth day, she would remove the under wear elastic and lift the plastic cover to taste test the sauerkraut. Usually it was ready to can by the eleventh day. She canned it by scooping it out of the kraut jar and into large pans that she would heat on the stove. While it was boiling, she stuffed it into quart jars, put on new lids, and turned them tight. The heat from the boiling sauerkraut sealed the canning jars. She let the cans cool in the wash house, and then carried them into the root cellar under the house and sat them on the shelves, along with her beautiful jars of green beans, pickles, peaches, corn, tomatoes, and lima beans.

Mom tried to teach me how to judge the sauerkraut, but I never acquired the skill that she had. She let me reach into the jar first and put a little bite of kraut in my mouth. She said, "Here, you need to learn how to tell when the sauerkraut is ready to can." I tasted it, but if I said it was ready, she would disagree after taking her taste. If I said it wasn't ready, she often said it was. As years have gone by, I am certain that she didn't disagree with me every time out of pure meanness. I believe she did want to teach me her skills, but was not exactly ready to hand over her knowledge and control of this and other food preparation and processing techniques. I still ponder those kinds of things even today.

This picture was taken in my brother, Warnie's root cellar. He and his wife, Dianna follow in the tradition handed down by Mom and other Hopkins Gap folks. (2005).

Fried Sauerkraut Recipe...

Ingredients
1 quart jar of sauerkraut
2 tablespoons of lard
¼ cup of water
Sprinkle of sugar

Use an iron skillet. Place lard in the skillet and heat until near smoking. Drain brine off the sauerkraut. Spoon it from the jar into the hot lard. Sprinkle sugar over the top and pour water on the kraut. Cover and cook. About 15 minutes before serving, remove the lid and turn the kraut. Fry it down until the water has evaporated. Serve.

Sauerkraut Dumplings Recipe...

Ingredients
1 quart of canned sauerkraut

Meat broth
Biscuit dough

Drain the brine off the sauerkraut and rinse (if desired).
Empty the sauerkraut into a fairly large cook pot.
Pour meat broth over the sauerkraut until there is about 1 inch of broth over the top of the kraut.
Bring to a boil and cook until the meat broth has time to flavor the kraut.
While the kraut is boiling, drop biscuit dough on top of the boiling kraut.
Cover and wait about 15 minutes before uncovering the pot.
You will find that the biscuits have steamed, risen, and cover the sauerkraut with a delicious cloud of tasty dumplings. It is ready to serve. For a tasty combination, serve it with mashed potatoes and pinto beans.

Sauerkraut and Pork Chops Recipe...

Ingredients
1 quart of canned sauerkraut
Meat broth
4 fresh pork chops
1 cup shredded cheddar cheese (mild or sharp)

Open and drain brine from sauerkraut
Pour kraut into 9 x 15 baking dish
Pour meat broth over the kraut
Sprinkle cheese on top
Place 4 pork chops on top of the cheese
Bake at 400 for 45 minutes (depending on how thick the chops are)

The "Dog Days" of summer...

We were not very far into summer until "Dog Days" started. They began around July 7 and didn't end until August 11. Grandma Molly always warned us about the dangers of dog days. First, she said we could not go in the river. Here it was the hottest part of the summer and the time when we were all working harder to put up food, than any other time of the year. I remember being absolutely furious with her, because Mom listened to every word she said as if Grandma Molly had a private line to God. Nothing would have felt better than rolling around in the swimming hole after a day of picking blackberries or making sauerkraut; but, it was off limits. We weren't allowed to go. Grandma said, "If you go in the river during dog days, you will get falls sores all over your body. If you cut yourself or kick your toe or anything, it won't heal." Of course, she had several horror stories about children who had died from dog days sores and others who never got rid of a sore toe until Christmas.

I think the truth of the matter was that the rivers were low because most years we had really dry weather during July and early August. When the water didn't run in the rivers, then the swimming holes were stagnant. Mom always told me that water had to run over nine rocks before it was pure. When I went with Uncle Shirley's children to check out the swimming holes, they did have a different smell when the water wasn't flowing in and out of them at a good pace. Having checked out the facts of the warning to stay out of the river, I heeded Mom's and Grandma Molly's advice.

The second thing we were told about dog days was that snakes were blind and aggravated during that time. The heat really bothered them because they were cold-blooded creatures. Being blind and bothered by the heat, they struck out at any warm-blooded creature that got near them. When we went to pick blackberries, it was always in our minds that we had to be more careful and watch for snakes. Hilda told me that when she was about eight years old, she went to the hen house one day to gather eggs during dog days. She walked close to the chicken-lot fence and there was a copperhead snake lying just on the other side. She said, "I heard something hit the fence and looked down. That snake was striking out in the air in all directions trying to bite me. If he hadn't been blind, that would have been my second copperhead snake bite."

All in all, dog days was a miserable time—a lot of garden work of picking, stringing, chopping, and canning, hot weather, little or no rain, and it lasted until just before school started. Really, for me, summer vacation was over at the end of June and I have always, to this day, felt that way. I am very much like a snake myself during dog days. I can't stand the heat, so it makes me aggravated.

Toward the end of summer, we had eaten all the fresh vegetables we wanted, and they were still hanging on the vines. That's when Mom made her famous Chow Chow recipe. She canned it in pint-size jars, and we enjoyed it as a garnish with pinto beans and meat.

Chow Chow Recipe...

Ingredients

2 medium cabbages	¼ bushel of green tomatoes
2 dozen large, firm cucumbers	6 large onions
18 small ears of corn	1 large head cauliflower
4 green peppers	1½ gallons vinegar
3 lbs brown sugar	½ ounce tumeric
2 ounces white mustard seed	2 ounces celery seed

Chop and boil vegetables in ½ gallon vinegar until they are tender; drain. Take 1 gallon fresh vinegar and add the sugar and spices. Pour over chopped vegetables and boil for 5 minutes, or until tender. Put into sterilized jars while hot and seal.

The end of summer brought the return to school for us children. Even though we dreaded school's opening in reality it was in many ways a relief from the hard work of helping Mom with the gardening and canning.

Chapter 8

Fall Harvest

Autumn begins with a subtle change in the light, with skies a deeper blue, and nights that become suddenly clear and chilled. The season comes full with the first frost, the disappearance of migrant birds, and the harvesting of the season's last crops.

—*Glenn Wolff and Jerry Dennis*

Hunting, gathering, and preserving food for the winter and spring slowed somewhat during the month of September, as we waited for frost to kill the potato vines and the sweet potato vines. In the meantime, while we children were back in school, Mom, Aunt Ethel and Uncle Shirley began the search for apples to use for apple butter and pears for canning and pear butter. After the first heavy frost, we began to harvest again. Meantime, Mom harvested her sweet potatoes, and the Irish potatoes were ready to come out of the garden.

Irish Potatoes

Potatoes are a poor man's friend for several reasons. They are very easy to grow, and they are a basic root vegetable that winters easily and simply. All you need is a storage area with a dirt floor.

At our house, Dad built a wooden box structure on top of our dirt floor in the cellar. It was big enough to hold about twenty-five bushels of medium to large potatoes.

Special seed potatoes are not necessary, because if you stick a potato in the ground, you can grow more potatoes. Potatoes are such a fine staple and can be used in every meal. They are a starchy food and provided energy for the hard work of subsistence living. Potatoes

This root cellar was built in a dirt bank and extends back under the ground. Grass is growing over the top. Potatoes and other root crops wintered best in this type of structure. (Courtesy of Wayne Cannoy).

existed long before the fine machinery that was invented to do the work once done by human hands.

Hopkins Gap families prepared potatoes in so many different ways that folks never tired of them. They were served one way or another at every meal. At breakfast, potatoes were fried and served with milk gravy or chopped up and served as hash browns with eggs and side meat. They were also fried or boiled for dinner and supper. For Sunday dinners, potatoes were usually mashed and served with fried chicken and gravy. In the summer time, potato salad was a favorite way to eat potatoes.

Fried potatoes were Dad's favorite dish. Sometimes he tolerated potatoes boiled in water with a tablespoon of lard and some salt and pepper or potatoes boiled with the skins left on them, but he preferred his potatoes fried. Mom knew to have a dish of fried potatoes for supper every evening with an occasional boiled potato substitute.

Fussin' over fried potatoes...

When Mom asked Dad what he wanted for supper on Saturday and Sunday, he would invariably say, "Fry me a pan of taters." Her response was sometimes harsh as she picked up the potato pan and tiredly walked down the cellar steps to the potato bin. She often couldn't keep from yelling, "Damn it, Norman, I fry potatoes every day of the week for you. You might give me a rest from peeling potatoes on Saturday and Sunday." But she peeled and fried his potatoes as he sat at the dining room table, playing solitaire and waiting for supper.

Mom didn't wash her potatoes before she peeled them. She could peel a potato as close as anybody I ever saw. She always told me that the vitamins and minerals in a potato were in the skin or right under the skin so if the peeling was thick, you had basically lost the "good of the potato." As she peeled each potato, she placed it in a pan of water that entirely covered the raw potatoes. Mom told me this kept the first potatoes she peeled from turning dark until she finished peeling the last potato.

She rinsed the potatoes again before she sliced them. Mom had sliced so many potatoes that she had ridges on the ball of her left thumb where the sharp peeling knife always nicked the skin and caused a callous to grow. She was so good at slicing potatoes that I often told her, "Mom, you could go to work in a potato chip factory." She answered, "I peel enough potatoes for your daddy. I don't think I want to earn a livin' peelin' and slicin' potatoes." Her slices were so thin they began to curl before she put them in the iron skillet to fry.

About half way through her slicing, she would put her iron skillet on the stove, add a heaping tablespoon of lard, and let it heat until the grease was just starting to smoke. At that point she carefully slid her potato slices into the hot grease.

The sliced potatoes, which had a little water on them, hit the hot grease with a loud sizzle. The water drops caused the grease to pop out of the pan. By watching that process several times, I understood why Mom had round grease burns on her forearms and hands every day of her life. The hot grease didn't seem to bother her. She put salt and pepper on the potatoes while they were sizzling, then she poured some water on top of them to spread the seasoning and cool the pan. She would then put a lid over the potatoes and begin to prepare the rest of supper.

She knew when the potatoes were ready to turn by the crackling sound they made as the bottom ones started to turn brown in the cast iron skillet. I learned this because if I was in the kitchen and she was busy with something else, she would tell me to turn the potatoes. "Peg, turn the potatoes over for me. They're getting' ready to burn," she said. Sure enough, when I turned them over, the bottom potatoes would be brown and crispy.

The result was a delicious mixture of crispy, crunchy potato slices and soft potato slices, steamed to perfection. On special occasions and for a different flavor, Mom sliced a large onion over the top of the potatoes once they were in the pan and starting to fry. This added a totally different taste to the fried potatoes. Dad called them "taters and onions" when he occasionally placed this order for Sunday evening supper.

While the potatoes were frying and Mom's back was turned, Dad would quietly slip into the kitchen, lift the lid off the pan, and sniff the potatoes to see if they were done. She often turned around and caught him and would yell, "Can't you wait?!!!" He would quickly retreat back to the table, pick up his deck of cards again, and play solitaire until Mom put the meal on the table.

Fried Potatoes Recipe...

Ingredients
6 to 8 large potatoes (depending on the size of the family)
1 teaspoon salt
½ teaspoon pepper

1 heaping tablespoon of hog lard
½ cup water

Using a sharp peeling knife, remove the skin from the potatoes without cutting too deeply into the potato. Place peeled potatoes in a bowl of cold water. Slice each potato as thinly as possible. Heat lard in 9-inch cast iron skillet until it begins to smoke. Slide the potato slices into the grease. Protect your hands from the popping grease. Add salt and pepper. Add water. Cover the pan. For crispy potatoes, stir the potatoes when they start to pop on the bottom. For soft potatoes, stir frequently. For a delicious variation, slice a large onion and add it to top of the potatoes before putting on the lid on the skillet.

Mashed Potatoes Recipe...

Ingredients

5 lbs. potatoes	¼ lb. butter
1 cup of milk	salt and pepper to taste

Peel potatoes and place in a large pot of water. Bring water to a boil and simmer potatoes for 15 minutes or until tender when pierced with a fork. Drain off the potato water and set aside for making gravy, soup, or bread. Keep potatoes on a very low heat for a moment, if they are soggy. Add butter and ½ cup of milk. Mash thoroughly with a potato masher. Gradually add remaining milk until the texture of the potatoes is like you want it. Add salt and pepper to taste. Mound in a serving bowl and add a dab of butter in a hollow in the middle. Serve with gravy.

When we knew Mom was making mashed potatoes, we all begged her to make a lot more than we could eat. My brother, John, especially liked fried potato cakes. He would plead, "Mom, will you make some extra potatoes so we can have fried potato cakes tomorrow evening for supper?" His wish was always granted when it came to his favorite foods.

Fried Potato Cakes Recipe...

Ingredients

Leftover mashed potatoes	½ cup of flour
1 medium onion, chopped	4 eggs, beaten with spoon
2 tablespoons lard	Salt and pepper to taste

Mix mashed potatoes, onion, flour, and eggs in a large bowl. Add flour until the consistency is right for forming cakes. With hands, shape the mixture into cakes about the size of a typical hamburger. Heat lard in large iron skillet. Place potato cakes into the hot lard and fry until brown and crispy on each side.

When we had Morris family reunions and Sunday afternoon picnics, Mom and Aunt Ethel would put their heads together and plan the menu. The weather was usually warm when these events occurred, so it was a great time for cold potato salad. Family and other church members come from miles around to get a serving of Mom and Aunt Ethel's potato salad. We rarely went home with leftovers, mostly just empty bowls.

Potato Salad Recipe...

Ingredients

10 lbs. potatoes	1 dozen eggs
4 large onions	1½ quarts mayonnaise
6 tablespoons sugar	1½ cups vinegar

1½ cups water   ¼ cup celery seed
Salt and pepper to taste

Boil potatoes with skins on; boil eggs until hard. Cool and peel eggs and potatoes. Cut potatoes into one-inch squares; dice up onions and eggs, and combine them all in a large container. In a separate container, stir together mayonnaise, sugar, vinegar, water, salt and pepper, and celery seed. Add creamy mixture to the potato, eggs, and onions. Mix well. Place in refrigerator until chilled. Allow enough time for dressing to soak into the potatoes before serving.

Boiled Potatoes with Parsley Recipe...

Ingredients
8 large potatoes   1 tablespoon lard
3 sprigs of fresh parsley   salt and pepper to taste
water

Peel potatoes and cut into chunks. Put lard into a sauce pan and heat until melted. Put potatoes in the hot grease (careful not to splash grease on hands).

Pour in enough water to nearly cover the potatoes. Add salt and pepper to taste. Boil until nearly tender. Chop up in small pieces and add parsley.

Serve with butter.

The Potato bin and my arachnophobia...

Because Dad loved potatoes so much, somebody had to go to the cellar and get potatoes out of the bin every day of the year and sometimes twice a day. I can understand now why Mom started sending me when I got old enough. She must have been very tired of maneuvering down those rickety stairs to the cellar. However, she also knew that I was deathly afraid of spiders. When she told me to go get her a pan of potatoes, I would stomp and cry until she threatened to whip me. "Mom, you know I am scared of spiders, please don't make me go down there." She would head toward me with her hand drawn back ready to whack me. Just as she was within reaching distance, I would turn on my heel, grab the tater pan, and head for the cellar steps. I considered it pure torture, or at least emotional child abuse, that I suffered nearly every day.

Arachnophobia has plagued me all my life, and I have often wondered about the source of the intense fear. I assume it came from living in the country in a house with many cracks and holes. When it got cold outside, it was nearly impossible to seal every crevice to keep the small creatures out. We always had mice in our house during the cold months. The mice lived in the cellar and in the walls and in the attic where I could hear them gnawing at night, but I rarely saw one in the house. The spiders, however, stayed in the house all year. In the summer they built nests under the couch and up in the bedsprings. They made webs in the corners of windows so they could catch unsuspecting flies.

The spiders I feared the most were the big, fuzzy-legged kind that were probably harmless, and just as scared of me as I was of them, but I was deathly afraid of them. In the fall when the weather turned cold, I would be sitting at the dining room table doing my homework and spot a huge one walking through the room like it owned the house. I would scream for somebody to come and kill it, because I would be frozen to my chair, afraid to move, assuming there might be another spider close by. I couldn't even stand to crunch them under my foot until I was about thirty-five years old. I always assumed they crawled over me at night when I was sleeping, and there wasn't anything I could do about it.

To make matters worse, Dad loved to take us to the drive-in movies when he was in a good mood and had a little extra money. It was always a last minute decision to go to the movies and a case of 'go now while you have the money before you have to spend it.'

There we were, Dad and Mom in the front, with four kids in the back seat and Warnie, the baby, on Mom's lap. As I think back now, I wonder how we looked to the people in the cars parked next to us. They probably got more fun out of watching us than they did watching the movie. The back seat was crowded with four growing kids, so we often got into "push and shove" fights. Mom would ask us to be quiet and watch the movie. Of course, we didn't always listen to her, so Dad would reach his fist into the back seat and blindly strike out at whichever kid got in striking range. He didn't reach back without letting out some pretty awful curse words. It was probably entertaining for the folks in the car next to us some times.

Occasionally we hit on a good western movie that we all enjoyed. Other times, we were exposed to some science fiction movies. One I remember was called "The Lost World." It was about dinosaurs running around eating everything in their path including large animals, grown people, and children. That movie gave me nightmares for many months afterward including full color and sound effects. However, the most horrifying drive-in movie experience for me was one of Dad's last minute choices entitled "Tarantula." The huge spider made a sound like chains rattling as it moved.

We had an outside toilet at that time, so at night before bed, I had to go out to pee. I imagined I could hear the chains rattling as the big tarantula rolled across the fields toward me. Even before the tarantula movie, I imagined the spiders that lurked on the underside of the toilet seat just waiting for a warm butt to crawl on.

Needless to say, I frequently didn't make it all the way to the outhouse. I sat down and quickly emptied my bladder in the path to the toilet. I couldn't go into the grass because there might have been a spider lurking there to bite me in the butt or crawl into my clothes to get into the house. One night Mom caught me squatting in the path, and she yelled at me, "You had better not piss in the path; you'll get a sty on your eye." With great difficulty, I cut off my stream and pulled up my underwear. It seemed to me that I could not win, so I asked her if she would go to the toilet with me because I was scared of spiders. She said, "No, I am not going to start going to the shit house with you. You need to get over bein' scared of spiders."

So it was in this context of extreme arachnophobia, that I grew old enough to go to the cellar for potatoes. There were spiders all over the cellar—in webs hanging from the ceiling, in the rafters hanging upside down in their webs with their eggs stuck into the corners, in the potato bin, and between the jars of canned food. I was afraid one of them would fall or jump on my head so it could ride upstairs where it was warm and dry.

As I grew older and smarter, I came up with a plan to save myself from being exposed to the mercy of the spiders in the cellar. It was an act of desperation because for the most part, I am not a mean person who would take advantage of those younger than me. My sister, Brenda, was my first unsuspecting victim. She was nine years old—three years younger than me. She never had any spending money whereas I always had a few nickels and dimes in my pockets from various jobs I did for Aunt Goldie and the neighbors or from picking and selling blackberries for a dollar a gallon. So, I offered Brenda a nickel if she would go to the cellar in my place. She gladly went down there for me, brought back potatoes or whatever I was supposed to get, and asked me for her nickel. My answer was, "I don't have a nickel right now, but I will pay you in June when school is out and I can work for somebody." She said, "Okay, but you had better pay me; I ain't gonna forget."

These occasions came up nearly every day when she went to the cellar in my place for a nickel to be paid in June. Brenda kept very careful records of my growing debt. Finally, June rolled around and I owed her seventy-five cents. She came to me to collect. Of course, I didn't have the money, or if I had it, I had other plans for it, so I asked her, "Did I say I would pay you in June of this year?" She looked at me in disbelief, but she had to tell the truth because she was incredibly honest then and still is to this day. "No, you didn't say which year it would be," she answered with disgust on her face. "Well then," I said,

"I could pay you next June or the one after that. I'll probably have the money by then." Since Brenda is an intelligent person, she caught on after the second June rolled around, and I owed her about three dollars. She realized she had been tricked and refused to go to the cellar in my place. My fear of spiders had not subsided, so I began to look around for another unsuspecting victim to go to the cellar for me.

Mom always babysat several of my cousins' children while they worked, so I began paying attention to my Cousin Joyce's little girl, Barbara. She was old enough to go to the cellar for me and since she also wanted a little spending money, she was a sitting duck for my trick. She still asks me to this day to pay her what I owe her—with interest. So for perhaps four or five years, I avoided exposure to the vicious spiders that lived in our cellar. Recently, I handed Barbara a sum of twenty-five dollars. I am not sure she was satisfied, as she began to calculate interest for fifty years.

Sweet Potatoes

Mom always harvested her sweet potatoes in late September and usually got about ten bushels from her two ridges. She sold some and gave some to Aunt Ethel and Uncle Shirley. I would take some home with me when I visited. She told my siblings, who lived nearby, that she was putting the rest of the sweet potatoes in her root cellar and for them to get a "mess" whenever they wanted them. My favorite way to eat Mom's sweet potatoes was baked. I would go home to visit and ask her to make me some baked sweet potatoes. She always complied. Later in her life, we discovered how good they were baked with the skin on them and eaten with butter.

Baked Sweet Potato Recipe...

Ingredients
2 pounds medium sweet potatoes
¼ cup butter
¼ cup maple syrup
¼ cup light brown sugar, firmly packed
¼ teaspoon cinnamon

Peel and cut sweet potatoes in ¾ inch slices. Cook until tender but firm. Place cooked slices in a buttered 2-quart baking dish. In a saucepan, combine remaining ingredients; cook until mixture boils. Pour over potatoes; bake at 350° for 30 minutes, or until hot and nicely glazed.

Aunt Goldie' Grape Vines

Aunt Goldie lived at the end of our road, about a quarter mile from our house. I absolutely loved to go over and visit her every chance I had to slip away from home. Mom often said, "You keep the road hot between here and there. I don't see why you want to be over there all the time." Well, she was perhaps not as tuned in to the good things I found at Aunt Goldie's house, or she was tuned in for different reasons. For instance, my "keeping the road hot" to Aunt Goldie's house had a definite pattern that was determined by the season of the year. In mid August, the grape vines under Aunt Goldie's kitchen window were bearing their delicious fruit, and I was as drawn to their nectar as the bees, the ants, and the yellow jackets.

There were two vines. One was a purple concord grape and the other a white grape. Uncle Rob had built sturdy arbors for the vines to grow on. They consisted of two tall posts buried in the ground with a board across the top that formed a cross. The posts were planted in the ground about twelve feet apart. On top of the posts, he built a lattice roof with two by fours. The vines climbed up the posts and over the lattice roof, providing a thick and luscious green enclosure. In September, clusters of big sweet and juicy grapes hung down from the enclosure, just within reach of my little hands.

Sling shot, round green plums, and temptation...

The grape vines were so thick that Aunt Goldie couldn't see me when I was under them. At the edge of the yard below the grape vines, she had planted some green gage plum trees that served as a cover for me as I walked up the road, entered her yard, and walked stealthily under the grape vines. As I walked under the plum trees, I remembered how I had enjoyed using the hard green plums as ammunition for my slingshot earlier that summer. I had crawled up in the tree and waited for Old Mrs. Varner to come up the road to get her mail and start back down the hill toward home. I was eleven years old, school was out for the summer, and I needed some type of excitement in my life.

I had noticed before that Mrs. Varner always read her newspaper on the way home. She held it wide open as she slowly walked along. It made a target I could not resist. So, from my hidden perch in the plum tree, I took aim with my slingshot, loaded with a perfectly round green plum, and shot it straight through her newspaper. Splat!!! It was a clean shot right through the comic section. Mrs. Varner was, of course, shaken by the attack that seemed to come out of nowhere. She stopped and looked all around. Then she looked on the ground to see what had made the hole in her paper. She didn't notice the green plum. I stayed very quiet in the plum tree. Finally she gave up and went on home cursing under her breath.

I couldn't resist doing the same thing the next day. Needless to say, the second time I shot a plum through Mrs. Varner's newspaper I got caught. She looked around on the ground until she found the plum. I will never forget her expression and the words she said when she realized where the plum had come from. She said, in a tight and angry voice with her lips curled into a threatening sneer, "I don't know who you are in that there tree, but I am going to report you to the mailman. It is a federal crime to interfere with a person's mail. You will be sorry for this mean trick." That was all the punishment I needed, because I worried for weeks that a federal agent would show up to take me away. That incident basically ruined the rest of my summer vacation.

Each time I used the green gage plum tree to hide my approach to Goldie's grape vines, my heart skipped a beat or two, for fear the agents were staked out and waiting for me.

The plum tree was a nice way to get to the grape vines without being seen. I slipped under the grape vines and filled my belly with delicious white grapes that ripened a bit earlier than the purple concord grapes.

As I ate the white grapes, I glanced over at the purple grapes noting that I would soon be eating them. They didn't ripen until after school started in September. I would have to sneak away from home on Saturdays to enjoy the purple grapes. They were starting to turn blue, but most still had a lot of green on them. When they were ripe, they had a slightly different flavor and texture.

Whether I was eating white grapes or purple grapes, I plucked them one at a time and staggered my choices so that any one clump of grapes would not give me away with too many empty stems. For however long it took for me to fill my greedy belly, it was just me, the bees, and the yellow jackets under the grape vines. It was heavenly with the heat of summer gone, a slight breeze blowing, and my nostrils filled with the sweet grape aroma. I also plucked the grapes one at a time because it was so exciting to place them against my lips and squeeze the delicious pulp into my mouth. With a little squeeze between my fingers, the grape hull parted gently and squirted the pulp and juice into my salivating mouth. I will never forget the taste of Aunt Goldie's grape nectar as it hit my tongue and slid down my throat.

I was careful not to drop the empty grape hulls under the vines, as that would have been a dead giveaway that a grape thief had been busy in the vicinity. I have never understood why I had such intense pleasure while eating the stolen grapes. Over the years I have reflected on the fact that I felt no guilt as I was slurping the grapes. Perhaps it was the joy of eating forbidden fruit, or it might have been that I was bored living so far out in the country and needed excitement in my life. I really do not know the answer.

When I had my fill of grapes, I went on in the back door that was shaded by a huge Bartlett pear tree, hanging full of pears, and visited with Aunt Goldie. If she was working on something, she would ask me to help her, and I always did. When I left for home, I went out the back door and exited once again under the grape vines. I always stopped and enjoyed a few more grapes before I left her yard.

I must admit, on a few occasions Aunt Goldie caught me in her grape vines. Her kitchen sink was directly under the window that looked out over the grape arbor. Once or twice she would be washing dishes as I left for home. She saw me go under the grape vines but didn't see me come out the other side. After watching for a few minutes, she would yell out the window, "Get out of my grapes. I am going to make juice out of them this week." The grape juice Aunt Goldie made was out of this world.

Grape Juice Recipe...

Ingredients
2 cups of washed grapes (white or purple, but never mix the two
    types of grapes)
½ cup of sugar for each jar
Enough boiling water to fill each jar (Aunt Goldie used ½ gallon
    jars)

Put lids on the jars (do not tighten completely).
Place the jars in a kettle with water in it up to the shoulder of the jars (do not let the water totally cover the loosely lidded jars).
Boil the cans for 10 minutes.
Remove the jars and tighten the lids.
Place the hot jars in a cool place and listen to the "music" of each can as it cools and seals. (The lids made a popping sound as it sealed).

Once the jars were totally cooled, Aunt Goldie carefully carried them to her cellar and placed them on the shelves. I helped her carry some of the jars to the cellar and enjoyed the display of purple and white grape juice in colorful contrast with her cans of green beans, pickled beets, peaches, and other fruits and vegetables she had canned earlier in the summer. My mind always fast forwarded to a cold winter morning, with the snow falling outside, picturing Aunt Goldie opening a can of grape juice and using her fingers to hold back the grapes that had risen to the top of the jar, while she poured out the delectable juice.

Pears

Aunt Goldie had a huge Bartlett pear tree just outside her back door and there were a few unknown varieties of pear trees growing in the fields—one in our back pasture, one outside our kitchen door, and one along the road between Aunt Goldie's house and our house. These trees produced small, hard pears that were not good for canning. Aunt Goldie's Bartlett pear tree did not produce enough for all of us to get as many Bartlett pears as we wanted. If Mom had extra money from her milk, butter, and cottage cheese sales, she would locate a bushel or two of Bartlett's to can. She canned them the same way she canned peaches. (See peach canning description on page 208). If the pear tree in our pasture and the one outside our kitchen door produced enough pears, Mom gathered those and made pear butter.

The mark of a ripe Bartlett...

I have a pear-shaped birthmark on the back of my head. How that birthmark got there is a sweet story of Mom's unrequited lust for a beautiful pear at the very top of a tree when she was several months pregnant with me. She told me the story many times. "Me and your daddy were drivin' into town from Goldie's house. There was a big Bartlett pear tree near the fence on Raleigh Shank's farm. I know I probably passed it two times a week and hadn't noticed anything unusual until that day. As we turned the corner at the hilltop and started down the road, I looked at that tree. I saw the afternoon sun glistening off something in the very top. I told your daddy to slow down so I could see what it was. I looked up and there was the most beautiful pear. The shape was perfect and the color was light green with some pink on the side where the sun was shining on it. Suddenly, I got a craving to eat that pear, and told your daddy to stop and see if he could get it for me. He got out of the car and tried to climb the tree, but he couldn't reach the pear. So he picked up rocks and threw them at the pear. He hit the limb it was hanging on a couple of times, but the pear would not fall."

"He finally gave up when he couldn't find any more rocks to throw. I have never craved anything as much as I did that pear. I couldn't put it out of my mind all day. You were born the following May. When the nurse handed you to me, I saw a pink pear-shaped mark on the back of your head. It was there even after your hair grew out, so I guess it is still there to this day."

Pear Butter Recipe…

Ingredients
About 20 medium pears
4 cups of sugar
½ teaspoon nutmeg
1/3 cup orange juice

Core, peel, and slice washed pears. Combine pears and ½ cup water in large pot. Simmer until pears are soft. Put pulp through sieve to remove excess liquid. Combine pear pulp, and other ingredients. Cook the pulp until thick enough to round up on a spoon. Stir constantly to prevent sticking. Pour boiling hot butter into hot jars, leaving ¼ inch headspace. Wipe rim and place lids and rings on the jars. Process the jars in a water bath for 10 minutes for pints and quarts. Yield is about 4 pints for this recipe. You can double or triple the recipe.

Apples

Apples were ready to harvest in October. The trees that had blanketed the rolling hills in pink and white blossoms, providing nectar for hard working bees, now hung low under their bountiful load of fruit. The ground under each tree was strewn with fallen apples from thunderstorms and wind but there were still more than enough apples on the trees for pies, dumplings, apple sauce, baked apples, fried apples, and a forty-gallon kettle of apple butter.

Aunt Goldie's apple trees, buzzards, and pigpens…

On one edge of Aunt Goldie's orchard there was a fenced in pig lot. The pigs enjoyed the shade of the apple trees, and the wormy fruit that fell to the ground; and, they in turn kept the weeds to a minimum.

On another end of the orchard the apple trees overhung the edge of the bluegrass field where Aunt Goldie pastured her cows. I spent many long summer afternoons in the bluegrass field with my cousins, Randy and George. When George found his cow chewing her cud while standing under the shade of an overhanging apple tree, he would climb up on her back, stretch out on his stomach, and take a nap.

Randy and I rolled around in the grass and would stop now and then to stare at the blue sky. We watched buzzards circling over Little North Mountain and talked about faraway places that he was reading about in his English classes at Mt. Clinton High School. Many times, Randy and I talked about what we would have to give up if we wanted to be a buzzard, floating high above the ground and letting the summer breezes carry us along. We talked about Mom's sausage gravy—Randy's favorite food—and apple butter rolls, egg custard pies, homemade light rolls, and all the food that was cooked on hog killing day. We would have to give up those things. Randy was courting then, and he talked about how he would have to give up his girl friends. I was about eleven years old and much more committed to the adventure of flying than I was to the everyday things in life.

I asked Mom if it was possible for me to become a buzzard so that I could float on the warm afternoon breezes, glide over Little North Mountain and look down on Hopkins Gap to see what our relatives were doing. Mom thought for a minute, then said, "What do you think buzzards eat?" I replied that I hadn't thought much about it. Then she explained, "Do you remember when Ole Jerse's calf died last year?" I said, "Yes, we all cried about it." She went on with her story, "Your daddy dragged the dead calf to the corner of the pasture and left it lay there. You kids went to visit the calf for a day or two, and then stopped going because you said the calf was rotten and smelled awful. You went back to visit the calf one more time. When you came back that day, you told me the calf was all gone except for some hair and a few bones."

Mom looked at me with a smirk playing around the corners of her mouth. "Do you remember what I told you happened to the dead calf?" Suddenly I had a flash back to that moment and heard her plain and clear as she said, "The buzzards ate it." She went on with her story, as I stood there picturing the buzzards tearing at the rotten calf, "When buzzards smell a dead animal, they swoop down and eat it. They eat so much that when they take off flying, they puke because their bellies are so full. I know some people who got puked on by buzzards. One time Conard Payne was walking up the road from the bluegrass field, and he scared a bunch of buzzards eatin' a dead sheep in Hirsh's field. They took off flyin' and when they got over top of him, they let the puke fly. It got all over his head, in his hair, and on his shirt. He was just a kid. He run to the house cryin' and screamin'. He stunk so bad. I had to clean him up, and I thought I would puke myself." By this time, I was afraid to ask whom else buzzards had puked on because my stomach was rolling like I was going to puke myself. I ran out of the house gagging.

What I learned that day convinced me that I no longer wanted to be a buzzard. But I still wanted to fly and feel the breezes under my wings, and carrying me above the land, so I asked Randy about other birds that soared like buzzards. He told me about eagles that lived in other parts of the country. I knew a little about them from school. I said, "Randy, do eagles eat rotten meat like buzzards do?" He answered, "No. Eagles eat fresh meat. They swoop down and catch rabbits and other small animals. They like their meat fresh." I decided that I would rather be an eagle.

As time passed, Randy and George grew up, got jobs, and no longer wanted to play in the orchard with me. I had a lot of advantages being the age that I was, because I had older cousins to play with. When those days were gone, my two brothers were old enough and daring enough to play with me. I taught them a lot of the stuff that Randy and George had taught me—like how to make bows and arrows and sling shots. We built Indian teepees out of small saplings and covered the outside with old burlap sacks. We played cowboys and Indians. We crawled through tunnels that Aunt Goldie's pigs had made under the taller weeds. We got muddy and a good portion of the brown stuff on our clothes was probably hog manure. When we got home for supper in the evening, Mom told us we smelled like hog shit. She yelled, "If I asked you all to crawl through hog shit to help me, you wouldn't do it." She was probably right about that. It was during those days that we plucked large feathers out of Aunt Goldie's chickens' tails and stole turkey feathers from the neighbors' flocks so we could make Indian headdresses.

Apple Pie

There are many, many versions of apple pie, but the kind that Mom and Aunt Ethel made usually started with fresh apples. They began the apple pie season with summer Rambo apples because they ripened early in the summer.

Fresh Apple Pie Recipe...

Ingredients
7–8 ripe apples from the orchard
1 cup of sugar
¼ cup of flour
Sprinkle of salt
Sprinkle of cinnamon and nutmeg

Peel, core, and slice or chop the apples into small pieces. Mix sugar, flour, salt and stir into the apple pieces. Set aside. Mix a batch of Mom's Pie Dough (page 141). Roll out dough to about 1/8th inch thick for the bottom of the pie. Spread into the pie pan and tuck into the bottom of the pan. Fill the dough with the apple mixture. Sprinkle the top of the apples with cinnamon and nutmeg.

Roll out dough to about 1/8th inch thick for the top of the pie. Dip fingers into water and wet the edges of the bottom dough with water. Spread over the top of the apples. Press the top and bottom dough together at the edges of the pie pan with a fork. Using the same fork, place a design into the top of the pie so it can get air while baking. Bake at 350, for about 50 minutes, or until crust is golden brown.

Apple pie and Mom's stroke…

In 1987, when Mom was sixty-seven years old, she had her first stroke. The stroke left her with aphasia. She was unable to organize her speech patterns so that her words would come out in a logical sentence. Her doctors prescribed speech therapy while she was still in the hospital, and she continued with the therapist when she came home.

Mom's therapist was very dedicated to her treatment, and was using all the appropriate methods to help her correctly sequence her words, but after a month or so he was not making any progress. He remained very patient, but Mom was getting more and more impatient. She would seem to be progressing for a few days, but then she would regress again.

In one frustrating session, the therapist was using a stick with notches cut into it. He asked Mom to place her finger in a notch as she said each word in the sentence, "The quick brown fox jumped over the lazy dogs." Mom could not get her finger and her words to work together with the stick. On his way to his car, the therapist, in desperation, asked Hilda what he might do differently to help Mom. She said, "Why don't you ask her to tell you how to bake an apple pie? I'll bet that would hold her attention. She really wants to be able to cook again."

The next visit, the therapist brought his stick with the notches in it, but instead of his usual sentences, he asked Mom to tell him the steps in making an apple pie. Hilda told me later, "Her eyes popped open wide, and she smiled and nodded her head."

The therapist had worked out a routine in which he could use his standard methods, but include a topic that interested Mom. He told her, "In a month or two I want you to serve me apple pie when I arrive for your treatment."

Week after week Mom worked on her speech problem with the steps in baking an apple pie. Hilda told me, "She sure made some messes at first; but she kept on tryin." She wanted to bake a pie for her therapist as much as she wanted to cook again for her family. The therapist watched her progress, and one day as he left the house, he told Mom, "I expect a slice of apple pie the next time I see you." Mom rose to the task and sent him home with a stomach full of apple pie after his next visit. She insisted he take a piece for his wife.

This was the beginning of Mom's return to her kitchen.

Mom and Aunt Ethel never wasted any left over pie dough. They used it either for a small pie for a grandchild or they would make apple dumplings. Recently, I was visiting Aunt Ethel as she was baking apple pies. She ended up with a small ball of pie dough. She looked around and thought for a while, and she said, "This is enough dough to make two apple dumplins'. I'll make one for you to take home with you. You can stop on the way home and get you some ice cream to eat with it. I'll make one with a sugar substitute for Shirl's supper."

Uncle Shirley suffers with diabetes and can no longer enjoy Aunt Ethel's wonderful pies made with sugar.

Aunt Ethel got busy and peeled two apples. She rolled out her dough,

Aunt Ethel uses her leftover pie dough to make a sugar-free apple dumpling for Uncle Shirley and one with sugar for me to take home. April, 2006.

cut it into two squares, and added her apples and other ingredients. Because there were only two dumplings, and one without sugar, she used two small pans to keep them separate as they baked. I asked Aunt Ethel "Is that how you usually make apple dumplings?" She said, "No, when I make a big batch for the whole family, I use another recipe." She then recited her "big batch" apple dumplings recipe to me.

Apple Dumplings Recipe...

Ingredients

Two cups sifted flour
2 teaspoons baking powder
1 teaspoon salt
½ cup lard
¾ cup of milk
dash of nutmeg

Six apples peeled and cored
½ cup brown sugar, packed
1/3 cup butter
1 1/3 cups hot water
dash of cinnamon

Stir together flour, baking powder and salt; mix in lard. Add milk; stir to form a ball of dough. Put some flour on the counter, knead the dough to shape then roll out to 1/8th inch thickness. Cut into six squares, about six to 8 inches each. Place an apple on each square. Top each apple with a little sugar, a dab of butter, and a generous shaking of cinnamon. Stretch dough to cover the apple and pinch edges for sealing. Place in pan greased with lard, sealed edges under. Combine brown sugar, butter, hot water, nutmeg and cinnamon; pour over dumplings. Bake at 450 degrees for 15 minutes. Turn heat down to 350 degrees and bake until done. Serve with milk or vanilla ice cream and fresh coffee.

Fried Apples Recipe...

Ingredients

8 to 10 apples	Dash of salt
½ stick butter	½ cup sugar

If available, use Red or Yellow Delicious apples or Granny Smith apples. Peel, core and slice the apples. Heat the butter to a low heat in an iron skillet. Add the sliced apples, sprinkle with sugar, and add a dash of salt to enhance the flavor. Let the apples fry, stirring and turning frequently until tender and just starting to brown. Serve immediately.

Baked Apples Recipe...

Ingredients

8 apples, peeled and cored	¼ cup butter
½ cup sugar	½ teaspoon cinnamon
1/3 teaspoon ground ginger	juice of ½ lemon
1 teaspoon vanilla extract	1/3 cup chopped walnuts
¼ cup water	

Place peeled and cored apples in a 9 x 13 baking dish with lid. In a small saucepan, over medium heat, combine butter, sugar, water, cinnamon, ginger, lemon juice, and vanilla. Bring to a boil. Drizzle over apples. Cover and bake 30 minutes in preheated over (350 degrees). Remove cover and continue to bake for 10 minutes or until apples are tender. Serve warm.

Applesauce Recipe...

Ingredients

4 large apples, peeled, 	2 tablespoons butter
    cored and chopped 	2 teaspoons lemon juice
1/3 cup sugar 	nutmeg to taste
¼ cup water

In a heavy saucepan, add apples, butter, sugar, lemon, and water. Cook over low heat stirring frequently, until apples are soft and pulpy. Add nutmeg to taste. Stir or mix to break up apple chunks if any. Serve warm.

Apple Butter Boiling

After dad died in March of 1994, my brothers and sister and I finally realized that Mom and Dad were not going to be around to pass on the family traditions. One of these traditions was the annual apple butter boiling. Mom and Dad both knew they needed to learn from Grandma Molly before she died, but somehow it seemed, we expected Mom and Dad would always be around to remind us that all the apple butter was gone from the cellar, and we needed to make more. We all got together and planned a day long apple butter boiling.

We found that the whole process of apple butter boiling takes about three days. We first had to locate enough apples to fill a forty gallon copper kettle.

Mom and her great-granddaughter Erica begin the long day of work. Four generations were present for this 1994 apple butter boiling.

We found we could get the apples we needed at an orchard about twenty miles away, near New Market. On the way to get the apples, Mom told us how lucky we were to find apples already picked and to be able to pay for them. She said, "We always went to the orchards and asked if we could pick up the apples off the ground to make our apple butter. Apples were only about three dollars a bushel, but we needed six or seven bushels, and that was a lot of money. The orchard owners let us pick up as many apples as we wanted because they were just gonna rot anyway. It took four or five of us all day to get enough apples."

The apples we purchased were not bruised from falling from the tree, so we could wait until the next day to peel and quarter them. As we leisurely peeled and quartered, Mom told us that because the apples they picked from the ground were often bruised, they had to start the peeling and quartering process the same evening after they had gathered all day. "We stayed up late into the night so our apples didn't waste." She continued, "The next morning we were up at 5:00 getting the fire going under the kettle. We knew we were looking at a good eight hours of stirrin'."

We all knew we had to gather some tools for the apple-butter boiling the next day, so off we went to the shed. We took a forty-gallon solid copper apple butter kettle down from a loft. As we looked at the kettle, we discussed its history in our family. I said, "I bought this kettle from Uncle Jim for one hundred dollars in 1974. He was selling off his equipment. I bought a pie safe at the same time for twenty-five dollars. He died shortly after he sold his things." Larry spoke up, "This kettle belongs to me now." In fact, I had traded him the apple butter kettle for building me a solid oak pie safe that would fit in a certain spot in my kitchen.

The kettle was covered with soot on the outside from the previous years' boilings. The inside was corroded and nearly as black as the outside of the kettle. We imagined the cleaning work ahead and groaned with dismay. Mom appeared on the scene about then and told us how to make the inside of the kettle shine like a new penny.

She went to the cellar and got us two quarts of tomato juice she had canned in August. She provided us with several soft scrubbing pads, and we went to work. In no time, the kettle was clean and shining.

On the wall of the shed, we found the apple butter stirrer hanging among cobwebs, with spider eggs hidden in the grooves and holes. The stirrer was made from poplar wood because it could not be made of wood with any acid content. The foot of the stirrer was as long as the kettle was deep and had three sections. The center portion was about an inch narrower on each side than the upper and lower thirds. The bottom section had five or six one-inch holes drilled through it to keep the apple pulp circulating. The foot of the paddle was also rounded to fit the bottom of the kettle. The seamless copper kettle and special paddle were designed to prevent the apple pulp from sticking to the bottom and burning. The handle is rectangular for a sturdy grip and at least six feet long so the person stirring is far enough away from the apple pulp when it starts popping out of the kettle. For each drop that lands on uncovered skin, there will be a serious blister. We carefully scrubbed the stirrer and laid it across the top of the kettle.

We turned our attention to the seven bushels of apples that we needed to peel and quarter before the next morning. With an old-fashioned apple peeler and five sets of hands, we started on what appeared to be an insurmountable task. To our amazement, in a few hours we were finished. We got to bed early so we would be rested for the long ordeal of boiling and stirring the apple butter. The next morning, we got up at a decent hour of 6:00 and started the all day job.

Larry was the first to go to the washhouse where he made a fire in the kettle stove. He had rigged a stove pipe going from the kettle and out the washhouse window so that the smoke from the fire could escape. The kettle stove was round, with a door in the front that could be opened to add wood as needed. The top of the stove had a round opening so that a large kettle could be placed on top of the stove with its bottom hanging directly into the fire.

When Larry set the apple butter kettle on the fire, he poured in several gallons of apple cider to keep the kettle from burning until the apples were ready. He also added twenty-four copper pennies to the mix. These had been cleaned the day before when the kettle was cleaned with scrubbing pads and tomato juice. The pennies were pushed around over the bottom of the

The first of the apples have been added to the kettle. Now the stirring must begin in earnest.

kettle as the stirrer went back and forth over the bottom of the kettle, and helped to keep the apple butter from sticking and burning.

The inside of the kettle was pretty. It was the color of a bright new penny. While Larry was getting the kettle hot, Hilda began to wash the apples and remove any bad spots that had appeared over night. She dumped the apples into the kettle in small batches at a time after she had cleaned them. Once the apples began to boil, the stirring began and did not stop, until every drop of apple butter was removed from the kettle at the end of the very long day.

Each person took a turn stirring the apples. The younger family members wanted to stir but they tired of the job in a short time. Mom was always watching to make sure the stirring was done just right. She warned us, "If the apples start to stick on the bottom, you might as well throw the whole batch

Mom is holding her great grandson, Lance's hips to show him the correct rhythm for stirring the apple butter kettle.

away. Burnt apple butter is no good for anything." She continued, "There is a certain way to move your hips that helps to move the stirrer. That way your arms don't get so tired."

As more and more apples were dumped into the boiling kettle, the washhouse filled with steam. Lance and Erica, the younger generation, were scared the washhouse was on fire. Erica said, "I can't see in here." Lance had a frightened look on his face and asked his granddad, Winston, "Do you think the building is on fire? I am gonna go get Great Grandma." Mom had gone into the house to start fixing her famous sausage gravy breakfast for the apple butter helpers.

Lance asked Mom to come back to the washhouse and check on the fire. When she stepped into the washhouse she said, "It's just steam from the apples boiling. But you do need to put more wood on the fire." Mom opened the door to the kettle stove and added some wood. She told Larry and Hilda, "When you put the wood in the stove, make sure it is not touching the bottom of the kettle. That will cause the apple butter to burn quicker than anything." We all took turns stirring the kettle, and during our breaks, enjoyed Mom's delicious breakfast of fried sausage, sausage gravy, homemade light bread, and stewed apples.

As the day went by, Mom entertained the three younger generations through the tedious and hard labor of stirring, by telling stories about the times she made apple butter with Grandma Molly. She repeated the little rhyme that the old folks recited as they stirred the kettle:

> *"Twice around the sides*
> *And once through the middle*
> *That's how you stir*
> *The apple butter kettle."*

She repeated her instructions on how to put wood under the kettle. She said she had learned that from Grandma Molly. I realized, as I listened to Mom that she was not only entertaining us, but she was passing on Hopkins Gap history and our family history to live forever in our memories. Once I recited the little poem as I stirred the kettle, memories came flooding back about the one or two times I had been present when Grandma Molly was supervising the apple butter boiling. That little poem was very familiar because it had entered my head from Grandma Molly's voice many years before. I wondered, that day in the fall of 1994, if my nieces and nephews who were helping, would always remember what Mom was telling them, as I had remembered my own grandmother's words.

Throughout the day, we took turns stirring and started a contest to see who could stir for the longest time. Hilda ended up winning the contest because she kept the stirrer going for a little over an hour. Winston was next with a time of forty-five minutes. The teenage generation lasted about fifteen minutes and had to be watched for "lazy stirring," as Hilda called it. When they started getting

Several hours have passed. The kettle is full of apples and the pulp is beginning to pop as the stirrer moves through the boiling apple butter.

tired, they would just let the stirrer flop over on its side. "Somebody take over the stirrer," Hilda warned, "or we are going to waste all of this hard work."

Mom was busy going back and forth from supervising us in the washhouse, to baking bread dough and meals for us in the kitchen. She had told us earlier, "I am going to make a batch of bread and hot rolls. We need to try our apple butter with fresh light bread." Nobody argued with her plan.

While Mom was making up her light bread, she rolled out some pie dough and made apple dumplings for dinner. She brought them out to the washhouse in a baking pan, with soup bowls, spoons, and a pitcher of fresh milk from the morning's milking.

"I saved some pie dough left over from the weekend," she said. "I am going to make a batch of apple butter rolls for you all to put in your lunches next week."

Apple Butter Rolls Recipe...

Ingredients
Pie dough
Apple butter

Use left over pie dough. Knead into a flat round shape. On a slightly floured surface, roll the dough out to a 1/8th inch thickness. Scoop apple butter into the middle of the dough. Use a tablespoon to spread the apple butter to within ½ inch of the outer edges of the dough. Add apple butter until it is approximately 1/4 inch thick on the dough. Gently pick up the outer edge of the dough and roll toward the center and to the opposite edge. Pinch the ends of the roll shut. Place on a greased cookie sheet and bake at 350 degrees until brown. Remove from the oven. Let cool then slice the roll cross ways. The result is lovely to look at and even more delicious to eat.

The apple butter gradually changed colors as the hours passed. It was not a particularly pretty sight. It changed from a golden color to an ugly grayish brown to a brick-red color toward the end of the day; Hilda and Larry began to wonder how we would know when the apple butter was done and ready for the sugar and seasonings. Mom's knowledge was again in urgent demand. She told them, "Go in the house and get me a flat saucer so I can show you when it is done."

Mom dipped into the boiling butter with a tablespoon. She put two tablespoons of apple butter on the flat saucer. She then took a knife and split the apple butter down the middle and separated it on the saucer. The apple butter stayed in two separate piles and none of the liquid wept out; that is, the water no longer separated from the pulp. She said, "See there. That's how you know it's done and ready for the sugar and seasoning. If those two piles had oozed any water, we would need to keep on cooking it for a while. Hilda, go get the oil of cinnamon and the sugar."

With Larry's help, Hilda poured the sugar into the boiling apple butter. The kettle came dangerously close to running over. Mom prompted the stirrer to stir harder to keep the butter from overflowing. Mom then added two small bottles of oil of cinnamon. The washhouse now smelled like a little piece of heaven, and the stirring was even more intense. Mom warned, "Now that the sugar is in, you need to be even more careful with the stirring. You have to keep the apple butter moving in the kettle."

The pennies were making a scraping sound as the stirrer pushed them around on the bottom of the kettle. The sound seemed more obvious now with the renewed effort of stirring. It reminded me of how runners suddenly get more energy when they see the finish line. The pennies were scraping louder, the stirrer was moving with more speed and perfect rhythm, and everyone was scurrying around getting the quart jars set up on the table. The funnel was in place, and the dipper lying nearby.

Mom said, "We can

The long day's work is about over, the fire is going out. Apple butter splats are obvious on the floor and walls around the kettle and kettle stove. The stirring continues until all the apple butter is dipped out of the hot kettle and stored in quart canning jars.

let the fire die down some now. We will need to get close to the kettle, and we don't want the apple butter popping on our arms as we dip it out. Hilda, hand me that big dishpan. I am gonna dip it full of apple butter then you can start putting it into the jars."

When only the last few inches of warm apple butter was left in the kettle, Mom's homemade light bread was passed around for everyone to dip in and sample the sweet fruits of their labors.

Chapter 9

Bringing Home the Bacon

Some have meat and cannot eat, and some would eat that want it;
but we have meat, and we can eat, and so the Lord be thanked.
—*Robert Burns*

By the end of October, all the fruits and vegetables were gathered, harvested, processed and safely stored in the cellar for the next year's meals. It was then time to "bring home the bacon." The cooks could relax a while, as it was mainly up to the men to fill the larder with squirrel and venison; although Aunt Ethel and I tried our best to help by deer hunting together every season. I contributed quite a few squirrels to the family table after I turned fifteen. Both men and women joined forces again in mid November to complete the hog butchering. The Monday after hog butchering at our house was the first day of deer hunting season.

Squirrel Hunting

Squirrel hunting became legal on October 1, but that didn't mean much to the folks in Hopkins Gap. We were hungry for fresh meat by August 1. At least that is when my dad and I started hunting squirrels. Squirrels were frantically eating and hiding acorns starting in August because they were, like my family, preparing for the upcoming winter. They were easy to hear and see as they moved around in the oak trees which were still full of green leaves. You could hear them rustling to grab a nut at the end of the leafy branches. Then they would move to a sturdier limb to eat the nut or came to the ground to hide it. While they were chewing away at the nut, we took aim with Dad's .22 rifle. We used bullets called .22 "shorts" because they were much quieter than .22 "longs." The shorts made a little "spat" sound when the trigger was pulled, and we were less likely to be caught by the game warden. Dad had a strategy to prevent being caught which always worked for me too. We stepped into the woods, stopped to listen for squirrels rattling the leaves, shot the squirrel, and moved to a different part of the woods to listen for the next one. In other words, we never stayed in the same spot long enough for the game warden to locate us by the sound of our gunfire.

Larry adopts a new identity...

Either my brother, Larry, hadn't learned the strategy of not staying in the same place in the woods or the game warden got lucky one day. Larry was hunting one Saturday in Dean's woods, with Dad's .22 rifle, when Ronald Wilfong, the game warden, walked up on him. Mr. Wilfong asked, "What are you doing, young fellow? What's your name?" Larry was standing there with a rifle and several squirrels, so it was quite obvious what he had been doing. Larry just looked at him and didn't say a thing. "What's your name?" Mr. Wilfong asked again. Larry found his tongue and answered, "I'm Ted Knight." Mr. Wilfong said, "Well, Mr. Ted Knight. How about you come with me? I'll carry the gun and the squirrels." He escorted Larry back to his car and drove him home to our house. Mr. Wilfong brought Larry through the yard to the kitchen door and knocked. Dad answered the door. Mr. Wilfong knew Dad quite well. He said, "Mr. Shifflett, I would like you to meet Mr. Ted Knight. I caught him hunting squirrels out of season with your gun."

Of course, Dad and Larry went to court, paid the fine, and

retrieved the confiscated .22 rifle. Larry was not charged for claiming to be Ted Knight. We all teased Larry for years afterward, about being Ted Knight on that fateful Saturday in Dean's woods.

My favorite time to hunt squirrels was in late September, after the hickory nuts were ready. I could hear a squirrel from a long distance, grabbing a hickory nut from a high limb and then moving to a lower limb to eat it. When he would take the hull off the nut it sounded like a hail storm hitting the limbs and leaves on its way to the ground. In no time, the squirrel was chewing into the hard shell to get to the tasty nut inside. The sound would then change to a fast, low, grinding noise. The squirrel sat very still and was focused totally on the grinding. That was when I would take aim with Dad's .22 rifle and shoot him through the head, so I wouldn't mess up the meat. I was a good shot and often returned home with five or six squirrels, all shot through the head. Mom always bragged about my aim, saying, "You bring home the cleanest squirrels. I don't have to pick the hair off the meat where the bullet hit. Your daddy don't seem to care if he shoots them through the legs or not." Mom's bragging always made me want to shoot more squirrels to please her.

Usually by the time squirrel hunting season opened on October first, Dad, Larry and I had already stocked the freezer with over one hundred squirrels. Mom and I did all of the skinning and cleaning. One of us held the squirrel by the back legs, while the other cut a slice through the skin at the bottom of the tail. Then one of us put our foot on the tail and pulled upward with the back legs. Usually the skin peeled off in a consistent pattern, down the back and off the front legs to the neck. We pulled the front feet loose from the skin. The skin separated in a v-shape over the squirrel's stomach leaving a pointed skin piece that was easy to grab. The skin came easily off the back legs. In a minute or less, we had a furless squirrel nearly ready for the pot. Mom made a variety of dishes using the squirrel's four legs, back and ribs.

Fried Squirrel Recipe...

Ingredients
4 squirrels   salt and pepper to taste
2 cups flour   water
½ cup of lard

Clean and cut squirrels into serving pieces, usually six pieces per squirrel. Put pieces in a large cook pot and cover with water. Add salt. Boil the squirrel pieces until tender when pierced with a fork. Put flour, salt and pepper into a deep dish and mix well. In an iron skillet, heat some lard to make about ½ inch deep in the skillet. Dip squirrel pieces in the flour mixture and put them in the hot skillet. Fry until crispy brown on each side, turning only once. Serve hot.

Squirrel Gravy Recipe...

Ingredients
Broth from boiled squirrels
2 tablespoons flour
3 cups of milk
Salt and pepper to taste
¼ cup water

Add milk to the squirrel broth and bring to a boil. Mix flour with water and add to the broth while stirring. Stir until the mixture gets medium thick. Add salt and pepper to taste. Serve with fried squirrel and warm bread.

Brunswick Stew with Squirrel Recipe...
Ingredients

4 squirrels	1 tablespoon salt
1 minced onion	6 potatoes
1 teaspoon pepper	2 teaspoons sugar
2 cups lima beans	6 ears of corn
½ pound of salt pork	4 cups sliced tomatoes
½ pound butter	

Cut squirrels into serving pieces. Add salt to four quarts of water and bring to a boil. Cook until tender. Remove meat from the bones and return it to the broth. Add lima beans, corn cut from the cob, and salt pork. Simmer for two hours. Add sugar, tomato and onion and simmer for one hour more. Ten minutes before removing from heat, add butter cut into pieces the size of a walnut and rolled in flour. Bring to a boil. Serve in soup plates.

Hog Butchering

Hog butchering has always held a particular fascination for me, and I have always tried to get home for butchering day. I was allowed to attend my first one in November, 1945, when I was four years old. As I think back to that day, I realize that Dad had just returned from World War II, and it was his first butchering for his growing family. Mom was three months pregnant with the fourth child, my brother John. We still lived in Pop May's rental house. Pop May was our neighbor and owned the house we lived in. He was tall and slender with a full head of white hair, always covered by a straw hat, and a white handlebar mustache. He had watched over Mom and us three kids while Dad was in the war.

I still have vivid memories of the sights, and especially the smells, that I experienced that day. I remember Mom doing a lot of extra cooking in the days beforehand, and I recall Dad gathering wood for the fires the butchering would require. Dad and my uncles made elaborate plans for the best way to get the butchering done.

I recall that there was snow on the ground and, I could barely contain my excitement. I begged Mom to allow me to go outside to watch the butchering. She finally relented and after many warnings and a "once upon a time" story about a little girl who slipped and fell into a kettle of hot lard and died a terrible death, she dressed me in several layers of clothing, and a one-piece snow suit that zipped all the way down the front.

It is not difficult for me to remember that day because shortly into the morning, I had to go to the bathroom, but I didn't want to leave the butchering. Having experienced some sixty years of butchering days, I realize that at four years old I would have been very busy watching everything. At a hog butchering, something new happens every moment. I am sure I didn't want to miss anything. I was very likely noticing the changing smells that go along with each step of the process. First, there was the unpleasant smell of hog manure wafting from the hog pens as my dad walked up to the fence and shot the first hog between the eyes with his single shot .22 rifle. The first few times I followed behind him and watched as he put the gun barrel several inches from the hog's head and pulled the trigger. The hog grunted and squealed, then fell over in the mud. One time I started crying. Dad yelled at me, "Stop cryin' 'cause that makes 'em die harder." That was the last time I watched him shoot a hog. I usually went into Mom and Dad's bedroom and held my hands over my ears until the hogs were all dead.

Once the hog was dead and its throat cut so

The men use ropes to turn the hog in the scalding pan so all the hair will come loose enough to scrape off (1974)

that it could bleed out, it was placed in a trough of scalding water to loosen the hair enough to be removed easily. I always stood by and watched as the men scraped the hair off with hog scrapers and with their hands. The scrapers made a rhythmic sound at times when the men were in sync with each other. They knew exactly how hard to dig with the scrapers so they didn't break the skin on the hog. Their hands were always red from the hot water.

As the steam rose up from the scalding pan, I got another unpleasant whiff. Scalded hog hair was never a welcome visitor to my little nose. When the hog was scraped clean, one of the men stuck a knife through the tendons on the hind feet and inserted an S-hook in each foot. The hog was dragged on

John Mason, my dad, and Uncle James remove the hair from a hog while Uncle Jim sets up the hog hangers in the background for the hog they have just finished scraping. (1974)

top of a set of three poles with hooks that corresponded to the hooks in the tendons. The hog was attached to the poles; and using the poles as leverage, the heavy hog was lifted off the ground and hung, head down from the tripod. Once the hog was hung, scraped down, and washed clean by the women, the head was removed. One of the butchers sliced into the bone around the hog's neck; and then with a hog hook, he twisted the head off. Uncle Jake, the head man, was waiting for the head so he could start his job as head cleaner. At that point, smells of hot blood would fill the air as the headless hog finished bleeding out. It was not a pleasant smell, but a slight improvement on the steam from the scalding pan.

The head butcher quickly went to work, and it wasn't long before the hog started coming apart. Using a very sharp knife, he carefully cut through the belly fat without cutting the membrane that held the intestines in place. The second cut was gentler, as he opened the membrane so the intestines would roll out.

Mom stood by with a tub to catch the intestines as they were sliced away from the ribs and sides of the hog, and they rolled out in a steaming mass. Mom said to the head butcher, "Make sure you don't cut a gut. I will have to throw the intestines away and won't have them to stuff my sausage. I have tried before to get hog shit off the guts, but there is no way to git rid of that smell." (The air blowing across those hot steaming guts smelled a lot like hog shit to me.) The butcher carefully removed the large intestine from the anus, and using some twine string, tied it shut. He gently cut the final membranes, and the guts fell into a tub that Mom had set down. Another large clean dishpan was placed by the tub. The butcher dug around through the guts and found the liver. He removed it and turned it over to cut out the gall bladder. The kidneys and heart were also removed, trimmed, and set aside to soak.

When the guts were out and the hog split down the back, one of the younger men was called to carry a half of a hog to the cutting boards. This was a test of manhood for the young man. A half of a hog weighed as much as three hundred pounds, and if the young man could successfully carry the weight across his shoulder, it meant he was ready to start learning to trim the hams and shoulders.

An iron kettle was designated as the puddin' kettle and it had a gallon or so of water boiling in the bottom. Mom said, "I want a good chunk of liver put in the puddin' 'cause that makes it good." The butcher got the pan with the liver, kidneys, and hearts, and Mom showed him how much liver to take off for the pudding.' He put the kidneys in the puddin' and started a tub for the sausage meat by slicing the heart into about four pieces. The heart went into the sausage meat.

As the head butcher started to trim out the hams, shoulders

and middlins, he tossed the fattest scraps of meat into the puddin' kettle and scraps with lean meat on them into the sausage meat tub. The head man removed the jowls and the brains from the hog's head, and tossed the meat scraps from his work into the puddin' kettle.

The younger men started setting up another kettle over a fire for the lard. As the men, women, and children cut the big slabs of fat into one inch square pieces; this was dumped into the kettle to be rendered into lard. The lard kettle had to be watched carefully and stirred often to prevent burning. One kettle would hold about twenty gallons of lard, and if it burned, it was a major loss for the family.

The lard kettle filled with sizzling chunks of fat. A piece of old tin roofing was used to keep the fire under the kettle so it didn't spread in the wind.

Lard was the grease that ran the entire Hopkins Gap homestead for the following year. Both men and women used the lard in various ways. The cooks used it in many recipes from soup, to pie dough, cakes, and homemade light bread. Mom's style of using lard was very typical of all the cooks. When her bread came out of the oven, she would brush lard over the top of the loaves and cover them with a cloth so that the crust would be soft and easy to chew. She seasoned her vegetables with hog lard—pinto beans, green beans, potatoes, and cabbage. She fried her greens and sauerkraut in lard.

When it was time to castrate the pigs for next year's butchering, Dad mixed turpentine and lard to rub into the holes where the testicles came out. Castration was necessary because the hormones that were secreted by the testicles gave the meat and lard an unpleasant, strong flavor after the hog was butchered. Mom rubbed her iron skillets with lard and baked them in the oven to "cure" them so food wouldn't stick when she cooked in them. After the butchering, the iron kettles were rubbed down with lard and stored for the next year. Cross cut saws and other tools used around the farm were also greased with lard to prevent rust.

Grandma Molly, in the older days, mixed lard and brown sugar to treat bed sores on Grandpa Austin and other bedridden folks in Hopkins Gap. Before Mom died, she suffered from leg ulcers caused by diabetes. She had me mix lard and brown sugar and put it on her ulcers. Lard was a priceless product and extreme caution was taken to make sure it wasn't wasted. Dad used to brag all the time about how much lard he got out of his hogs, "That old sow made four tanks," he would say to anybody who would listen.

Suddenly, the odors of butchering began to improve when the puddin' kettle started boiling. By now everything but the "hogs' squeal" was rolling around in the kettle as the broth boiled and bubbled. The hog's tail, scraps of meat, chunks of liver, and other hog body parts were tossed into the boiling pot. I watched one of the butchers tie a string around a long skinny piece of meat that he planned to snack on later. He kept an eye out so Mom didn't see him. He dropped the meat into the puddin' kettle and let the string hang over the side. Later in the morning, I heard Mom fussing about how she didn't have the right number of "fish" (a local name for the finest cuts of tenderloin). She accused the butchers of stealing the fish. The men laughed at her and told her she was stingy. They tried to tell her she couldn't count or was crazy. She argued, "No, I ain't crazy. We butchered eight hogs, and we should have sixteen fish. We only have thirteen." Then she stomped away, and I am sure she felt very helpless at that moment. By the next year's butchering, Mom had worked out a strategy for saving her best meat. She ordered my dad to grab the fish and the larger tenderloins as soon as they came out of the hog. Over the years, she was often called names such as "old tight wad" and "old tight-assed Myrt" for guarding her best cuts of pork.

I knew which butchering helpers had put the best meat in the kettle, but I decided to wait and tell her later. Besides, I still had to pee through all these stages, so I stood around in misery, wishing

I was a boy and could just go behind the barn, unzip and go to the bathroom without undoing all those layers and freezing my little behind.

Finally, my curiosity and my full bladder got me into trouble. During one of the most exciting moments—maybe it was when they cut the second hog's head off, or when they chopped down through the hog's backbone with

Mom and Dad are carrying the tenderloins and the fish toward the house for safekeeping (1974)

an axe, or when Uncle Jake cracked a hog's skull open with his axe to remove the brains, or when Grandma Molly put a hog gut into her mouth and blew it up like a balloon—I don't remember the exact moment—but I must have wet my pants and only noticed when I started to feel the cold. I told Mom, and, of course, she got upset because she was busy with Grandma Molly, teaching her how to clean the small intestines of the hog for stuffing the sausage.

Mom yelled at me, "I told you to stay in the house in the first place. I'm going to put some dry clothes on you, but you can't come out here again." I stayed in the house for a while and watched Aunt Ethel and Aunt Hazel cooking the butchering dinner. They had every cook pot in the house bubbling and steaming on the wood stove. The windows were steamed up with streaks of water running down the panes. While in the house, I noticed the smells were altogether different and very inviting. There was the delicious smell of frying apples—sweet and buttery—mixed with the pungent smell of sauerkraut dumplings and pinto beans. I thought I would starve to death before dinner.

On the porch table, just outside the kitchen, was a three-layer banana cake with curly white icing, along with at least twenty pies. There were apple, cherry, peach, and blackberry pies, along with fancy pies of egg custard, coconut cream, chocolate and lemon meringue.

One of my favorites was always there—raisin pie with an elaborately designed lattice crust.

A big coffee pot steamed on another table at the end of the porch in case the butchers got cold and hungry. The men would send one of us kids into the house to tell the cooks to bring them a slice of pie and some coffee. The cooks dutifully and pleasantly carried hot coffee and slices of pie to the hard working men. It always pleased me to see everybody getting along with each other on butchering day, because that wasn't always the case. In the days leading up to the hog killing, Mom and Dad often got into one of their heated discussions about Uncle Jake, dad's brother, or about "not mixin' whiskey with hog killin'."

Aunt Ethel and Aunt Hazel were frying fresh liver and tenderloin, just removed from the hog. Interestingly, frying the fresh meat with Aunt Ethel became my job at future hog killings. When I thought enough time had passed and that Mom had forgotten her orders for me to stay in the house, I slipped out the door and back to the warmth of the butchering kettles. I just made sure I got to the house in time to get out of my clothes before I wet them again.

As I look back on those wonderful occasions, I see that many important things were going on besides killing the hogs and preserving the meat. Raleigh May was the head butcher and meat trimmer. We always called him "Pop" May. He would quietly and patiently show Uncle Jim, Uncle Shirley, and my daddy each step of the process by letting them help him. Grandma Molly passed down her knowledge to Mom by showing her how to clean the hog intestines. After Mom got up the nerve to blow up her first hog gut, she became quite good at cleaning hog intestines. She became the gut cleaner after Grandma Molly was too frail to help with butchering.

My presence introduced a third generation to watch and learn the process of butchering hogs. In the next few years, my brothers were old enough to stay warm by the kettles as they watched and learned. Over the years I watched and eventually took my place at the November hog killing. During that time, I watched Uncle Shirley and Uncle Jim become the head butchers. My daddy learned how to season sausage from Pop May, and with some creative additions of his own, he became the expert on sausage seasoning and mixing the cure for the hams and shoulders.

As each ham, shoulder, and middlin' was carved to perfection out of the hogs, Dad took them into his little meat house. This little building was built especially for curing pork. It was only about five feet wide by eight feet long. It was raised about eighteen inches off the ground, and had two steps up into the door. The outside of the building was covered with corrugated metal nailed directly to the two by four framing. The roof was also corrugated metal. On the back wall inside the meat house, Dad built shelves and left cracks between the boards for air circulation. He laid his meat on the shelves which he called meat boards.

The meat house had a window on each side that could be opened for ventilation if needed. There was a wonderful smell in the meat house depending on the time of year. Immediately after butchering, there was the smell of salt and sugar mixture—very inviting. Along about February, the smell changed to a sweet moldy odor as the meat was curing. These were smells that I associated with Dad. In the days after he died, I went in the meat house and felt very close to him. On butchering days, I would visit him in the meat house, as he rubbed the fresh meat with sugar cure mixture. He would proudly show me the size of the hams, and the lean streaks in the middlin' meat. He often said, "This is going to taste good next year. We'll cut one of these hams in about six months." We had some of our best conversations in the meat house.

A tornado hits the farm...

Approximately a month after Dad was buried in March of 1994, a small tornado came through our farm. It picked up the butchering building, carried it across the yard fence, and smashed it to pieces. Dad's meat house was not spared by the tornado. It was picked up and turned upside down in nearly the same spot it had set all through the years. Mom called me and told me the story. My first comment was, "Oh God, Dad's pissed about something." I thought he was angry that he had died and left his uncut hams and shoulders for others to eat and enjoy.

Very soon after the tornado, Uncle Shirley and Aunt Ethel arrived and over the next week or so, helped my brothers and Mom clean up the mess left by the butchering building. When my school was out for the summer, I went home to see what I could do. Mom wanted to immediately rebuild a butchering building because she said Dad would want her to replace it.

I pointed out that my brothers should start butchering at their homes, so we would build a new butchering building at Larry's home instead. After she weighed the pros and cons of that solution, she looked at me and said, "I want the building put back exactly where it was, just like your daddy would have wanted it." Over the next month, my brother Warnie and I built a butchering building in the exact same place as the previous one. The only thing we changed was to make the new building somewhat bigger.

———————————————————————————————

Dad rubbed the sugar cure mixture into each piece of meat, being sure to push it into the crevices around the shank bone, and placed it on a layer of clean white flour sacks that Mom had placed on the meat boards earlier in the week. In a day or so, the sacks would be soaked with bloody water. Dad would show me, "See the sugar cure is drawing out the juice from the meat so it can cure. If that juice stayed in, the meat would spoil."

Sugar Cure Mixture Recipe...
Ingredients
For each 100 lbs. of bone meat:
8 lbs. of fine salt
3 lbs. of brown sugar
3 ozs. Salt peter

For each 100 lbs. of side meat or middlin'
6 lbs. of salt
2 lbs. of brown sugar
2 ozs. Salt peter

Mix well in a large container. Rub on fresh meat making sure to get the cure in all cracks and especially around the bone. Repeat as needed and more often if the night air is above freezing.

Each year, Mom would ask Dad to set aside four middlin's to make into pepper belly. That was the very best bacon.

Pepper Belly Cure Recipe...

Ingredients
2 slabs of middlin'
¾ cup brown sugar
1 lb. black pepper
3 bottles MSG
2 cups of salt
(Double the ingredients for four slabs of middlin'.)
Mix well and rub on the meat. Repeat as necessary depending on the night temperature. If above freezing, repeat every other day until the weather is below freezing at night.

Panhaus

Panhaus is made with the broth from the meat scraps after the meat has been dipped out of the pudding kettle. It is the last event of hog butchering day. The men take turns stirring the mixture so it doesn't burn. Stirring is easy at first but becomes more strenuous as the panhaus begins to thicken. Once cooked, the panhaus is placed in small pans to cool. A portion is retained for the family, but a large part of the panhaus is sent home with the butchering helpers, as a token of appreciation for their assistance.

Panhaus Recipe...

Ingredients

1 gallon corn meal   salt and pepper
½ gallon flour   5–7 gallon broth
1 gallon ground meat

Remove all meat chunks and bones from the puddin' kettle leaving the broth. Grind about 1 gallon of the meat and return it to the broth. Bring the broth to a rolling boil. Salt and pepper to taste. Slowly pour in corn meal and flour until the broth thickens. Maintain a rolling boil. Stir swiftly and constantly until the mixture thickens and does not stick to the sides of the kettle. Taste just before removing to make sure the mixture does not taste like cornmeal. When satisfied with the taste, remove the kettle from the fire. Put the panhaus into containers for storage.

My brothers, Larry, John, and Warnie stepped away from the kettles and stood beside Uncle Shirley and Uncle Jim while they trimmed the hams and shoulders into works of art. Larry and John learned their future roles as meat trimmers and head butchers at the side of the best butchers in Hopkins Gap.

At the end of butchering day each man who had helped kill and clean the hogs went home with a "mess" of meat" and a pan of panhaus. Dad told each helper, "Before you go home, stop in and let Myrt give you a mess of sausage." When Mom wrapped a "mess" of sausage, she took note of the size of the helper's family. If it happened to be Branson Conley, she recognized his "mess" should be larger than other "messes"

Larry Shifflett helped butcher at Uncle Shirley's house. He is in the middle stage of learning to be a head butcher. Here he is learning how to remove a hog's head while his wife, Hilda, waits with a bucket to take the head to the head cleaner.

because he had a lot of children—fifteen in all. Branson's "mess" was bigger than John Mason's "mess," because John had only himself and his mother in his household for many years. Butchering day turned out to be a time of feasting for the families in Hopkins Gap.

Hog butchering at my home usually marked the first butchering of the season. The following Saturday Uncle Shirley would butcher, then Uncle Jim, then Skip Crawford. Many of the same helpers were called to be present for all the butchering. In that way, everybody got their hogs killed and processed before Christmas, and there was fresh pork throughout the fall for most of the families in Hopkins Gap.

After all the men left at the end of hog butchering day, my brothers got out their high-powered rifles and began to shoot at targets so they would have their sights lined up for the opening of deer season on the following Monday morning. They had all grown beards and let their hair grow long. They claimed the extra hair kept them warm on cold mornings. I never believed that. I thought it had something to do with feeling more rugged and manly for the big hunt. They started growing their beards in August.

The day after hog butchering was Sunday. The fresh sausage, tenderloin, puddin' meat, backbone, and hog feet were left in the butchering building to cool out before they were canned on Monday and Tuesday. The women did the canning. Mom saved her canning jars from year to year and always washed them the week before butchering, and had turned them upside down and ready on a table in the canning area of the butchering building. In later years, she had a small gas stove in one corner. She used that to place her copper boiler over the burners for canning.

This past year, November 2005, was the first year since 1940 that the Shifflett family did not kill hogs. My brother, Larry, the current head butcher, was very ill and could not raise hogs and organize a butchering. My brother, John, called me just before butchering day and said, "Did you know Larry is not butchering this year?" I felt the impact of his statement in my stomach, "Oh no," I answered, quietly. John told me, "I am going to buy him a Turner Ham for Christmas, but that still won't be the same."

Just across the fields from Larry's house, the butchering fires didn't burn under the Crawford family kettles, because the head butcher in that family, Skip Crawford, died September

Here is Skip Crawford as a young man who tended the fire under the kettles as he learned his future role as head butcher for his family.

21, 2005. Skip also learned the skills of head butcher at the side of Uncle Shirley, Uncle Jim, and my dad. With Larry's death on September 11, 2006, the tradition of butchering ended for the Shifflett family.

At the gathering after Larry's funeral, both the Crawfords and the Shiffletts expressed sadness that so many years of family tradition have come to an end.

Tenderloin

Tenderloin from the hog was considered a delicacy to Hopkins Gap folks. It was the finest meat from along the backbone. If bones were left in it, it was pork chops. Mom and Dad kept some tenderloin for slicing and frying for several weeks after butchering day. The remainder was canned in quart jars for winter eating.

Fried Tenderloin Recipe…

Ingredients

Pork tenderloin   flour

Salt and pepper   lard

The amount of each ingredient is determined by the number of people to feed. Slice tenderloin into 1/3 inch thick slices. Mix flour, salt, and pepper in a shallow dish. Dip tenderloin slices into water and then into flour mixture. Be sure to coat both sides of the meat with the flour mixture. Heat enough lard to be about ¼ inch deep in a skillet. Heat the lard until near smoking. Place floured slices in the hot lard. Fry until crispy brown, turning only once. Use drippings in the pan to make milk gravy. (Recipe on page 115.)

Pork Backbone Recipe…

Ingredients

Pork backbone   salt and pepper

Water

Boil pork until tender, in enough water to cover the backbone pieces. Serve as whole pieces. Meat falls easily from the bone. Very good served with noodles. Retain the broth from the backbone for vegetable soup or ham potpie.

Pigs Feet and Hocks Recipe…

Ingredients

Pigs' feet cut off at the hock   water

salt and pepper   vinegar

Vinegar

Remove the pigs' feet at the hock (first joint up the leg). Put in hot water to clean. Take a razor and shave off the hair. Place in a pot of water seasoned with salt and pepper and boil until the meat is falling from the bones. Place on a large platter for serving. Add vinegar to each serving. Eat all the meat (the hock provides large slivers of lean meat) and the jelly substance. Once the meat is cleaned from the bones and eaten, suck the bones to remove any extra meat and the marrow.

Potpie

Using the broth from the boiled ham or pork shoulder, Mom made my absolute favorite dish for cold winter months. I never felt as warm and comfortable as I did after eating several servings of potpie. This dish, for me, represented security, safety, continuity, and total comfort. Mom's potpie was very different from what most people think of as potpie. It did not have a crust, but was more like soup made from boiled dough.

Since Mom died, I visit Aunt Ethel when I am hungry for potpie. She goes to the basement and gets a ham hock from her freezer. In the past she would have gone out to the meat house and cut the end off a ham—a meat house similar to the one my Dad used to cure his hog meat. Aunt Ethel still cures her hog meat in a meat house, but after the first cut on a big ham, she places the remaining pieces in her freezer.

Aunt Ethel cuts a large onion into her boiling meat broth.

Aunt Ethel sifts her flour, preparing to make the dough for the potpie.

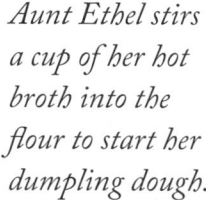

Aunt Ethel stirs a cup of her hot broth into the flour to start her dumpling dough.

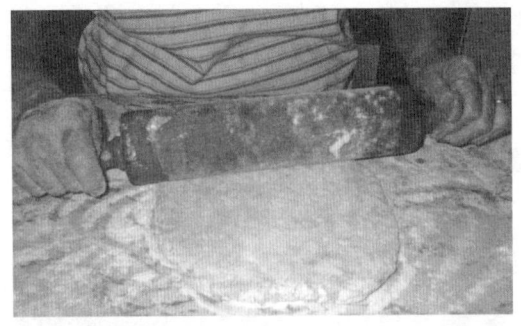

Aunt Ethel uses her ancient rolling pen to roll her dough flat so she can cut it into strips.

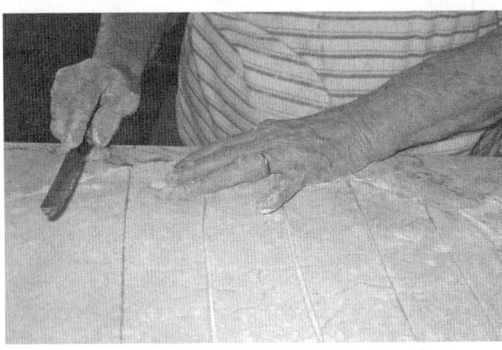

She slices her dough into wide noodles. These noodles are dropped into the boiling meat broth.

Ham Potpie Recipe...

Ingredients for broth
1 ham hock   water to cover

Boil the ham hock for at least three hours on the stovetop or for one hour in a pressure cooker. If boiling on a stovetop, check the water level to make sure it is above the meat. Add more water as needed. When the ham is tender, place it on a platter to use as the main course alongside the potpie.

Ingredients for noodles
Ham broth   1 large onion
3 large potatoes, chopped in   pan of all-purpose flour, sifted
    1-inch chunks

Slice the onion into the boiling broth. Sift flour into a large pan and form a hole in the middle of the flour. Dip a cup into the boiling ham broth and pour enough into the flour so that a ball of dough can be formed. Once the dough is formed, roll it out onto a tabletop. With a rolling pin, roll the dough flat until it is approximately 1/8 inch thick. With a knife, slice the dough into strips of about two inches wide. (The width is up to the individual cook. Mom sliced her dough into 1-inch pieces). The strips are then sliced in the opposite direction to lengths of about three inches. Drop the noodles one at a time into the rapidly boiling meat broth.

Add the potato chunks. Boil until the potatoes are tender, about 20 minutes. Serve.

Hunting Season

The main purpose of hunting season was to bring home meat for the winter. A secondary purpose was to bring in some extra money by selling the skins of small animals such as raccoons and skunks. Every homestead maintained one or two well-trained raccoon hounds for the sport of hunting as well as for the income from skins.

Uncle Shirley and Skip Crawford pose with their coon hounds and a beautiful display of raccoon skins. (circa 1950)

The Sunday after hog butchering, my brothers packed their camping gear, hunting gear, fresh meat from the butchering, and a huge pot of pinto beans. They left for the mountains so they could be at their designated deer stands long before daylight on Monday morning.

I tried my hand at deer hunting for quite a few years. Aunt

Ethel and I would arrange a day or two to hunt together. She drove us back into the Hog Pens, to Uncle Shirley's hunting cabin, where we would spend the night so we could be in the woods early in the morning. She always packed the food and, for me, she fixed sausage sandwiches with mustard and dill pickle slices.

One time Aunt Ethel and I were walking up a trail when we saw a deer cross the path just in front of us. She said, "Peg, you shoot him." I answered, "No, you shoot him." The deer just stood there while we were being polite to each other. We both raised our rifles and shot at about the same time. Both of us missed and the deer trotted off, probably smiling to himself. After that, Aunt Ethel and I always had a discussion about who would shoot first, so we didn't have to discuss it with our target standing in front of us.

Sometimes during deer season a lucky hunter would shoot a wild turkey. This was no easy feat since wild turkeys are the smartest quarry in the mountains and have to be shot "on the fly." This quarry gives the lucky hunter a lot of bragging rights.

Squirrel hunter kills first deer illegally with .22 rifle...

One year while I was still at home, I faithfully got up at 3:00 a.m. every morning of deer season and headed deep into the Allegheny Mountains with my brother, Larry. We hunted hard and long with absolutely no luck at all. On Friday of that week, we decided to stay home and catch up on our sleep. Later that day, Larry suggested that we take our guns and head to the woods to hunt for some squirrels. Larry said, "Maybe we will have more luck if we just hunt for squirrels. He took a sixteen gauge shotgun and I took Dad's .22 single shot rifle.

It was about noon when we got into the woods. We soon found that nothing was stirring. It was really too early for squirrels to begin their afternoon foraging. We just ambled along for a while, shooting through squirrel nests to see if we could run them out into the open. We even tried to kick up a rabbit or two by jumping up and down on brush piles. In other words, we were making a lot of noise just playing around. All of a sudden, we heard a dog barking in a field just below where we were standing. We looked around and saw that the dog was chasing a deer. Suddenly, the deer stopped to look back at the dog. It was at least one hundred yards from where we were standing. Larry said, "Look at that, damn it. I didn't bring my deer rifle." I said, "Let me try to shoot it with the .22 rifle." Larry said, "You will never hit it from here, but

go ahead and try." I aimed Dad's trusty rifle, pulled the trigger, and the deer fell dead in its tracks. Then I got scared. The deer was so far away I couldn't tell if it had horns, and doe season didn't start until the next day. I said to Larry, "Let's run like hell. I just killed a doe I didn't think I could hit from this far off. You're not supposed to shoot at a deer with a .22 rifle. He said, "No don't run. Let's go look." When we got close to the dead deer we saw that it was a male with spiked horns. "Look at that," Larry said, "how in the hell did you hit him that far away. You got him right under his left horn." We both sat on the ground in disbelief until we realized we had to field dress the deer and had a long way to drag him to get him home.

I was very proud that I could contribute to the meat supply that winter. All of us together brought home four bucks. We skinned them out and Mom put the meat in the freezer.

Fried Venison Steak Recipe...

Ingredients

1 pound venison steak	1 teaspoon salt
¼ cup of flour	¼ cup of lard
½ cup of water	½ teaspoon pepper

Soak the meat in vinegar water for 24 hours. Drain, rinse, and salt the meat. Roll in flour mixed with pepper. Heat lard in a large skillet until near smoking. Place meat in the hot lard. Add water, cover and simmer until the meat is tender. Use the drippings for venison gravy. (Use recipe for milk gravy on page 115.)

In order to use all the meat of a deer, Mom would cut the shoulders into cubes and can it. During the winter, she opened the shoulder meat and made venison stew.

Canned Venison Recipe...

Ingredients

Shoulder of venison	salt
Water	

Cut venison into cubes. Put meat in large shallow pan; add just enough water to keep it from sticking. Cook meat slowly, stirring occasionally until medium done. Add water to cover. Bring to a boil. While boiling, pack hot meat loosely in clean hot canning jars. Cover the meat in the jar with broth, leaving 1 inch head space. Process in a pressure canner at 10 pounds pressure: pints for 75 minutes and quarts for 90 minutes at 15 pounds of pressure.

Venison Stew Recipe...

Ingredients

2 cans canned venison or
    3 lbs boneless venison   2 large onions, chopped
Flour   2 large garlic cloves, minced
Salt and pepper   3 tablespoons of lard
¼ teaspoon dried tarragon   2 cups beef stock

Cut meat into 1¼ inch cubes (if not canned). Dust with flour, salt, and pepper. Brown the meat on all sides in lard over medium heat. Add onions and remaining ingredients. Cover and simmer approximately 1½ hours or until tender (if meat is not canned). Cover and simmer approximately 45 minutes if meat is canned.

By Christmas time, Hopkins Gap folks could look forward to plenty of food throughout the winter months. The cellar was full of canned food, the potato bin would be running over, and when freezers became popular, they were also brimming over with food. Attention was now turned toward celebrating Christmas. Our family practiced a ritual that Grandma Molly taught Mom. To ensure that all the food we had gathered, processed, and stored would bring good health to our bodies, Mom always baked a fancy apple pie on Christmas Eve and placed it outside where the dew could fall on it overnight. We all ate some of the pie on Christmas day. Grandma Molly and Mom believed that the dew that fell on Jesus' birthday was pure and if consumed by the family, it would bring good luck and good health in the upcoming year.

The months of December, January, and February were quiet in terms of food gathering and processing. The cooks turned their attention to other household duties. Mom did most of her sewing during the cold months while we were in school. She sorted through her barrels of colorful feed sacks to make our school clothes, her dresses and aprons, and other items such as kitchen curtains and sewing machine covers. Mom used the feed sack scraps to piece together comforter tops. She stuffed the comforters with fleece she bought from stores such as Woolworth and J. C. Penny. While I helped her stuff a comforter, Mom related a story about her mother, Mary Lamb Morris, and how she stuffed her comforters. "Mom went along the fence rows and gathered sheep wool from the barbed wire—you know, where the sheep had rubbed against the wire and pulled out some of their wool. She put it away until she had enough to stuff a comforter. Real sheep wool was warmer than the stuff I buy now."

I recall my sister and I pointing to pieces of feed sack on our comforters and saying, "That was my school dress in the sixth grade or the fourth grade, and that was Larry's first grade shirt." Those were some very peaceful moments in my life.

Chapter 10

Meal Time: Puttin' It All Together

*"Food is the most basic forum for
discussing things like love and the
absence of love; how we hurt ourselves
and how we heal ourselves."*

—*Laura Benanti*

      Hopkins Gap folks, like most folks, always ate three times a day. Each meal was served at a time that met the scheduling needs of family members. Any time I sat down for a meal with my relatives, they expressed great pride in the food set before us, as it was usually filled with the products of their own labor. They ate a variety of fruits and vegetables depending on the season of the year. Their meat consisted mainly of pork, squirrel, or venison when available. They ate a natural and healthy diet from their efforts of hunting, gathering, planting and preserving. Modern day nutritionists and doctors would certainly have reservations about their use of lard, but they probably burned a lot of the saturated fat they consumed from lard as they worked toward setting the table with future meals.

Breakfast Menus

Breakfast menus were determined by when the chickens were laying. During their molting time in the fall and early winter, when eggs were not available, some typical menus would include:

Fried pork middlin'
Milk gravy
Light bread
Canned fruit
Homemade butter

Cornmeal Mush with milk
Fresh pork sausage
Light bread
Homemade butter
Canned fruit

Pan cakes with warm
    syrup or honey
Fresh tenderloin
Tenderloin milk gravy
Canned fruit

Corn cakes with warm syrup
Fried panhaus
Milk gravy
Canned fruit

It goes without saying that the above menus were served with all the milk we wanted to drink. When the chickens were laying during the spring and summer, Mom had a variety of recipes for breakfast.

Canned sausage, fried
Fried eggs
Light bread
Canned or fresh fruit

French toast with warm syrup
Fried pork middlin', sugar cured
Homemade butter
Canned or fresh fruit

Poached eggs
Corn flakes with milk
Canned sausage, fried
Homemade butter
Light bread

Soft-boiled eggs
Fried pork middlin', sugar cured
Milk gravy
Oatmeal with raisins
Homemade butter
Light bread

Breakfast at Home

Mom always started breakfast by frying the meat in one of her iron skillets. The smell of coffee perking and meat frying served much better than an alarm clock to get us out of bed for work and school. When the meat was done and she took it out of the pan, she laid it on a fairly large, oblong plate that she called the meat plate. She left the grease from the meat in the skillet and slid it off the fire. She would then set the meat plate on the back of the stove to stay warm while she went to the barn to milk her cows.

When Mom got back to the house and had strained the milk and put it away, she finished cooking breakfast. She moved the skillet back over the fire and heated the grease again. Once it was hot, she added some flour. She stirred the flour until it was sufficiently browned. Between stirrings, she gathered the remaining ingredients for gravy. She took a large dish from the cabinet and mixed equal amounts of milk and water. When the flour was browned, she poured the milk and water in the skillet.

Mom knew by the smell when the flour was browned just right. In her later years when I was helping to care for her, she asked me to make sausage gravy or tenderloin gravy for our breakfast. She sat at the dining room table, and using her nose, told me exactly when to add the milk and water to the browned flour. Many times I have heard her diagnose a dish of bad gravy by saying, "She didn't let her flour get brown enough."

After stirring continuously until the gravy began to bubble, Mom added salt and pepper for seasoning and stirred for a few seconds more. Using her dishcloth or her apron to protect her hand from burning, she picked up the skillet. She poured the gravy back into the large dish.

The air was tinged with the faint odor of cows, fresh milk and cool mountain air from Mom's early morning sojourn to the barn. The scent of milk gravy had an aroma of its own, as it blended with fried meat and coffee percolating on the stove. The kitchen was warm from the cook stove, and, added to all the other smells, was the faint perfume of wood smoke and pine kindling. This was enough to wake the dead in Gospel Hill Cemetery across Little North Mountain.

Breakfast with chicken slop...

January and early February were rough times to have breakfast at my home. Mom began a different way of feeding her laying hens because she wanted to have her chickens to start laying eggs before anybody else in the neighborhood (and perhaps in the world). For this goal, all of us children suffered.

The kitchen and dining room was filled with mouth-watering aromas of the finest breakfast foods. We were all sitting around the table enjoying the fruits of Mom's labor in front of the hot stove. As soon as Dad walked out the door to go to work, Mom walked out to the back porch and picked up a bucket that contained table scraps, potato peelings, and anything else that had once been edible. The contents were in the early stages of rot and smelled like it. To this mess, Mom added some whey that she had saved from making cottage cheese the day before. She added a scoop of laying mash from a sack on the porch.

She stirred the contents, carried the bucket into the kitchen, and plopped it on top of the stove. At first, I just wondered what she was doing and thought nothing of it as she usually had good reasons for what she did.

Suddenly the contents of the bucket started to steam, and we had started to hold our noses while we tried to finish eating. The smell was nearly indescribable. The overall effect was sour, but we could pick out the various rotting foods as each one heated up—whey, half rotten potato peelings, sweet-sour rotten apple peelings, and hot laying mash. I asked, "Mom, what are you cooking? I think I am going to puke." As usual, Mom answered with a question, "Do you like nice fresh eggs for breakfast, egg custard pie, egg custard, deviled eggs, and banana pudding?" I replied, "Of course I like them," realizing that I had just set myself up for one of Mom's lectures. She delivered as expected.

She said, "Everything you eat started out in manure. You know I grow sweet potatoes in pure hog manure. We always try to find some horse manure to put on the garden every fall. When I go to the barn to milk, I have to clean manure off the cow's teats before I can milk them. Hogs wallow in manure and mud puddles all year until we butcher them. My layin' hens love hot slop, and it makes them start to lay sooner than anybody else's chickens, so we can have plenty of eggs and I can sell some." "Okay, okay." I said, in a loud voice. "I get the picture. I don't need any more examples."

Throughout my life I came to understand that I had to suffer some really bad smells in order to get to the good ones. All of my favorite foods came out of situations where the smells were nearly unbearable. The meat we ate came from the stench of the hog pens. The smell of delicious fried chicken we ate at Sunday dinners came from the awful odors of cleaning those chickens on Saturday. Mom had to wash the manure off the cow's teats before she squeezed out the delicious sweet milk. I absolutely loved fresh eggs from the hens that pecked around our yard.

The hens laid more eggs if they were fed hot slop made from table scraps in the early laying season. That slop had to be heated somewhere, and the kitchen stove was the only place available. After I realized this, I didn't mind the bad smells as much since they were always outdone by the good smells.

Mom finished cooking breakfast while all of us, including Dad, ate the first round of gravy bread. Sometimes she made a big cake of warm bread to go with the gravy and often she had homemade light bread or light rolls on hand. No matter what type of bread Mom had made, Dad and us kids broke off a chunk, crumbled it on our plates, and poured milk gravy over it. We ate it with a teaspoon so we didn't miss a drop of the gravy. My dad used a tablespoon to shovel the gravy bread into his mouth.

In a smaller iron skillet, Mom would heat lard for frying fresh eggs from the hen house. Each person had a preferred style of eggs, so she would ask each of us two questions, "How many eggs do you want this morning, and how do you want them fixed?" My dad always wanted four eggs, fried sunny-side up, with the grease dipped over the top of his eggs while they were frying. By Mom's standards, he ate his eggs raw. Mom fussed with him all the time, "Norman, I don't see how you can eat half-raw eggs." He paid no attention as he put another fork full, with egg white stringing from it, in his mouth.

On the back of the stove sat a steaming pot of oatmeal with raisins. Many days I went to school having consumed a plate of gravy bread fixed just like my daddy, two eggs fried over easy, a bowl of oatmeal with raisins swimming in fresh milk, and a small side dish of fruit. We had to walk a quarter of a mile to meet the school bus in those days, and that breakfast really "stuck to my ribs" as Mom always said.

The cook rebels...

Mom was responsible for cooking every meal, and I am sure that was true in most Hopkins Gap homes. Occasionally, she told me and my sister to help her cook some foods, but Dad and my brothers never hesitated by the cook stove long enough to figure out how it worked or how she prepared their food. I remember one morning when Dad and Mom were arguing over some simple little problem they had.

Mom said to him, "I am tired of cooking for you. You don't appreciate it anyhow." He answered, "You go on to the barn and milk. I'll get my own breakfast." So she slammed out the back door and down the path to the barn with her milk buckets on her arm. Dad got an iron skillet out of the cabinet and put it on the woodstove to heat. He always ate four fried eggs for breakfast, so he went into the refrigerator and got his eggs. He cracked them on the edge of the stove and dropped them into the skillet. He never realized that he needed to put some lard in the pan so his eggs would fry. His eggs stuck to the skillet, and he couldn't turn them over. He kept trying to turn them as the egg whites began to burn and fill the kitchen with a horrible smell. Finally, he grabbed a plate from the cabinet and dumped the egg mess on it with a splat. He grabbed his plate and went to the dining room and sat at the head of the table. He started to eat his eggs. The whites were scorched on one side and raw on the other. The yolks were not cooked. As he got a bite onto his fork and headed to his mouth with it, the egg white and yolk strung from his mouth to the plate. He gobbled them up really fast and left for work.

Mom was furious when she returned from the barn and found her favorite skillet with scorched eggs all over it. She said, "I ought to leave this messy skillet and hit him over the head with it when he comes home this evening."

Special Breakfasts

Several times during the year, Mom served special breakfasts. Two foods she liked to serve on special occasions were fried oysters and fried salt fish. She always served fried oysters on Christmas morning.

Fried Oysters Recipe...

1 box of saltines	2 cups of whole milk
6 eggs	1 teaspoon Old Bay seasoning
salt and pepper to taste	1 cup of lard
½ gallon of oysters	

Crush crackers into a fine meal using a rolling pin or a food grinder. Place in a large dish. Add Old Bay seasoning, salt and pepper, and mix well. Break eggs into a dish, add milk and mix well. Remove oysters from container and check them, with fingers, for pieces of broken shell. Dip each oyster into the egg and milk mixture, then into cracker meal. Dip them again into the egg mixture and the cracker meal. Place each oyster into the palm of the hand and pat the cracker meal, egg, and milk mixture around the oyster. Place the oysters on a plate and refrigerate overnight.

Heat a large iron skillet adding lard until it is at least ¼ inch deep in the pan.

Heat grease until just before smoking. Place oysters in the hot skillet and brown each side turning only once. Serve with tomato catsup.

Christmas Eve with Mom and Dad...

No matter where I lived for as long as Mom and Dad were alive, I always returned home for Christmas. The one exception was Christmas of 1986 when I decided thatI needed to be independent of this family obligation. Instead, I flew out to California with a friend to drive Highway 1 from San Diego to San Francisco. I felt so guilty that I called Mom on Christmas morning. We both cried. She told me, "Your place is at home with your family today." After that, I always planned my "independent-from-family" excursions at other times during the year.

Mom saved her Christmas wrapping for me to do on Christmas Eve. I worked at the dining room table; Dad sat in the living room and watched and listened to Christmas carols being sung on television by various groups. I positioned myself at the table for the wrapping so that I could see and hear the carols with Dad and still visit with Mom as she worked in the kitchen "rolling" her oysters for Christmas morning breakfast.

When Dad thought that Mom was very involved in her oyster rolling, he would slip into the bedroom and pull a box or bag from under the bed. He would quietly hand me the gift that he had gotten Mom for me to wrap. After so many years of the same pattern of events, no conversation was needed. I knew exactly what to do. I wrapped Mom's present from Dad and put it under the Christmas tree.

Just like clockwork, Mom came out of the kitchen, opened the door on the bottom of the corner cabinet in the dining room, and pointed to a bag or box. I wrapped Dad's gift and placed it under the Christmas tree.

By the time I finished wrapping Mom's gifts to her grandchildren, she had her "rolled" oysters in the refrigerator. All three of us sat in the living room and listened to Christmas carols until midnight. I felt very close to Mom and Dad on these occasions.

During the winter season, on occasional Sundays, Mom served salt herring for breakfast. Salt herring, or salt fish as we called it, was the food that demonstrated Mom's devotion to feeding her family what they liked to eat for breakfast. She could not stand the taste of salt fish, and her hands cracked and stayed sore for days after she cleaned them for the rest of us to eat. However, she knew how much we liked them, and she refused to disappoint us.

As I got older, she showed me how to clean the fish, and it turned out to be my job to scrape off the scales and remove the bones. After I left home, Mom planned to serve salt fish for Sunday morning breakfast based on when I was going home for a visit. She called before she bought the fish, "Peg, when are you comin' home? I want to get some salt fish and have you clean them for me." We made arrangements that way so that she could have me clean the fish on Friday night when I arrived. She then soaked them in cold water to remove some of the salt until she was ready to fry them for breakfast on Sunday morning.

Fried Salt Herring Recipe...

Ingredients
Salt herring
Flour
Salt and pepper
1 cup of lard (depending on the number of fish to be fried).

Remove the bones from the fish, scrape off the scales. Place them in a large pan of cold water deep enough to cover the fish. Soak fish for 24 to 36 hours. Change the water about every 12 hours. When ready to cook, drain the fish and dip them into a mixture of flour, salt, and pepper. Be sure to coat both sides of the fish with flour. In a large skillet, place enough lard to melt to about ½ inch deep. Heat the lard to near smoking. Put floured fish into the hot grease. Fry on both sides until crispy brown, turn only once. Remove fish from the grease and drain them on a cloth or paper towel. Serve very hot.

Dinner

Throughout my lifetime, the noon meal, or dinner, as it was called, was not a large production because Dad worked every day, and we went to school. On Saturdays when we were all at home, Mom did prepare a more complete dinner for us. Sunday dinners were usually eaten after church in Hopkins Gap.

During the weekdays, Dad ate his dinner in Harrisonburg. He walked from the Rockingham Milling Company several blocks to Layman's or Hobe's Restaurant on Liberty Street. He ate a plate lunch of two or three vegetables and meat. Sometimes he walked on a bit further to eat at the Daily Lunch on Water Street. In the early school years, Mom packed our school lunches. She always put in a nice sandwich of chicken or ham, a piece of fruit or a little jar of home-canned fruit. Not long into our school years, a cafeteria opened, and Mom no longer had to pack our lunches.

On Saturdays when everybody was home, Mom always fried potatoes for Dad and served some type of meat, such as fried sausage cakes or ham with sliced tomatoes in the summer or homemade pickles in the winter. If she had leftover pinto beans from the evening before, she "stretched" them so there would be enough to feed all of us. To "stretch" her leftover beans, she added more water and "rivels." Rivels were little pieces of dumpling dough that expanded and cooked in the bean broth. The menu always included fruit; either fresh or canned depending on the season.

Pinto Beans with Rivels Recipe...

Leftover Pinto Beans
1 cup of water
1 ½ teaspoons baking powder
¼ cup melted butter or lard

1 cups all purpose flour
½ teaspoon salt
1/3 cup milk

Add water to leftover beans and place on stove to heat. Sift dry ingredients.

Pour milk and melted butter or lard into a measuring cup. Do not stir. Pour all at once into dry ingredients. Mix dough with fork until mixture leaves sides of bowl and forms a ball. Pinch off small pieces (rivels) and drop into the boiling leftover beans. Boil slowly for about 12 to 15 minutes until rivels rise and are fluffy inside. Serve with homemade butter and light bread.

In the summer when school was out, Mom fed us a variety of food for the noon meal. Depending whether it was early summer or late summer, she always served us something fresh from the garden. We ate onion and butter or radishes and butter sandwiches on light bread. We had plenty of lettuce from the garden to add to these delicious mixtures. Later in the summer, we ate tomato with butter or mayonnaise sandwiches.

___

Peanut butter and tomato sandwiches...

My absolute favorite sandwiches were the ones that my cousin, Randy taught me how to make in late summer the year I turned twelve years old. These were tomato and peanut butter sandwiches. He told me, "You have to have a fresh tomato from the garden that has been nicely warmed by the sun. The tomato has to be big enough so that you can get two thick slices out of the middle that will cover a slice of bread. You need two slices because one sandwich will call for another one. The best peanut butter and tomato sandwiches are made with yellow tomatoes. Here, let me show you," Randy explained.

He took me out into Mom's tomato patch to search for a yellow tomato that was the right size. He explained, "You can use red tomatoes, but I want you to have the best when you try your first peanut butter and tomato sandwich. "

We found a big, warm, unblemished yellow tomato. "Now, let's go wash it," he said, "and I will show you step by step how to fix the best sandwich you will ever eat." I held the tomato under the cistern spout while Randy turned the crank to bring up some water. "Rub your hands over it to get the dirt off when the water comes out," he told me. I would have licked the dirt off the tomato if he had asked me to because I thought Cousin Randy hung the moon.

We took the tomato into the kitchen. Randy went into the refrigerator and got the homemade butter and a jar of mayonnaise. The peanut butter was in the cabinet. He cut four slices of light bread and carefully laid them out on the table.

He behaved like a scientist in a laboratory as he moved through each step. He carefully spread a layer of peanut butter on all four slices making sure to cover the bread all the way to the crust. He then spread a thin layer of homemade butter on top of the peanut butter on all four slices. Next, he opened the mayonnaise jar and with a spoon, put a dollop of mayonnaise on all four slices of bread. He took the knife and spread the mayonnaise on top of the butter. "Now," he said, "I sprinkle each slice of bread with salt and pepper on top of the three layers." Finally, he got out Mom's sharpest butcher knife and sliced two center slices out of the tomato. He placed one on each sandwich and carefully positioned the top slice of bread over the tomato. "Now, there's one more step," he said, "Get me two plates." I reached into the cabinet and got two plates. He placed the sandwiches on the plates and cut them in half." He turned the plate for me to see the halves. "Look here," he said, "Now that's a peanut butter and tomato sandwich."

I could see all the layers he had placed on the bread. The peanut butter was starting to blend with the butter and mayonnaise and ooze out around the beautiful, thick and juicy slice of yellow tomato in the middle. "Take a bite and see what you think," he said to me. He only had to say it once. I bit into the first half of my sandwich and found myself wishing it would never be all gone. I had never tasted anything like it. To this day, I enjoy peanut butter and tomato sandwiches every summer.

Randy died in 1972 as a very young man. He had a rare blood disease that ended his life within five months after he was diagnosed. Not a year passes that I don't make and eat peanut butter and tomato sandwiches and think of him. None of my sandwiches ever taste as good as the first one he made for me.

Supper

It is difficult for me to write with certainty how every family in Hopkins Gap ate their evening meal. I am describing my observations of my immediate family and the kinfolk who welcomed my family to their supper tables. I also have talked with other folks who grew up in Hopkins Gap and asked them to share their supper table experiences with me. I found a lot of similarity in their experiences and mine.

The evening meal was called supper. In most homes it was served sometime between five o'clock and six o'clock. Everyone was usually at home by then. About the only time the men and older boys came in late was during hunting season. At these times supper was kept warm on the back of the woodstove or heated up after the woodstove was replaced by the electric range.

Supper Menus

Supper menus varied by seasons of the year. In all seasons, supper menus consisted of foods gathered from the wild; foods such as potatoes from the root cellar, foods canned the past summer, and cured meat from the meat house. These two supper menus were typically served in the spring season.

Boiled pork shoulder	Lettuce salad from the garden
Fried potatoes	Radishes from the garden
Wilted dandelion greens	Fried ham
Pinto beans	Pinto beans
Home-canned pickled beets	Fried potatoes
Light bread	Spring onions
Homemade butter	Homemade butter
Home-canned peaches	Light bread
	Fresh wild strawberries

Later in the summer when the garden began to produce vegetables, supper menus were varied and plentiful. We had fresh green beans, new potatoes, cucumber and onion salad, stewed summer apples, blackberries, corn on the cob, tomatoes, and cabbage to add to the basics of homemade butter, light bread, and pinto beans. Summer supper menus consisted of combinations such as these:

Sliced middlin' fried	Cold fried chicken from
Creamed new potatoes	Sunday dinner
Green beans	Boiled new potatoes with skins on

Corn on the cob	Pinto beans
Sliced tomatoes	Sliced tomatoes
Cucumber and onion salad	Sliced cucumbers
Light bread	Cole slaw
Homemade butter	Light bread
Fresh peaches, sliced	Homemade butter
	Fresh made applesauce

When Mom knew she had a busy week of canning coming up, she often made some dishes that she could serve for supper without a lot of effort. On Saturday and Sunday she prepared big batches of potato salad, cole slaw, and green beans. All she had to do for supper was open a can of pork ribs from the cellar, warm them up and put the food on the table. It was on days like these, when she was busy canning, that she would make a huge family pie that she hoped would last for two suppers. The family pie filling consisted of whatever fruit she happened to be canning that week. It might have been blackberries, peaches, or pears. Later in the fall she made fresh apple family pies.

Winter supper menus were quite different. All the garden produce was gone except turnips and turnip greens. Mom made frequent trips to the meat house and the cellar when she started thinking about what to cook for supper. The meat in winter supper menus varied more because of the recent hog butchering. Some of the products of the hog butchering had to be consumed soon after the butchering; such as the pork liver, loose sausage, sliced tenderloin, and panhaus. Hunting season added additional variation to the meat dishes.

Fried Sausage patties	Fried venison steak
Fried potatoes	Cooked potatoes and turnips
Pinto beans	Turnip greens, boiled
Sauerkraut and dumplins'	Pinto beans
Canned peaches	Canned pears

Homemade butter	Homemade butter
Light bread	Light bread

Boiled Ham bone	Fried squirrel and gravy
Ham potpie	Fried potatoes
Pinto beans	Pinto beans
Pickled cucumbers	Pickled beets
Homemade butter	Warm bread
Light bread	Homemade butter
Canned peaches	Applesauce

At my house, we ate supper at 5:00 p.m. This time was established by the fact that Dad arrived home from work at 4:30 p.m. He had time to slop the hogs and make sure we had done our after-school chores to suit him. I remember watching the clock and dreading 4:30 in the afternoon, because we never knew when Dad would come home in a bad mood because of stress at his place of work. I don't know what my brothers and sister did, but I watched him from the front window as he got out of the car. I would look at his face and watch him walk toward the kitchen door. If he was in a good mood and saw me in the window, and he would take his cap off, set it sideways on his head, and grin at me. Most days he was in a good mood.

If he was in a bad mood, he had his cap pulled down over his eyes, and never even looked up to see me at the window. I ran into the kitchen and told Mom, "Dad's in a bad mood today." On these days he always found something wrong with how we had fed and watered the chickens, even though it was done the same way every day. If he was in a really bad mood, we would get a whipping with his leather belt or his fist planted firmly in our backs. Needless to say, on these days we ate supper while being very upset, and I worried about my whole family.

Stomach linings at supper time...

When I was in the sixth grade, we studied the human body in health class. There were two colored pictures of the human stomach in my health book. The teacher explained that when a person was calm, the stomach lining looked like the nice pale pink picture; but when a person was upset, the stomach lining was a blazing red. She had us read what the two pictures meant. The book warned about eating a meal while upset. It said that the food we ate would not digest properly and the result could be stomach ulcers.

My older cousins, Ruby and Randy, and Uncle Jim and Aunt Goldie had already suffered from bleeding stomach ulcers. They had spent time in the hospital where they were given blood transfusions and placed on special diets that were hard to follow because the foods were different from what we usually ate. I was scared to death of needles because when I was really young I watched Pop May pull up a chunk of skin on his leg and stick a needle in it, to help control his diabetes. He always grunted when the needle went in, and the spot bled just a little when he pulled it out. I knew it had to hurt, so I did not want to have blood transfusions because of stomach ulcers—or any other reason for that matter.

Every time I went to the supper table upset, I thought about the pictures in my health book; and, in fact, I still think about them to this day. I thought about stomach ulcers and worried about me getting them. I also worried about my brothers and sister. But we had to go to the table to eat when Mom and Dad did, so there was no avoiding putting food into a blazing red stomach.

Seating Arrangements

The seating arrangement at the supper table was always the same, and it silently portrayed the "pecking order" in the family. The Joe Morris family represents the typical Hopkins Gap seating arrangement around the table.

Joe Morris, Millie Morris, their granddaughter and other family members prepare to start a meal at a typical Hopkins Gap table. The table is covered with oilcloth, the plates are set with the fork and spoon on the plate. There are no napkins beside the plate. The plates are not a matching set. Some are white, and some have flowers. Joe Morris sits at the head of the table with his wife, Millie next to him. The family members are sitting on oak split-bottom chairs. Joe and Millie have replaced their ice box with an electric refrigerator.

While it is not possible to identify the food in the dishes in the picture, I am certain the arrangement reflected a long family tradition. My cousin Joyce recently told me, "I still set the table like Mom and Daddy did. I always put the meat and beans at the head of the table closest to Skip when he was livin', and I still do. Every food and everybody has a certain place at the table." In my home, we had the same everyday arrangement for the supper table.

This sketch represents the seating arrangement at my home. It was consistent at all main meals.

My dad's seat at the table was defined as the "head of the table." Mom always sat to his right because she needed to get up often and go to the kitchen for whatever folks needed. Mom's seat was close to the kitchen. As the oldest child, with the most responsibility next to Mom, I sat at the opposite end of the table from Dad. Brenda, my sister, sat next to Mom.

Guests were always expected and prepared for with a permanent place at the table. There was a space next to Brenda for any guest that may drop in. The guests might include Aunt Goldie who was widowed and lived alone. She would often drop in for supper. Many times Mom called and invited her to have supper with us because she had cooked some dish that Aunt Goldie liked. However, after Larry married Hilda when she was fourteen, the guest's spot became her permanent seat. Hilda was learning how to cook and to be a proper wife for Larry, so she often got up to go to the kitchen and bring what people needed back to the table.

If more than one guest dropped in, we would squeeze them in at my end of the table. Brenda, and later Hilda, moved closer to Mom. I moved closer to Warnie, and he moved closer to Larry. We often entertained from one to five people by squeezing in plates and forks around that end and side of the table. We never squeezed a guest in at Dad's end of the table.

Very often, our supper table looked like this. Somehow, there was always enough for everyone to fill up.

Sometimes the guests were the parents of the children Mom babysat for while they worked. My cousin, Randy, and his wife, Joann, often stayed for supper when they came to pick up their children, and now and then my cousin Joyce would stay to eat.

The arrangement of my brothers, at the rear of the table, is the result of a conflict between John and Warnie. John is right-handed and Warnie is left-handed. The original arrangement placed Larry, the oldest son, next to Dad with Warnie next to Larry in the middle and John at the end. That arrangement placed Warnie's left hand next to John's right hand, so every time they tried to eat, their arms bumped together. There were many fights between them over bumping arms. The fights resulted in Dad getting up from his place and going behind the table and hitting both of them on the sides of their head with his fist. One day Mom had a brainstorm and moved Larry between John and Warnie. The problem was solved.

Food Placement on the Supper Table

The layout for the various food dishes was always the same. Food was placed strategically on the table. Boxes with letters, on the diagram below, represent the food dishes.

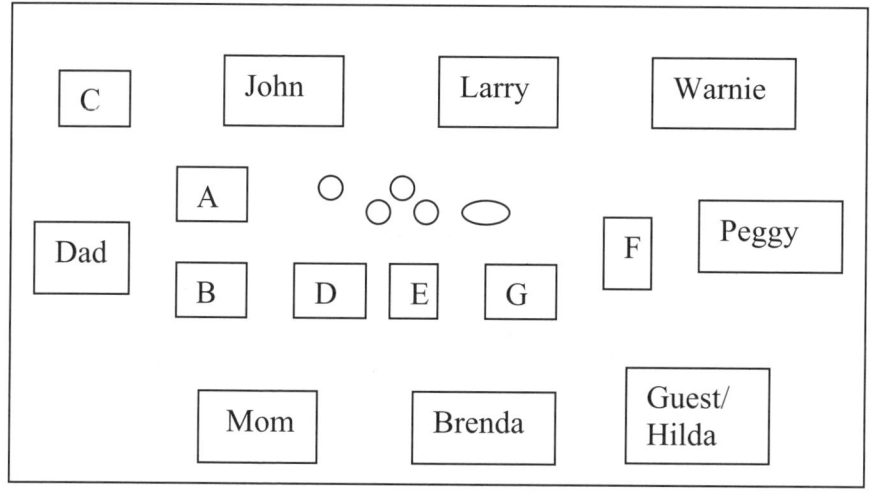

Box A was usually a meat dish. The meat dish was always next to dad's place at the table. Hilda recently told me, "All the important foods were around Dad's plate." As in most Hopkins Gap families, he was responsible for providing the meat.

The meat dish was the first food to be distributed around the table. The dish was not passed around the table in the modern way. Each of us, including Mom, held his or her plate close to Dad so that he could put a piece of meat on it. Mom received the first piece after Dad took his portion. Dad would sometimes take two or three pieces of meat at one time. We all fearfully watched him with our mouths watering. When he started forking two or three pieces of meat from the plate, we looked at each other and rolled our eyes. Mom would say, "Norman, leave some for everybody else." His response was usually, "I fed these hogs all year. I'll take as much as I want."

I always scrutinized the meat plate for the piece I wanted hoping all the while that Dad wouldn't pick that one. After being disappointed time after time, I learned to "want" a piece of meat that was a layer or two down in the pile and then figured out how to get that piece. I stood beside Mom when she was forking the meat out of the frying pan onto the meat platter. I picked out my piece and had her to put it at least one layer down in the meat pile so I would have a better chance of getting it after Dad took his portion and Mom took hers. She knew exactly what I was doing and would sometimes tease me by pretending she was taking that particular piece of meat. Not a word was said as we negotiated that little maneuver. I often wondered if Larry, Brenda, and John had a little system worked out to get their favorite piece of meat.

Box B represents a dish of beans—flavored with ham broth and salt and pepper. They were cooked for hours until the beans were falling apart and the broth was thick and soupy. Typically, the beans were pintos, but sometimes Mom substituted navy beans or Boston beans.

While Dad distributed the meat, we took a slice of homemade bread or a hot roll from the bread plate (box C) at the end of the table, and broke it into pieces on our plates. Then Dad took each of our plates and scooped beans and broth over the bread. Mom would start dishing out the potatoes, which were either fried or boiled (box D). The only time we had mashed potatoes was on Sundays, with fried chicken and gravy. My daddy had to have fried potatoes or boiled potatoes for supper every evening during the week and twice on Saturdays because he was home for dinner.

Box E was the major variation in the supper meal. That dish tended to be whatever vegetable was in season. In the early spring, it was likely to be wild greens that Mom had picked from the field or road side—wilted lettuce, dandelion greens, rock lettuce, creasy greens, or water cress gathered from Muddy Creek. Sometimes it was "weed greens"—a mixture of all of the above, along with other wild greens added to them. In the summer, it would be boiled or fried cabbage, creamed cucumbers, sliced tomatoes, cole slaw, or corn ears.

Box F represents the fruit. Mom most always opened a quart of peaches or pears that she had canned the past summer. She counted the days during the seasons when she would not have fresh fruit and tried to can at least enough quarts of peaches, pears, or applesauce so we could have some fruit every day.

Box G is a dish that we always had on the table. It also contained seasonal foods. In the spring it was filled with radishes from the garden. Mom cleaned the radishes and cut one strip of the red from around the middle. I never understood why she did this, and I never asked. Radishes were a great complement to fried potatoes. We just picked them up and bit off chunks, as we ate our potatoes. Other times, the dish might contain small onions that were pulled from the garden, stripped of their outer layers, and chopped off, leaving about four inches of the green tops on them. We all ate these with our pinto beans by just chomping off a bite or slicing them directly on top of the beans. Sometimes we put a lot of butter on a slice of bread, wrapped it around an onion, and ate it like a sandwich, along with our beans.

In the summer, dish G was often filled with cucumbers that Mom peeled and sliced in half. We picked those out with our hands and put a lot of salt on them. These were very good with potatoes and green beans. As the fall and winter season rolled around, this dish contained cucumber pickles or canned pickled beets from the previous summer. The small circles in the center of the table represent the vinegar cruet, salt and pepper shakers, the teaspoon holder, a butter dish, a pint of jelly, and a dish of apple butter.

Not only was supper a time to consume the evening meal, but the day's events were talked over and family issues, both good and bad, were often discussed and sometimes resolved. Supper time was often the only time each day that the man of the house sat down with his wife and children around him. From his seat at the "head of the table," supper time was an opportunity for him to carry out the powerful position of head of the household and main provider for his family

It always bothered me that the man of the house sat where he did. The location of the "head of the table" was usually at the end of the large rectangular table. I questioned positions and pecking order at the supper table in the same way I was curious about why men sat on one side of the church and the women sat on the other. (In the church situation, I thought maybe the men had a better view of the preacher from their side. I tested that question by sitting down on the men's side after church while everybody had lined up to shake hands with the preacher after the sermon. I didn't find any obvious reason why the men sat on that side of the church.)

I found it ironic and frustrating that Dad was the head of the house when Mom did just as much work as he did, or more. He went to bed before she did, he got up after she did in the morning, and ate breakfast she had cooked for him. He left for his job that was basically the same from day to day. He came home in the evening, ate the supper she cooked for him, did not help clean up the dishes, and sat down to rest until his bedtime.

On the other hand, Mom's work started before daylight. In between caring for the children, cleaning the house, gathering and processing the food, she cooked three meals each day and cleaned up the dishes. Later on, as we children became more independent, she took in laundry to help with the expenses. Even during her work for other people, her mind was busy all day as she planned the activities necessary for the next meal, for the next week's meals, and for the next year's food supply. Mom's bedtime was sometimes hours after the rest of us had gone to sleep. Her work varied from day to day and season to season.

This type of thinking brought up, in my little head, two questions about the supper table. Was there something special about that end of the supper table that made it the "head of the table?" Did it have a special notch or carving? Were the table legs stronger at that end so they would hold most of the food dishes that sat close to the man? Does the man sit where he can see out the windows? Does he sit with his back to the wall? Who determined that his seat was "the head of the table?"

My second question sought the answer from a different angle. Did the man sit at the "head of the table" just because he was a man? If that were true then the "head of the table" could be located anywhere around the table. It could be on the side of a rectangular table. At the first meal in a different house, did he just sit down someplace around the table, and that spot was forever the "head of the table?" Did his wife put him there the first time? Did he have a better view of his children from that end of the table? In other words, was it the "place at the table" or "the man" that was important? It was a real life "chicken and egg" question for me.

All I know for sure is that, at least at our house, nobody sat down at "Dad's place" to eat supper. Being a curious child just like I was in church, I sometimes sat down at the "head of the table" just to see what would happen and how I would feel. My presence there tended to upset the rest of the family. My brother, Larry, said, "You better get up from there. You know that's Dad's place." Brenda and John would chime in, "You are gonna get it if Dad sees you at his place." If Mom came in from the kitchen, she told me, "Git in your own chair. Are you tryin' to start something?"

I could hear Dad behind the kitchen stove washing his hands and face in the wash pan before he came to the table. I knew he was about ready to take his place when I heard him pull the towel off the rack above the wash pan. The towel rack made a special noise as it smacked back against the wall, so I ignored Larry's warning until I knew Dad was just about to appear around the corner. Then I jumped up and took my seat at the opposite end of the table. I was very glad that end was not known as "the tail of the table."

Most often, while seated at the head of the table, the man of the house looked over his family with great pride as he led them in discussions of the events of the day. My dad worked very hard. We all knew he was tired from lifting sacks of feed all day, working with lazy co-workers, waiting on customers, and dumping dusty ingredients into the mixer for yet another batch of chicken, cow, or turkey feed. He came home covered with feed dust. It hung on his clothes, in his hair, and on his eyebrows. He breathed the dust into his lungs, and it eventually killed him. When he was in a good mood, my Dad teased each of us children as we ate our supper. He made funny sounds with his jaws and winked at us. On these occasions, he talked about important subjects that were of interest to all of us, such as the upcoming hog butchering or hunting season. He would brag about his potato patch and speculated about how many bushels he would harvest from his crop.

By supper time, Mom was always tired from her long day filled with the chores of making the morning fires, milking the cows, cooking and cleaning, caring for special needs of each family member, and taking care of all the unexpected events in her day. Some evenings she came to the table after "drenching" a sick cow or helping to birth a calf. Many times in my younger life I watched her grab a cow in the nostrils with her left hand and pull her head up and hold it. With a large bottle of medicine in her right hand, she placed the neck of the bottle in between the cow's teeth and poured the contents down the cow's throat. Even the veterinarian that cared for her cows was amazed at her ability to care for her cows. On other occasions, she followed her cows around the pasture until they lay down to give birth. She carried a dry burlap sack in her hands. She watched, and if they needed help, she wrapped the sack around the calf's feet and pulled on the calf every time the cow had a contraction. I started helping her with this when I was about twelve years old. Later on, Hilda helped. What I recall the most is the strength required to move that little calf even one inch.

From her seat next to Dad at the supper table, Mom had two additional jobs. She was always the gatekeeper who determined the amount of information given to Dad about daily activities. When we brought our report cards home from school for a parent's signature and our grades were good or had improved from the last report, she told Dad at the supper table, "Norman, you need to sign report cards after supper so the kids can take them back to school tomorrow." On the other hand, when our grades were not good or had gone down since the last report, the report cards were kept hidden until Dad went to bed. Mom signed them herself on these occasions and made sure we carried them back to school before he saw them. She always told the one who had gotten the bad grades, "Now I am gonna sign these report cards for you this time to keep you from getting' a whippin', but you need to do better for the next six weeks, or I will have to tell your daddy."

Occasionally Dad brought the stresses of his day to the supper table. Sometimes he expressed it, not by crying or calmly discussing his feelings, but in the only way he had been taught to save face and be strong for the family—through anger and threats of violent physical behavior. On those occasions, Mom had to be on guard at the supper table. She had to get up from her chair and place herself between Dad and one of us kids to protect us from his anger.

My dad was a victim of "shell shock," or post traumatic stress syndrome, from serving in World War II. He was never treated for this problem that he brought home with him after serving the country in Germany. In fact, I'm sure the psychological consequences of war were not even recognized at that time. He could not stand to be around a lot of noise such as multiple conversations going on at the same time. Loud noises scared him so that he would jump and get into a position to protect himself from bombs and gunfire. These occasions humiliated him and made him angry.

Later in life, Dad had the misfortune of watching his second son leave for a tour as an infantryman in the Viet Nam War. When we took John to the airport to leave, Dad told me to drive the car home. He had never before trusted me to drive his car when he was riding with me. He sat in the back seat and cried. It was the first time I saw him cry. The second time he cried was when Aunt Goldie died.

My Dad was not a drinking man, but there were two times in his life that he came home from work drunker than a hoot owl. The first time, I was about three or four years old. When he staggered to the front door and couldn't open it, Mom jerked the door open and met him with her fist in his face. I ran into the bedroom and got under the bed and didn't come out until supper.

Finally, the origins of my arachnophobia.....?

While I was waiting for the fight between Mom and Dad to be over, I am not sure what I saw under the bed. I do believe, however, that under that bed is where I got my initial fear of spiders. I do know that later in my childhood, Mom asked me to help her clean the bed springs on a warm and sunny Saturday in early May. She took the mattresses and springs and carried them out on the porch where she wiped the dust off the coils in the springs with a rag and beat the dust out of the mattresses with a broom. There were always spider webs and empty spider egg sacs in the coils that had hatched out the summer before. I think that on that very day, for the first time in my life, I had to choose between two scary situations, so I chose to stare at the spiders until the yelling had calmed down and supper was on the table. Now that I think about it, I am certain that was the beginning of my arachnophobia that stayed with me until this very day.

The second time Dad came home drunk was much later in our family life. It was when my brother, John, was in Viet Nam. I was grown up by then and living at home while I was in college, but I was still curious about what kind of mood Dad was in, so I always watched out the window for him to come home from work.

One evening I saw his car coming from the opposite direction that he usually came home. He was driving really fast down the hill toward the house. The dust from the dirt road was swirling in clouds around his car until you could hardly see it. The gravels were flying up and hitting the fenders. He didn't make it all the way up the hill to where he usually parked. He jerked the steering wheel toward the bank. The car stopped with two wheels on the bank and leaning sideways. I watched Dad as he fumbled with the keys trying to turn the motor off. Then he tried to get the car door open. Finally, he fell over on the front seat and made no effort to get out of the car. I ran to the car thinking he might have had a heart attack. When I opened the door, the smell of alcohol nearly knocked me down. I closed the door very quietly and went into the house to give Mom the news. She very calmly said, "Just leave him alone. I'll go get him in the house when supper is ready." My memory went back to how she had greeted him at the door when I was a child, and I expected her to grab a skillet or something else and go beat him black and blue. I thought to myself, "Wow, time sure does change some things." I imagine she was glad that it was only the second time in twenty-eight years that he had arrived home drunk.

Mom delayed supper until the sun went down over the mountain and darkness had settled in. Then she went out and got Dad out of the car and helped him into the house. I heard her fussing with him as they came around the back of the house toward the kitchen door, "You ought to be ashamed of yourself. You could have run off the road and killed yourself and somebody else. You get yourself in here and eat so you can sober up." Then she said something that I could never forget. She told him, "I got a letter from John today, and you're in no shape to read it. He hasn't had his shoes off for three weeks. The war is really getting' bad."

Mom had boiled potatoes with the skins on them. The dish was setting on the dining room table. As Dad staggered in through the kitchen to the table, he reached over into the potato dish, grabbed a potato, and before Mom could stop him, he threw it at Larry who was sitting behind the table eating his supper. The potato hit Larry in the chest and flew into pieces all over the dining room. Dad yelled, "I know you all want to pick a fight with me, and if I had my boy John here with me, we would beat the hell out of all of you." He fell into his chair at the head of the table and passed out again with his head on his plate. I am sure we all had blazing red stomach linings during that supper.

As I look back on that incident, I realize I had been a witness to my dad's expression of grief and worry about his son, John, being in Viet Nam, suffering the same fear that he himself had felt in Germany. He was worried that John would never come home or come home seriously wounded. He may have been thinking about the "shell shock" that John would suffer from for the remainder of his life if he survived the war. The feelings of helplessness and despair are probably what led him to think he could numb his sorrow by drinking.

Although we were fairly isolated in our little community, the events from the outside world did creep in and affect us. I know that my dad loved all of us very much, and most of our family meal times were quite pleasant. Unfortunately, it is the ones that made me feel uncomfortable that I remember best.

Epilogue

I long to accomplish...humble tasks as though they were great and noble. The world is moved along, not only by the mighty shoves of its heroes, but also by the aggregate of the tiny pushes of each honest worker.

—*Helen Keller*

As the cover picture of this book tells us, the cooking lessons continue today. Just as Mom taught Hilda and her granddaughters, Aunt Ethel has taught her daughters, her granddaughters, and now her great granddaughters. Just as Mom did, Aunt Ethel will continue to pass on the traditions to whoever will listen. For as long as she lives, she will take out her old tools for cooking from their storage places and use them when the cabbage heads are ready to burst, when her green beans are ready to process, and when the blackberries are ripe. Because Mom and Aunt Ethel, and all the cooks of Hopkins Gap, were busy feeding their families, the food traditions and recipes remained in their memory and were never written down. They have always been passed on by demonstration, until I awakened to the fact that the cooks are dying and taking food traditions with them to their graves. Unfortunately, many food traditions have been lost.

With the untimely death of my brother, Larry, on September 11, 2006, the last of the traditional hog butchers in my family is gone. This fact came as a shock to me the day of Larry's funeral. As I drove over the mountain to the cemetery, I passed the home of Skip Crawford's widow, my cousin Joyce, and saw his scalding pan (used to scald the hair off of a hog) lying at the corner of the yard with a "for sale" sign on it. Skip Crawford died on September 21, 2005. He was the head butcher in his family.

When I talked with Joyce later in the day, I said to her, "That scalding pan should sell like a hot potato this time of the year with November butchering coming up soon." She replied, "No, I'm having a very hard time sellin' it. One man came by and offered me half of my asking price. Nobody uses scalding pans anymore. People skin their hogs now. Only one family in Hopkins Gap, the Conley's, still butcher the old way, and they have their own butchering equipment." I began to think about the implications of skinning hogs instead of scalding them to remove the hair. The skin of the hog was very important in the processing of fat into lard. The skin became "cracklins" after the lard was pressed out of it. This meant that folks no longer make "cracklins." I realized at that moment how much and how rapidly the old ways are changing.

Very few families plant a large garden in the summer. Unfortunately those traditions have been replaced by prepackaged and frozen vegetables available at a number of grocery stores. Years ago, very few women worked for wages outside the home, with the exception of my Aunt Hazel and Aunt Goldie, and now, most women hold jobs outside of Hopkins Gap. Many of the men have ingeniously devised ways to maintain the tradition of hunting in the fall and winter months. In August, 2005, I visited Aunt Ethel to learn how to make ham potpie. A group of men were paving her driveway. When they came in the house for refreshments, I discovered it was her son and many of my first and second cousins who were working together. They had formed their own paving company so that they could work in the spring and summer and have the fall and winter seasons for hunting. Many of the men of Hopkins Gap choose to be self-employed; mainly because they want to hunt squirrels, deer, and bears during the hunting seasons.

Friends and families still drop in unannounced at meal time but not predictably so. One of the most significant signs of change in family relationships is Aunt Ethel's frustration when she thinks about her Sunday dinner, "I never know how much to fix. If I cook a big meal, nobody comes. If I cook for me and Shirl, here they all roll in, and I have to fix more. So, I mostly just cook enough for a bunch of people. It is easier, and me and Shirl can eat leftovers for the next week."

As the fact that food tradition and family relationships in Hopkins Gap are changing stares me in the face, I have come to realize how very fortunate I have been all my life. I was given a legacy of food traditions, recipes, and Hopkins Gap history through association with Dad and Mom, Aunt Ethel and Uncle Shirley, Aunt Hazel, Grandma Molly and Lena, Aunt Goldie, and many others.

This book is a final tribute to their hard work and efforts to teach what they knew through demonstration. Their lives were affected by worldly events, such as wars that took men away from their families. Some men never returned, and some came back with deep psychological wounds. My dad suffered from shell shock after he returned from World War II. In spite of his psychological wounds, he never missed a day of work for thirty-eight years because he just didn't feel like going to work. The only time he missed work was when we had thirteen feet high snow drifts that blocked our road. Each week, he gave Mom all but five dollars from his pay check. He needed a little money to buy his lunch each day.

Dad never hesitated to plant his potato patch every spring and try to reap more potatoes than he had the year before. He died in March of 1994, and Larry stepped into his potato patch, planted, and cared for a large crop of potatoes. Larry measured his bushels; and, remembering from the year before, he bragged that he had harvested one or two bushels more than Dad's last crop.

The cooks, the hunters, and the gardeners of Hopkins Gap "accomplished humble tasks as though they were great and noble." Many of the children born to my generation in Hopkins Gap have been high achievers because of the humility and the pride instilled in them by their parents, grandparents, and aunts and uncles. Mom and Dad felt proud when they showed off their canned food, and full potato bin. Their pride showed in their eyes. I feel the same pride as I finish this book and dedicate it to the great cooks, hunters, and gardeners of Hopkins Gap.

List of Recipes

Apple Butter Rolls. 276
Apple Dumplings 268
Apples, baked 269
Apples, fried 269
Applesauce. 270
Bacon, Pepper Belly Cure 293
Banana Pudding 142
Beans, green. 199
Beans, hay 200
Beans, Pinto with Rivels 317
Beets, Harvard. 221
Beets, pickled. 221
Biscuits, buttermilk 122
Blackberry Dumplings, steamed 205
Bread Pudding. 143
Bread, light 116
Bread, warm. 122
Brunswick Stew with Squirrel. 283
Butter, Sour Cream 110
Cabbage, boiled. 230
Cabbage, fried 230
Cake, Cold Oven. 56
Cake, Prune with Buttermilk Icing 145
Cheese, stovetop 114

Cherry Dumplings, steamed 190
Cherry Pudding Cake 192
Cherry Winks 191
Chicken, fried 129
Chow Chow 243
Corn bread, buttermilk 125
Corn Bread, Old-Time Buttermilk 124
Corn bread, sweet 126
Corn Cakes 150
Corn on the Cob 222
Cottage Cheese 113
Creasy Greens 152
Cucumber pickles 218
Cucumbers, sour cream and onion. 219
Dandelion Greens 156
Dandelion Salad, wilted. 157
Dandelion Wine 160
Doughnuts, Yeast. 56
Egg Custard 140
Eggs, deviled 145
Eggs, pickled 139
Grape Juice 259
Gravy, fried chicken. 130
Gravy, milk 115
Green Beans 199
Lettuce, wilted 176
Morel Soup 166
Morels with Sour Creamed Potatoes. 167
Morels, (toadstools) fried 165
Mushrooms, canned 207
Mushrooms, fried 206
Mustard, Kale, and Beet Top Greens. 177
Oatmeal Cookies, Grandma's 55
Oysters, fried. 313

Panhaus 294
Peach Jam 210
Peach Whirligigs 210
Peaches, pickled 207
Pear Butter 262
Pickles, bread and butter 218
Pie Crust 141
Pie, butterscotch 144
Pie, egg custard 140
Pie, fresh apple 265
Pie, Lemon Meringue 144
Pig Feet and Hocks 298
Pork Backbone, boiled 298
Pork Tenderloin, fried 297
Potato Cakes, fried 250
Potato Salad 250
Potato, new breaded 215
Potatoes with Parsley, boiled 251
Potatoes, creamed new 215
Potatoes, fried 248
Potatoes, mashed 249
Potpie, Ham 300
Salt Herring, fried 316
Sassafras Tea 164
Sauerkraut and Pork Chops 241
Sauerkraut Dumplings 240
Sauerkraut, fried 240
Snow Cream 149
Squirrel Gravy 282
Squirrel, fried 282
Strawberry Jelly Rolls 183
Strawberry Shortcake, wild 183
Sugar Cure 293
Sweet Potatoes, baked 256

Tomato Bread 228
Tomato Juice 226
Tomato Preserves. 227
Tomato Sauce 227
Tomatoes with Macaroni. 228
Tomatoes, canned 226
Tomatoes, fried green 225
Vegetable Soup 229
Venison Steak, fried. 304
Venison Stew. 305
Venison, canned. 304
Watercress Soup 154
Wild Turkey, roasted 155

References

Beard, James. *American Cookery*. Boston: Little, Brown and Company. 1972.

Benanti, Laura. *Online Quotes*. http://en.thinkexist.com/quotation/food-is-the-most-basic-forum-for-discussing/412892.html.

Bennett, Lori. *The Morris and Crawford Families of Hopkins Gap—Fulks Run*, Virginia, 1992.

Blake, William. *The Complete Poetry of William Blake*. Editor, David E. Erdman. CA: University of California Press, 1992.

Burns, Robert. Attribution: *Robert Burns (1759–1796), Scottish poet. Poetical Works, vol. 2, ed. William Scott Douglas (1891). "The Selkirk Grace," (c. 1790).*

Carson, Rachel. *Silent Spring*. Boston: Houghton Mifflin Company. 1962.

Chernasky, Lisa, and Renee Comet. *The Artful Pie: Unforgettable Recipes for Creative Cooks*. Vermont: Chapters Publishing Ltd. 1996.

Dabney, Joseph E. *Smokehouse Ham, Spoon Bread, & Scuppernong Wine*, Nashville, TN: 1998, p. 4).

Dennis, Jerry and Glenn Wolff. *The Bird in the Waterfall: A Natural History of Oceans, Rivers, and Lakes.* New York: Harper Collins, Publishers, Inc. 1996.

Farr, Sidney S. *More than Moonshine: Appalachian Recipes and Recollections.* Pittsburgh: University of Pittsburg Press, 1983.

Fisher, M. F. K. *The Art of Eating.* New York: Macmillan. 1990.

Keller, Helen. *To Love This Life.* American Foundation for the Blind. http://www.google.com/search?sourceid=navclient&ie=UTF -8&rls=GGLG,GGLG:200612,GGLG:en&q=American+foundat ion+for+the+blind%2E.

Kostikan, Barbara. *ZQuotes.* http://www.zaadz.com/quotes/ Barbara_Costikyan.

Longfellow, Henry Wadsworth. *Online Quotes.* http://en.thinkexist.com/quotation/then followed that beautiful season...Summer/412892.html.

Ritchie, Jean. *Singing Family of the Cumberlands.* Lexington, Ky: University of Kentucky Press, 1988.

Schinz, Marina. *A Tuscan Paradise.* New York: Stewart, Tabori & Chang. 1998.

Sohn, Mark F. *Appalachian Home Cooking: History, Culture, and Recipes.* Lexington: University of Kentucky Press, 2005.

Ward, A. R. and W. P. Trent. "Lesser Poets of the Middle and Later Nineteenth Century—Owen Meredith." *The Cambridge History of English and American Literature.* New York: G.P. Putnam's Sons, 1907–21; New York: Bartleby.com. 2000.

Author's Notes

The Book Cover

The background of the book cover is my mom's feed sack apron, one of many that she wore throughout her life. It is faded across the belly and has a few stains here and there as testimony to her hard work in front of her kitchen stove. The picture on the cover is of Aunt Ethel Morris teaching her great granddaughter, Kylie Morris, how to make an apple pie.

The Stories

A few of the stories included in *Mom's Family Pie* were also published in *The Red Flannel Rag*. I repeated them here as they related to food.

The Recipes

I admit that I have not tried each of the recipes included in this book. Therefore, I cannot guarantee that they will turn out exactly as a cook might expect. As all good cooks know, recipes are affected by different ovens, altitudes, contents, and other factors. As Aunt Ethel and Mom always told me, "Try them several times until they come out like you want them."

About the Author

Peggy Ann Shifflett (B.A., M.A. James Madison University, 1969; 1971; Ph.D., Texas A&M University, 1980) is a retired Professor of Sociology and Chair of the Department of Sociology and Anthropology at Radford University where she taught from 1986 to 2005. Professor Shifflett studied anthropology and folklore at the University of North Carolina, Chapel Hill. A native of Rockingham County in Virginia's Allegheny Mountains, she has devoted her life to understanding rural America and Appalachia. She has studied the aged in rural Appalachia, Appalachian folklore, sociology of the family, and rural homeless children. For her book, *The Red Flannel Rag: Memories of an Appalachian Childhood*, she received the 2005 Elmer Lewis Smith Award for preservation of Shenandoah Valley folklore. This award is given by the Shenandoah Valley Folklore Society.

Professor Shifflett has written and published two textbooks in introductory sociology and many research publications in the journals of her discipline. Professor Shifflett can be contacted for questions and comments at pshiffle@radford.edu or Redesther2@verizon.net.